The Joy of
Entertaining

The Joy of Entertaining

by

Virginia Colton

3M Books

St. Paul, Minnesota

Published in Canada by Prentice-Hall Canada Inc.

Scarborough, Ontario

The Joy of Entertaining
by Virginia Colton

A Production of Tribeca Communications, Inc. and Media Projects Incorporated
Distributed in the United States by the Putnam Publishing Group
First published in Canada 1983
by Prentice-Hall Canada Inc.
1870 Birchmount Road,
Scarborough, Ontario M1P 2J7

Acknowledgements

Principal food photography by Gus Francisco and Allen Baillie.
Principal recipe development and food styling by Diane Mogelever.
Photographs courtesy of the Horchow Collection: pages 4, 7, 8 (left), 9, 10, 44, 67, 68, 69,
    70, 74 (right), 77, 91, 94, 104, 137, 140, 143, 169, 180, 191, 228, 234.
Photograph on page 131 courtesy of Epicure Batterie de Cuisine.
Photograph on page 184 courtesy of Dansk International Designs.
Book design by Jacques Chazaud
Editorial production services by Cobb/Dunlop Publisher Services, Inc.

Library of Congress Cataloging in Publication Data

Colton, Virginia.
    The joy of entertaining.

Includes index.
1. Entertaining. 2. Cookery. 3. Menus. I. Title.
TX731.C636   1983   641.5   83–654
ISBN 0–88159–600–0

Canadian Cataloguing in Publication Data

Colton, Virginia
    The joy of entertaining
    Includes index

    ISBN 0-13-511668-6

    1. Entertaining. 2. Cookery
    3. Menus   I.   Title

    TX731.C64   642'.4   C83-098516-6

Printed and bound in the United States of America

First Edition

1 2 3 4 5 6 7 8 9 10

Contents

Author's Introduction

When the point of entertaining is to give pleasure to other people, a book that encourages the host or hostess to enjoy his or her own party may seem, at first, a little strange. But there is really nothing odd about it. Think about parties you've been to in the past, and concentrate on one where you had a particularly good time. What made that party so pleasant? Was it the food? The free-flowing bar? The way the table looked, and the way the house was "dressed up" for company? Superficially, it was probably most of those things, but surface impressions alone don't guarantee a pleasant time at a party. We all attend parties that seem to have everything going for them, and yet they don't quite succeed. A subtle feeling of tension seems to be in the air, and the guests never quite unbend.

Why should the atmosphere at one party be festive and relaxed, at another chilly and strained? The attitude of the host or hostess is what makes the difference. If he or she is nervous and ill at ease, some of this rubs off on the guests, and can destroy a convivial mood. Guests enjoy themselves when you do—when you have the situation comfortably in hand and are free to please them, and be genuinely glad to see them.

That is not to say you won't ever be nervous. Any experienced actor or actress will tell you that a little stage fright is a good and natural thing. But tension so extreme that you can't perform—what professional athletes call "choking"—is a totally different ball game. It stems from a feeling that you're not up to what you're about to do. Unease at your own party comes from that same feeling of inadequacy, and it is that lack of confidence that this book aims to help you overcome.

The centerpiece of most parties is the food—well prepared and smoothly served. The *Party Menu Cookbook* is the heart of this book. We'll help you plan each party meal, shop for it, cook it, and serve it. (You'll get guidance, too, in setting up a bar, organizing equipment, and prettying up your house, but food is still the main event.) You will find suggested menus for just about any occasion that might call for a party, complete with recipes for a wide and interesting range of featured foods. If you are a novice, or have entertained infrequently, we recommend picking out a menu or two, and then perfecting those you choose until you can serve them with assurance. (Try out unfamiliar dishes first on family or close friends; a party is no place to test recipes!) It's advisable also to stay with complete menus, at least at first, as that saves worrying about what goes with what. More experienced partygivers will use the book differently—switching foods from menu to menu, developing a series of specialties. (You can't serve deviled crab forever, can you, no matter how delicious, not even to the most indulgent of friends.) Whether you follow one of these menus or develop your own, whether your party is large or small, I hope you will use this book to discover *The Joy of Entertaining*.

Virginia Colton

Part I

⚡⚡⚡

Guide to Party Planning

The Thought that Goes into Good Parties

Y ou might not get any two people to agree exactly on how to give a party. That's a matter of style, and different for each individual. But if you were to ask a hundred people, or a thousand, what makes a party *successful,* their answers would be very nearly unanimous. Give or take a choice of phrase, they'd tell you that a successful party is one where everyone has a good time, including the people who are giving it.

A good party may be easy to define—and to recognize—but it must not be quite as simple to achieve, or people wouldn't be so apprehensive about entertaining. That isn't true of everyone, of course. Aren't there hosts and hostesses who simply breeze through their parties, relishing every minute, making things work with no strain whatever? Don't you believe it. That calm, easygoing couple whose dinner party you so enjoyed last week put a lot of thought and effort into the whole event. You didn't notice it (which is the whole idea) because they had things so well planned and organized that everything went off without a hitch.

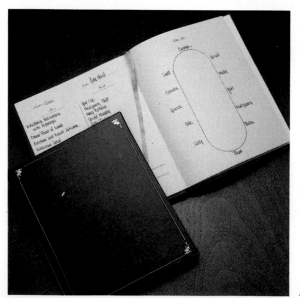

Hostess book.

If planning sounds like drudgery

Planning and organization may be the key to successful entertaining, but to many people they sound positively ominous, making work out of what is supposed to be fun. Try substituting a word like "thoughtfulness" for "planning." The dictionary defines thoughtful as "alert to possible effects or consequences, considerate of the needs of others." A thoughtful host or hostess, planning a party, is thinking about and providing for the well-being of guests.

All parties aren't big

One reason some people flinch at the prospect of entertaining is the vision it conjures up of a huge and complicated event. There *are* big parties, of course, and they *can* get complex. But entertaining can be something as small as setting up a cheerful tray to tempt the appetite of an ailing child, or doing the same for yourself when you're feeling low or tired.

As for big parties, size is relative. What's important is that you don't take on more than you and your home can comfortably handle. If you had a mansion with a full-time, full-fledged staff, you could take any number in stride. Since you don't, you must base any size decision on what you *do* have. Consider, with your budget and facilities, your skills and time, how many you can gracefully seat, cook for, and serve.

Observing, or breaking, the rules

Another factor that can inhibit a potential partygiver is the "rules" concept—the necessity of dealing with cut-and-dried precepts handed down by some authority or other about what should or should not be done. Fortunately for us, entertaining today is more casual than it was in the past, its style determined by concern for guests rather than other people's opinions. In this, as in all aspects of entertaining, what is needed is some sense of proportion. When some prescribed code of conduct is a pointless ritual, at least in our day, feel free to disregard it. Some rules, however, have helped hostesses for generations, and could do the same for you. When in doubt, ask yourself whether the step in question would make things go more pleasurably for all concerned. If the answer is yes, you might be wise to take that step.

What planning can do for you

Besides smoothing the course of your party, advance thinking can save you a lot of grief, time, and last-minute emergencies. What is the sense of finding a marvelous recipe, and building a menu around it, if you haven't *planned* to have all the ingredients when you need them?

If the larger amount you are making calls for a super-size bowl, what will you do if you haven't remembered to borrow or buy one? How will you feel if you've asked too many people for the size of your table, so that both guests and table look squeezed—or if you've washed all the vases and forgotten to order flowers? Forethought would avoid all these problems and others like them, and with them the nervousness and embarrassment unresolved problems can cause.

No amount of planning, of course, can guarantee that nothing will go wrong, but it can cut possible mishaps to a minimum—and to those you can handle. If you've seen to everything you possibly can in advance, you can roll with whatever trivial punches may remain.

How Much Planning Depends on the Occasion

Small and impromptu parties

What we have in mind here is any meal for, let us say, one to four people that would be routine—or might not happen at all, except for a generous impulse. It might be a solitary lunch where you treat yourself like a guest, a surprise tray for a houseguest or someone who's temporarily bedridden, coffee and cake with a neighbor who happens by, or an invitation for friends to share a big batch of your special chili. You may never have thought of such occasions as parties at all. By our definition of "parties"—meals prepared with extra thought and effort and intended to give special pleasure—they most certainly are, or should be.

Parties of this kind take very little planning. Those that are purely spontaneous, of course, can't be planned at all. It does help, though, to have a larder that's always prepared to welcome an unexpected guest or an extra person for lunch—and that is accomplished with a specific kind of planning.

In the case of a breakfast tray, or solo lunch, all that is required is the wish to give (or get) pleasure, and some ingenuity about what might accomplish that result. A houseguest would be charmed by the gesture, whatever the fare. The appetites of most "patients" will improve if you stay around for a visit while the food is eaten. You'll get more pleasure from your own company if you serve yourself a meal at a properly set place, complete with silver and napkin.

Aside from aesthetics, it is often practical to take a party attitude toward solitary meals. Too many people fuss less about meals when they are alone than they would for guests. This isn't just bad for your state of mind; it can be damaging to your health. It's downright beneficial to relax and enjoy your meals, which you are far likelier to do if they are served with style.

V.I.P. breakfast tray.

In the coffee-and-dessert situation, or the extension of an invitation to chili (or any other dish you prepare in quantity), the party might begin as an impulse: to put on the pot or pick up the phone. Or the notion to ask so-and-so over might occur to you as you are about to bake a cake or go grocery shopping. It's the thought that counts, as they say about giving. Put that thought into action, carry it through to the meal itself, and you have created a party.

When two to four add up to an event

Some small events celebrate very big occasions indeed. They may not need elaborate planning, in the sense of juggling a mass of details, but their importance to you imposes its own demands. More than any impersonal gathering, however socially significant, you want these celebrations to be deeply satisfying and memorable.

Many examples come to mind, and you can undoubtedly think of a dozen others—every life has its own ceremonial occasions. For young (and not-so-young) couples, there are anniversaries to observe and reunions to rejoice in. Homage is surely due a new mother just home from the hospital, or the baby's godmother flying in for the christening. When friends you made on vacation will be coming to town, you'll want to do something special.

Planning, in these situations and others like them, is largely a matter of menu planning—selecting foods that are a tribute to occasion and guests. It is greatly to your advantage that you know the events and their dates in advance. Also, with the possible exception of newly-made friends, you

A bedside carafe and a small arrangement of fresh flowers, two of the little touches that help to say "I'm glad you're here."

know the guest or guests to be honored well enough to have some sense of food likes and dislikes. There is the matter, too, of beverage preferences: whether coffee should be decaffeinated, or you should serve tea instead; if wine would be welcome, or a lacing of liqueur in after-dinner coffee. For menu directions you might like to take, refer to pages 146 to 155. If you should find one that is tempting but unfamiliar, you will have time to rehearse it before the big day.

Since you won't face any of the planning necessities that a big party entails—invitations and the wait for responses, decisions about location and timing, scrambling to put together adequate cutlery or china or glassware—you can afford to be a bit leisurely about table decorations, and the small touches that so flatter a house and compliment its guests.

What you can afford in the way of expenditure is up to you. A meal need not break the bank to be delicious and memorable; wines need not be vintage, or flowers exotic. On the other hand, this may be the time of all times when you want to splurge—perhaps the best time, considering the small number of people. And leftover roast makes marvelous hash!

Managing meals for four to eight

When the guest list increases well beyond the number of people in the average household—four to eight would be double the number in many—you might suppose that planning would become much more complex. Over a certain number that would be true, but this group can still be classified as small. If that sounds contradictory, it is easily explained.

Salad bowl and cruets.

The cooking and serving equipment in most households is ample to handle up to eight people. There are always bigger-than-usual pots and pans and platters that, given a good washing, can do all the necessary kitchen duty. China, cutlery, and glassware are also likely to be equal to the task. It's a rare household that doesn't have, stashed away somewhere, what it takes to accommodate eight. The most that might be needed, for a gala lunch or dinner, would be some supplementary serving pieces or utensils—soup tureen and ladle, wine carafe and coasters, salad bowl and servers, a set of steak knives.

Suitable recipes need not be an obstacle. Most that are designed to serve four or six can be adapted upward to feed a few more. For some that were developed to do precisely that, see the menus for four to eight on pages 156 to 194. They may very well feature foods that are new to your cooking repertoire. If so, perhaps it's time something was added. Trying your hand at a new dish renews your interest and sharpens your skills. You shouldn't do this without rehearsal, though; meals rise and fall with recipe successes and failures so it's best to plan a trial run.

The menus, as you will see, run a gamut from extremely relaxed to quite elaborate. Dinner for close friends might be served buffet-style and eaten in the living room—a warm and intimate way to share a meal. This is not recommended for acquaintances or business associates; a seated meal is best for people you know only slightly, or when the event is in someone's honor. Even in these more formal instances, however, the living room is a pleasant site for drinks before dinner and coffee at its close.

Aside from their social desirability, each of these approaches, in its way, simplifies serving.

Invitations to so few people can be telephoned. If a party centers around a particular individual or couple, they should be sounded out first and other guests approached when a mutually convenient time has been arranged. Though it is not always suitable, telephoning has the definite advantage of providing opportunities for quick responses.

It sometimes happens that a guest who has accepted must cancel at the very last minute, leaving you with a party planned to the final detail but minus one, or perhaps two, of its crucial number. This is regrettable, but needn't be fatal. Call a good and understanding friend (or two or three, if necessary), explain the situation, and the chances are that he or she, or they, will come running to the rescue.

For these parties one facet of planning *will* need attention: unless you habitually keep an exceptionally well-stocked bar, you will need to set up the makings for drinks.

Finally, when you're deciding what needs doing to put your house in shape and your guests at ease, don't neglect the mundane matter of a place for coats—and for guests' cars as well.

This butler's tray makes an attractive impromptu bar.

Appropriate menus and recipes

You will find menu ideas and recipes designed especially for solo meals and comparatively small groups on pages 136 to 155. Helpful, too, will be the collection of tea and coffee parties, and sweets and sandwiches suited to them, that begins on page 224. But don't pass over other menus and recipes merely because their stated purpose is different from what you have in mind. If a recipe or menu combination appeals to you, it can be turned to any purpose you please, usually with only minor modifications.

The planning advice that follows this section concerns progressively larger and more formal parties, and preparations for special occasions. There is a germ of wisdom in it, however, for any kind of party, so we suggest that you check through it, making mental notes of suggestions that seem sensible. This will put you ahead of the game when you want to plan something more elaborate, the kind of party that calls for considerable forethought and organization.

Guidance Every Step of the Way

Of course you must take some advance steps in preparation for any party, however small. It is when parties get larger and more formal, or are somehow special in character, that planning means thinking through, and following through, every last detail.

This can, and we think should, literally mean scheduling every step that is to be taken. If that sounds like work, it does take a little effort. But such a timed "checklist of chores" avoiding reliance on memory, is your best insurance that nothing will be overlooked. And it will reward you handsomely in all-around enjoyment and pride in your own performance.

We have alluded to some of the steps—guest lists, invitations, menu planning, equipment needs—as they came up in our consideration of smaller, simpler parties. What follows is a review of all possible planning steps, from the original impulse to give a party to seeing the last guests out the door. Not all will pertain to every party, but they should at least be considered, and you can do that better when you understand what they are.

Party-planner's quiz

Before you can begin to plan, or know how much and what kind of planning you need to do, ask and answer some basic questions.

1. What kind of party do you want to give?
2. When should it take place?

3. Whom will you invite?
4. Where should the party be held?
5. How will you handle food?

All of these decisions are interrelated, and so cannot be made independently or necessarily in the given order. A later decision may even make it necessary to rethink an earlier one. If you should find, for example, that a couple you especially want to come to your Christmas buffet will be out of town until New Year's, should you change your party date? Or make plans to see them later, perhaps at a more intimate dinner?

A review of all the basic questions, and what they can involve, should help you to come up with answers that suit your circumstances. When you've done that, you're ready to get on with your planning.

1. The kind of party

"Kind of party" can mean many things, but the meaning that comes first to mind is: the event itself—dinner or luncheon party, breakfast-brunch, cocktail party, open house, tea, and so on. Where planning is concerned, however, names alone are not very instructive. A dinner or lunch can be small and comparatively simple to organize; our first three menu collections (pages 136 to 145) are testimony to that. No elaborate guest lists, mode of invitation, equipment needs, decisions about timing or location. Even those of some formality require only more meticulous menu planning and table design.

Planning becomes more intricate when the guest list grows longer (eight and up for sit-down meals, according to many entertainment professionals; some say that in these servantless times, no table should be asked to take more than eight). A change to buffet service may be in order for a large group. Teas and coffees can be unplanned and intimate or, as when they serve some larger social purpose, gatherings of great formality.

Each variation connotes a sharp difference in serving style—another powerful influence on planning. Personal considerations can sometimes dictate serving judgments. Take, for example, finances. You may feel that a meal of several courses, perhaps calling for (or strongly suggesting) several wines, is a bit beyond your means. The menus for eight that begin on page 171 take that into consideration, including relatively expensive meals and two that are less so. Meal types are luncheons *and* dinners, both fall-winter and summer, which further expands your range of choices.

There can also be a problem of time or the lack of it. For people whose working or otherwise busy lives limit their leisure—and that can mean host *or* guests—the Sunday brunch is a blessed invention. It has very nearly joined the ranks of breakfast, lunch, and dinner as a conventional meal. See ideas for this sort of party starting on page 215.

Some occasions, because of traditions associated with them, seem to allow little latitude in style. Thanksgiving dinner, Christmas dinner, children's birthdays—say the words and you can almost recite the menus.

Though our menus for events like these bow respectfully to many conventions, they also offer you a new notion or two.

When a party takes place is not a matter simply of time of day; that is quite often a foregone conclusion. So also is time of year, particularly for holidays such as Easter or Christmas and for others, such as Thanksgiving or the Fourth of July, that have come to have customary styles of celebration. Timing, in day-to-day terms, means *when* people are likely to be available to attend the party. You may have the Fourth of July in mind, but will anybody be around to join you? It can mean *when* a guest of honor is not otherwise engaged; *when* a wedding is scheduled to occur; *when* your new, or newly renovated, house is ready for warming.

2. Party timing

As with the wedding date, the time may not be your decision at all. If you are elected to host, or hostess, a club luncheon—or a reception, or a congratulatory cocktail bash for the winners of a tennis tournament—the date is predetermined and you can only proceed accordingly.

Summer, incidentally, may have its drawbacks in some ways, but it offers a good many compensatory advantages. You can give many more kinds of parties, broader in scope and numbers and more easygoing in style. When people can wander in and out of the house, you will hardly notice the traffic. If the fair weather should turn foul, you can always cover the buffet table against a few scattered sprinkles or, with the help of a willing guest or two, move the whole works inside.

For parties that are obligatory, or those that mark big days on someone else's calendar, choice of guests may not be entirely up to you. It may even, with one or two exceptions, be imposed. Usually, however, the selection is yours and yours alone. It is wise to get going on at least a tentative list as quickly as possible; the number of people has a bearing on every other step. Literally first, and the step that sets the others in motion: the sending or phoning of invitations, a week or two in advance of the party date, three to four when it's a formal party or a date that, for many, is likely to be filled if you procrastinate.

3. The guest list

Then there is the question of how many people you and your home can handle. Suppose it turns out, let's say, that the list, no matter how you trim it, comes to ten or twelve, and you can't possibly seat more than eight. You might have to consider a buffet rather than a sit-down dinner.

Then again, your seating problem might be solved (if table size is all it amounts to) by renting two or three smaller tables, each seating, say, four to six. Many experienced hosts and hostesses swear by folding card tables fitted with round plywood covers that equip them to seat six or eight. When they are not in use, the tables are folded up and stored away with the "stack" of covers, which take up very little space (even less if they are hinged).

Before you hail multiple tables as the ideal solution, remember that they would require a space large enough to hold them—rare in present-day apartments and even in houses, spacious dining rooms having fallen from fashion.

You might, finally, take the opposite attitude toward the numbers: forget all about trimming or accommodating, let the list get even longer, and switch to a cocktail party—serving finger foods or substantial ones, as you prefer. Properly planned, this can be the least expensive way to cater to a crowd, and to write off a slew of social obligations.

If you are more concerned about *serving* a group of people than you are about seating them, this task can be greatly simplified by planning a meal-in-one-dish instead of one with several separate courses. Such dishes have progressed far beyond the standard American clichés (macaroni and cheese, or tuna and noodles); interesting ideas from all over the world have found their way into our cuisine—just have a look at the Index.

Quantity counts, but what about the proposed guests as people? When you've done your numbers, you must still reflect on them as a combination. As well as you can predict, are they likely to be compatible?

Contrary to a popular assumption, it is *not* best to people a party with one age group, one profession, one marital status. Shoptalk is notoriously dreary, and narrow shared experience is no better. Shake the mixture up a bit. You may be amazed at how much the guests find they have in common.

If you know of any personality problems, do steer clear of those. There are the couples who snarl and the singles who sulk. You may even feel some responsibility for heavy drinkers who, having failed to completely wreck your party, might really finish the job with their cars.

Smoking has become a hot issue, with nonsmokers increasingly vocal and smokers just as loudly defending their rights. Best not to invite the vehement few from either side, or certainly not together. Those who feel less strongly either way can still be relied upon to be considerate of one another.

4. The best place for the party

Naturally you would like to have your party in your home, but as you glance around, you wonder whether its size and facilities are equal to anything more than a small, casual dinner or a few people in for drinks.

Limited space can be a hindrance, but there are ways to expand the usefulness of even the smallest apartment. If a seated meal is impossible because of the cramped quarters, you can position a table along one wall, and serve a help-yourself one-dish meal. Another simplifier: have the first course in the living room along with drinks. This frees the kitchen and dining area for cooking and dishing up out of sight of the guests, and finishing the table as time allows.

If you've always thought a huge cocktail party was out of the question, think again. Just as with an open house, people drop in and drop back out again at their convenience, making way for newcomers. Keep the food simple and easy to replenish, away from the bar so the traffic will flow. To make certain that people don't overstay their welcome, limit your offerings to tiny cocktail sandwiches, appetizers, and other such finger foods, the kind that whet appetites rather than sate them.

When parties can be held outdoors, the capacity of a house virtually doubles. Guests have wandering room, and a few will always prefer to hover in the house. Bad weather need not necessarily mean taking the party indoors. A cleaned-up garage or carport can offer temporary shelter.

Although the question of food is listed last because the answer depends on earlier decisions, the menu is really the prime party consideration. The meal is the high point of most parties, and critical to their success, even if the offering is only do-it-yourself sandwiches. If it is to live up to expectations, every stage of the menu must be planned, from selection to service, with attention in between to perfecting unfamiliar recipes.

5. Providing for food

How to think about menus. Naturally, we assume (and hope) that you will be using the menus in this book (*Party Menu Cookbook,* pages 135 to 278). That being so, most helpful here would be some guidelines for making a choice.

- The cookbook is divided into kinds of parties, each described as to type and size. If you have a particular party in mind, glance through these menus and see whether you find one to your liking. Look also at menu plans that are similar except for the number of guests (not too many more or fewer!) and of course specific foods.
- A menu can be hard to evaluate, especially for novices at entertaining, because it has so many parts. Try, instead, looking among the main dishes in the index for foods that you like or recipes that sound interesting, then trace them back to their menus.

Either way, you will have picked out a possible menu approach. Now see how well your selection stacks up in all of these ways.

Is the cooking within your abilities? Perhaps you should find something simpler, or plan to modify the menu slightly. Of course, if your interest is strong enough, you can always master the necessary skills ahead of time by practicing, and then you'll have a new specialty to show off.

Do you have the required equipment? First in line is cooking equipment—too expensive these days to buy impulsively. Then there is serving equipment and adequate silverware and china. Each course calls for its own, even at a buffet. Part II (*Getting Organized*) goes into detail about all the needs and possibilities.

Can you picture a place for the party? There is the question of table size to think about for a seated dinner or lunch, and the feasibility of several smaller tables (perhaps rented) if your one dining table is too small for the prospective number. A buffet calls for a good-size table, generally longer than it is wide, positioned so that traffic can flow along or around it. Where will the guests sit to eat the buffet fare? Where can you set up a bar?

How will the planned party fit in your budget? If you can't afford both the menu *and* the number of guests, you may have to compromise one way or the other. Food is not cheap, but a delightful meal, even a distinguished one, can be quite economical. Check the one-dish specialties; there surely will be several made with your favorite foods.

Planning is done course by course. That doesn't mean, however, the four or five courses that were "proper" in the past. A meal of three courses, or even two, is proper today and far easier to cook and serve.

Start with the entrée, or main dish. It might be a fine cut of meat, or poultry, or fish. Just as correctly, it could be a casserole or stew, a thick and hearty soup, a substantial sandwich, a seafood or other main-dish salad. If you or someone else in the family has a specialty, consider building a menu around it. Many a great meal has begun with the talents of an "amateur chef."

Vegetables are a usual accompaniment, though potatoes or rice often take the place of one vegetable. If you make one starchy choice, avoid starch in the second choice; that's one of the principles of balance.

The first course. Why in the world is the first course listed third? Because it is an "accessory" to the main dish and its accompaniments and must be compatible: light (clear soup, fresh fruit, chilled vegetable juice) if the main meal is somewhat heavy, and not repetitious (avoid seafood cocktail, for instance, if the main dish is fish). This course literally is an appetizer, and should sharpen the appetite, not so satisfy it that there is none left for the meal itself.

The salad today is very often the second vegetable, sometimes served separately after the meat/vegetable or other entrée; in its stead, some hostesses serve a raw vegetable array—celery, carrot sticks, radishes, etc.—with the main course; a small salad may appear as a first-course appetizer, in which case any other salad is skipped. Any salad is appropriate—tossed, individually arranged, molded. A salad that can be tossed and served at table is convenient. Individual salads are less so, unless, of course, they are individual salad molds, ready and waiting in the refrigerator. Finally, of course, you can serve no salad at all, but don't choose this alternative without forethought—salad is often an incomparable balancer.

Breads or rolls are up to you. Aromatic and warm, they are always a welcome addition. Your final decision may be based on the rest of the meal. If you feel bread or rolls would enhance it, provide them in your menu. If you have time, do try to bake your own. Don't feel apologetic if yours are bakery- or store-bought, though packaged breads, with a few exceptions, leave much to be desired. Most communities have good bakeries offering quality baked goods.

Deciding on dessert. If this is your favorite course, you will be disappointed to learn that this choice, too, must defer to other foods on the menu: fruit gelatin or sherbet to close a meal that features a rich, highly seasoned main dish or potatoes or a vegetable in a cream or cheese sauce; cobblers and cakes and puddings only after such lighter entrées as a main-dish salad or simply prepared fish or poultry. If you must have the chocolate mousse, or deep-dish pie with heavy cream, go back to the beginning and rethink your elaborate entrée and its accompaniments.

Coffee is not a course, in the true sense, but it should appear after every dinner party. It can be regular or decaffeinated or both; if the guest list is small, this is a preference you might determine in advance. Guests might also be asked whether they would like coffee or tea. During the summer months, people often prefer coffee or tea iced—a simple conversion to make.

Those principles comprise the general possibilities, with some present-day simplifications: the salad need no longer be served separately (unless you wish); fish, once a separate course, is now counted among the main dishes. Within the guidelines some simplifications are implied: an excellent, and appropriate, lunch can consist of just soup and a sandwich with a light sweet for dessert. Salad and dessert make a fine summer luncheon, "salad" in this case meaning one with substance in the form of chicken or seafood, cheese, or fresh fruit. If your stew or casserole or other one-dish combination contains vegetables and perhaps potatoes (chicken and meat pies are a perfect illustration), you need worry no more about that aspect of the meal.

If you have thought about your skills, equipment, facilities, and budget as you read about courses, you will have eliminated "obvious impossibles" along the way. But you still must take another look at the combination you've come up with in the light of these additional considerations:

- Is it a balance of rich and simple, heavy and light? Since this was stressed in several places, your score here is probably high.
- Servings should be ample but not excessive; take care not to make far too much. You should be generous, but never wasteful.
- Could you, in all honesty, do with fewer courses? Remember it's no longer necessary to serve so many, and you'll only be making extra work for yourself.
- Visualize the colors and textures; we do, after all, also feast with our eyes. Will it be a pleasing mixture? Might the combination of foods be a bit busy for your china?
- If your menu passes that test, it should also do well on the next: is there variety of foods and flavors?

If that seems like a lot of thought to put into any menu except a formal one, consider a simple soup-and-sandwich lunch for two. If the sandwich is creamed chicken on toast, wouldn't a clear bouillon be better than a creamed or chunky soup? Wouldn't the plate look more appetizing with, say, the addition of currant jelly or a spiced crabapple? Wouldn't the tartness of either one complement the relative blandness of the creamed dish?

Steps that stem from the menu. Knowing the meal you plan to serve, you can begin to think about needs directly related to it: *cooking, serving, and table-setting equipment, decorations for your table and home, provisions for a bar.* For guidance with these, we suggest a review of Part II.

Even if your kitchen is the size of a phone booth, you will be fascinated by what's in store to *cook and serve* with. Beginning with the basic pots, pans, tools, and appliances, the sections go on to the greater glories of equipment for special purposes and specific dishes, and the marvels of far-flung cuisines—Oriental, Italian, Mexican and South American, Greek and Middle Eastern. You may never venture far beyond the tools and dishes you've mastered, but if and when you want to, you will know how!

You will find *party tables* approached from a number of angles: table plans and seating arrangements for meals of many kinds and styles; table and serving equipment from fundamental to fanciful; table decorating ideas (plus some for the rest of the house); and finally, for inspiration, a full-color gallery of table settings reflecting a variety of tastes.

Bar essentials are as different as the parties, differences fully explored in Part II. Bar needs, from liquor supplies to bartending tools, are reviewed party by party. Various bar plans are suggested, from a portable tray for before-dinner drinks to a fast-moving setup for a huge cocktail party. You will also find a buying guide for selecting liquor and deciding quantities to order, as well as buying strategies.

Invitations and final menu

Up to this point your party has been an idea in your head, with only possible guests and tentative menu committed to paper. When your guest list is firm, and your food plan taking shape, you are ready to make your first move: extending invitations.

Extending invitations

This is an area with as many exceptions as there are rules, and few experts seem to agree even about what the "rules" are. Base this judgment on common sense, within the flexible guidelines that follow.

Timing

Invitations should be extended, whether telephoned or mailed, at least one to three weeks ahead of the event, as many as four weeks ahead in some circumstances. Allow the longer lead times when the proposed day is a traditional one for parties or falls in a customarily hectic social period. Three weeks is minimum when the occasion is strictly formal. Allow enough time for responses beforehand when you must know exact numbers, and maybe sexes, before you can move ahead with menu and seating. (The sex question can come up at parties where you will want a "balance." Almost no one any longer feels bound by this constraint, but it still occurs occasionally.)

It is proper to send strictly formal invitations when you are asking people to a formal party such as a dinner, dance, or reception. (For formal luncheons, telephoning is permissible.) Formal invitations may be printed or engraved, as you prefer. Bear in mind that printing can take several weeks, engraving even longer. Your printer or stationer will have several styles to show you, but they won't wander far from a strictly prescribed form.

Printing will probably be your choice; engraving, though it used to be the only option, is now confined to official functions, and to what amount to "state" occasions in an individual's social life: milestone anniversary, wedding, debut, bar/bat mitzvah. Formal invitations are conventional in every way: paper type and color, lettering, form. Every detail is decreed, negatively for the most part. *No* abbreviations (except such forms of address as Dr., Mr., and Mrs.); *no* punctuation (except the standard comma between day and date, town and state); *no* capital letters (except for proper names). The arrival time is spelled out, never expressed in numerals; instead of the familiar 7:30, for example, the invitation would say "seven thirty" or even "half after seven."

Below the body of the invitation, at the lower left, there will be an R.S.V.P. (or r.s.v.p.; either is correct). Such pertinent additional information as "Black Tie" or "Dancing" (capitals permitted) appear at the lower right. If an individual or organization (a charity, for instance) is being honored or benefitted, this fact may be part of the printed information or handwritten at the top. (A further stipulation here: "honour" is the form, the "u" being restored to its once unchallenged place.)

All these considerations can be sidestepped by means of a convenience most stationers stock: fill-in formal invitations, forms engraved and suitably worded with space for supplying the data that pertain to your particular party. Response cards are available as well, made to match the invitations. They *can* nudge prospective guests more compellingly than an R.S.V.P., a consideration when you need to know numbers early and accurately. They are rarely necessary, however, since most people take an R.S.V.P. seriously. If you should decide to include return envelopes, they should be self-addressed and stamped.

For all informal occasions, you can mail or phone invitations as you wish. If the guest list for the event is extensive (typically a cocktail party or open house, where numbers above 100 are not unheard of), telephoning is out of the question. Making up a mailing list, complete with initials and zip codes, may be a time-consuming bore but more efficient than making 100 phone calls. (Even if you are mailing invitations, incidentally, record the telephone numbers on the list along with the names and addresses; they could come in handy, should you have to followup by phone if all responses have not been received.)

An R.S.V.P. is not usual on invitations sent to a mammoth mailing list, but there is something you can do if you would like some notion of numbers: you can add "Regrets only" at the bottom, with your telephone number (and the hours you can be reached) and base a reasonably good estimate on those who call to tell you they can't come.

Informal invitations can be printed, but this takes time that could be put to better use. In equally good taste, and instantly available, are pre-printed fill-ins, sold by any quality stationer. They range from dignified to diverting, just like parties. You can also use notepaper or fold-over informals, initialed if you like this style of personal identification.

When the decision to write or phone is either/or, each has its advantages. A written invitation acts as a memory-refresher for date, place, and kind of party. What a telephoned invitation offers is speed: faster certainly than a mailed invitation, it also usually evokes an immediate response, or a promise to call back right away after a short consultation. A combination of both is conceivable when some guests are "key" (to be honored, important to you personally, etc.). You will want to phone such people to be sure of their availability before mailing invitations to the others.

If the promise to call back isn't kept, or there are other people you don't hear from, you will have to send a reminder, another kind of card kept by stationers. One easy-to-use, elegant type is an engraved fill-in. Or you can, as before, write a reminder on notepaper, informals, or even a postcard. Nothing elaborate—just a note that says something as simple as "Don't forget lunch at Jane and John's, Friday, the 1st, around noon." A face-to-face invitation, of course, is just like a telephone call and demands a reminder, the words having been written on air. A reminder is a courteous and sensible idea, as well, to follow up on invitations that are sent a very long time in advance.

Specifying time

Here you can face something of a dilemma, though not with lunches or dinners, where an arrival time is given and guests understand the importance of being punctual. The confusion arises with a party that has, by its nature, an open-ended sound: brunch, a cocktail party, an open house, or housewarming. Unless you make it clear that the party has a definite end as well as beginning, there are those who will linger indefinitely. But if you give *both* times, start and finish, many people will feel free to show up any time in between—disastrous if what you are serving is a timed-to-the-minute brunch. It would be rude to serve before everyone arrives, but your brunch would be doomed were you to wait. Perhaps what is wisest, in that situation, is to give only an arrival time and plan to hold off on serving for a half hour or so.

Information you might want to add

Over and above such pertinent facts as "Dinner Jacket" or "Dancing," or an address or phone number for directing responses, there can be other kinds of information that guests should be given in advance. For an outdoor party, you might want to set a rain date or suggest bringing a light wrap or a swimsuit. It would be courteous to note, for example, on all or some of the invitations, that the person being honored is a new neighbor, business associate, old college chum, etc. On an informal invitation, you can jot down any asides that you think might help people get a "feel" for the occasion and be more comfortable or enthusiastic about coming.

Always buy or order a few more than your maximum number of guests. There will inevitably be a few refusals and you will probably want to send additional invitations to make up for the loss. (Don't throw away your rough, early guest lists. You may want to reinstate some names you were forced to eliminate.)

Number of invitations

For a large party, send more invitations than the hoped-for final number of guests—up to one-third again as many. That would be, for example, 75 if you'd like to end up with 50, 150 for a final 100. The reason? The experience of many has shown that only about two-thirds of those invited actually come to parties of this size.

Be as organized about this as you possibly can. You don't want your records of who accepted and who didn't on a dozen scraps of paper; it is with these numbers and names that you will be planning your menu and bar service, developing a seating plan, and calculating the need, if any, for new equipment.

Keeping track of responses

Some people are quite happy with duplicate guest lists. If you think this solution would suit you, just have photocopies made of the original, unmarked list—as many as you think you will require. Index cards are another idea. Though not as easy to see at a glance, they do provide more writing space than a list, enough for everything you might want to record, and they can be shifted into any desired order. A possible alternative that could be seen at a glance and also rearranged: a looseleaf address book in which each entry goes on a separate, hole-punched card. There is less space on these than on index cards, but plenty for the relevant information.

The menus in our *Party Menu Cookbook* (pages 135 to 278) take most necessities into account—season, degree of formality, number of people, balance, practicality, even expense. There are some general principles, however, that you should keep in mind before going ahead with any menu.

The menu: final decisions and follow-through

• The season makes a difference in the foods you should choose. Some are actually dangerous in hot weather and others *can* be if proper precautions are not taken. The precaution is usually keeping the food in question chilled, without prolonged interruption, from preparation to service. (Preparation *through* service in the case of those that will be out on a buffet table.) Foods on the "be careful" list include any dishes made with eggs or cream, such as cream pies or custards, also fish and meat (including even such processed types as cold cuts and frankfurters).
• You will take fewer chances of foods "going begging" if you stay with those that are familiar to you (having cooked and served them before).

- Don't plan on a dish that you haven't mastered to your own satisfaction—and someone else's taste. Better to postpone it to a later occasion if you are not quite sure.
- All dishes should be ones you are equipped to serve, or can provide for by the time of the party.
- Don't give up on a dish because you have no way to keep it hot and hesitate to invest in a hot plate or tray. For a large party, you will probably need to buy a few things, and such a unit could be a tremendous convenience at future parties. Borrowing may be a possibility, too—ask around.
- Consider, in making selections, how guests will be situated. Few people can manage on their laps or on a tray what they could at a table. In those instances you should avoid anything that requires strenuous cutting, or involves potentially sloppy sauces.
- Never put sauces or other liquids, especially hot ones, in containers they can soak into or through. Paper plates and cups are very risky, even when they are coated; the coatings have been known to dissolve.
- If you contemplate modifying a menu—changing vegetables, or substituting a different sauce—try to stay within the original type, in order to maintain the menu's intended balance.
- Plan to serve food on dishes that suit the amount you will be serving as well as the type of food and its appearance; an ample slice of cake can look stranded on too large a plate. If you fear that your cake or pie might not stretch as far as you had hoped without looking meager, serve some ice cream to keep it company. Ice cream is reliable and generally liked, and can be picked up on short notice even on a Sunday. Or you can keep a supply in your freezer.
- Quantities are not as predictable at a large party where uncounted numbers of people come and go (such as a cocktail party or open house) as they are with a specific guest list and controlled portions. Have plenty of what you plan to serve and be ready to come up with more—something different if need be—to keep your guests contented.

Reading and following recipes

Read recipes with great care—not once, but several times, each time in search of additional information or guidance.

- For your first recipe reading, have paper and pencil on hand. Jot down a list of the ingredients you need, the equipment required for preparation and, in your mind's eye (the recipe rarely specifies this in so many words), the platters, bowls, plates, or other dishes in which the various foods might be served.
- Be precise about the ingredients, listing not just the names but the amounts. It may be that you have enough of some of them already, so that only the others need go on a shopping list. (See *Maintaining an emergency larder,* page 31.)

- If you are not sure what kind of equipment should be used, or wonder whether there's something newer or more efficient that you might consider buying, look through the cooking equipment section of Part II. It is broken down into types and purposes, with descriptions short and to the point to make it easy to check through.
- Serving equipment, too, is dealt with in Part II. Among these items, you might find it enlightening to see what is available for keeping foods warm or cold—problems that seldom arise in preparing and serving everyday meals.
- The recipes will draw attention to what should, or can, be done ahead. Consider this information carefully. Work done ahead makes party-day cooking and serving infinitely easier.
- Recipes customarily specify the number of servings that they yield; many people mistakenly assume that this automatically means number of people. You *might* serve four people with four servings; or you might only serve two, if you planned on offering seconds. Also, not everyone defines a "serving" in the same way, some serving with a more lavish hand than others. "Serving," in recipes as in commercially processed foods, means a reasonably generous portion.
- Don't double a recipe unless permission, and directions, are given—or you know, from long experience, exactly what you are doing. When a recipe is for a mixture—as a salad or soup—you can certainly double the lettuce or the chicken or the tomatoes or the broth, but be more careful with seasonings and dressings. It is best to start with the prescribed amount, then add more judiciously, "to taste." Some recipes—cakes, custards, or gelatin desserts, for example—require the right proportions of eggs to milk, or liquid to dry ingredients, or gelatin to fruit juice, or the recipe simply won't work. With the simple exception of mixtures, take only the recipe's word about doubling—when and how.
- Be painstaking about measurements. If you don't have the necessary implements to be exact with flour, butter or margarine, sugar, baking powder, vegetable oil, milk, you really should make the small investment for the sake of accuracy. Part II explains what you need for each purpose if you are uncertain about what you should have.
- Another don't: never substitute ingredients, at least not significant ones. Use cake flour if that is what the recipe calls for; no liquid brown sugar if the instructions say "brown sugar, packed." A change of spices can be harmless (though the taste won't be the same), as can a few more nut meats in brownies or some coconut on a cake—almost anything except key ingredients.

Schedule the cooking of the various recipes so that everything turns out right, and is ready at the proper time. In the *Party Countdown* on page 26, a hypothetical cooking schedule is spelled out from the original menu decision to the last steps just before serving. It is interwoven with basic party preparations to show the whole progression and, within it,

Timing a menu's parts—

exactly what needs to be done from week to week and day to day as party time draws nearer. Essentially, it is a checklist of chores—indispensable, we believe, for any big party whether you are experienced or not. For the basic party steps, our schedule might suffice; to time the steps for an actual menu, it would be better to draft a shopping/cooking schedule of your own. The following principles should help:

- Read every word of each recipe in turn and list as you go the ingredients needed and the amounts called for, the cooking equipment and utensils required. When you have checked your own food and equipment supplies, the lists of what remains to be supplied will become your shopping (or perhaps borrowing or renting) lists.
- To your lists, add any telephone numbers or addresses you will need to run down what is missing.
- Schedule shopping trips, telephone calls, etc.
- The first "cooking" steps to be scheduled are those that should, or can, be done ahead.
- The preceding steps simply get you ready to cook. One other advisable preliminary: rearrange your working area so that it is as convenient as possible. It will help to clear the way if you set aside everything that will ultimately go to the bar area. Plan as much free counter space as you can; shuffle appliances around so that the ones you plan to use will be within easiest reach.
- To plan the preparation and cooking you will be doing on the day of the party, back up from the dish that will take the longest time; then "build in" the others within that time frame. For example, if your main dish will take a total of three hours to prepare and cook, and you expect to serve at 7:00 P.M., plan to begin preparations at 4:00 P.M.
- Consider, at this point, whether you have thought of every preparation step that can be taken in advance—and whether two or more steps might be accomplished as one. For instance, might vegetables for the main dish be cleaned, sliced, or chopped and refrigerated—and salad greens be taken care of at the same time? You can work ahead on anything that will not suffer from being prepared in advance and could be a nuisance to fit into the schedule for some major cooking operation. Certain recipes will benefit from some standing time: many salad dressings, for example.

Whatever kind of schedule you decide to make for your own use, we do recommend that you look at the two-part scheduling in the Party Countdown. It is important to be realistic, when you are focusing intently on cooking, about the other things that must go on at the same time. And it is good insurance against any of them slipping your mind to list them in a time frame as we have done. It can be more detailed or less so as you prefer, but it should at least take note of every aspect of the party that requires your attention. Nothing will do more to get you organized, and keep you that way as you go along.

Elements for elegant entertaining.

Preparing a Party Countdown

What follows is a representative party schedule that touches upon all the preliminary steps you might have to take for a party of your own. It weaves the two kinds of steps—basic preparations and food shopping/cooking—into the same time frame. This lets you see, at a glance, what is going on within each period in the progression: weeks in the beginning and finally days and hours. To permit mention of all possible steps, the countdown assumes a fairly large party, at home, with a somewhat elaborate menu.

This hypothetical "checklist of chores," which is what basic preparations amount to, might work in any real situation. Certain ones simply would not apply—something you would know automatically. A make-believe menu, however, is quite another thing. When you reach the point of scheduling the cooking for an actual party, you will need to construct a countdown for that particular menu.

The timing of the countdown begins with the first "outward" steps: extending invitations and making the menu firm. In practice you might have to begin your actions some weeks earlier: *if* invitations are to be printed or engraved; *if* the party locale is to be outside your home and you have to choose among several possible sites; *if* you plan to engage the services of a caterer, or do extensive renting of equipment.

PARTY COUNTDOWN	Basic party preparations	Food & cooking schedule
2 to 3 weeks in advance (4 weeks if highly social or formal event, traditional party day, etc.)	*Invitations* out (mail or phone). Set up a way to keep track of acceptances and regrets.	*Menu* decision is firm and recipes marked or clipped so they are easy to find for follow-up.
Shortly after invitations have gone out	Make *bar* decisions (kind of drinks, how and when served). Work out a *table* plan, seating arrangement, table design (setting and decorations). Decide how the *house* will be decorated. Make up your mind about *entertainment* and list sources, if suitable.	With menu and recipes in hand, list required *ingredients* (also any foods to be served "as is," such as relishes), *cooking equipment,* probable *serving pieces and utensils.* Check your *larder* to see what ingredients and staples you have; make a food *shopping list* of the balance. (Divide this, if you wish, into foods that can be bought ahead and ones that, for reasons of freshness, you want to purchase shortly before the party.)

PARTY COUNTDOWN	*Basic party preparations*	*Food & cooking schedule*

Check *liquor* supplies, *bar* equipment.

Check *table* equipment, basic and decorative. List needs such as candles, place cards (separate list for florist) and equipment, such as vases, candelabra, etc., that require special cleaning.

Add *guest* needs (soap, tissues, towels) to shopping list.

Consider the adequacy of *table and chairs:* must anything be rented?

Look the *house* over for any major jobs that need doing.

To your *telephone source list* (which already includes liquor store and florist), add any or all of the following, as applicable: temporary personnel agency, baby sitter, housecleaning service or cleaning person, laundry, dry cleaner, barber shop or salon, talent agency, ice supplier.

Check your *equipment* to see what you need to buy/rent/borrow, if anything. Look up and write down the phone numbers of possible sources. List items in need of more-than-routine cleaning or polishing. *Appliances* should be tested now, or not too much later, if they have not been used in a while. Be sure the dishwasher is in good working order—it, of all appliances, is indispensable at a party. (If you do not have a dishwasher, consider hiring someone to handle that chore.)

Examine your *work area* to see whether it can be made more convenient.

In *party area,* be sure electrical outlets are available where needed, plus heavy-duty extension cords for any heating appliances to go on the table.

Add to your shopping list any food items needed *for the bar:* lemons, limes, nuts, chips, etc.

Also add any miscellaneous *kitchen needs:* paper towels, plastic wrap, aluminum foil, dishwashing detergent, cleaning products, rubber gloves, etc.

Put on the shopping list items for *guests'* convenience or comfort (tissues, guest soaps, etc.) and *table* setting or decoration (candles, place cards).

PARTY COUNTDOWN	Basic party preparations	Food & cooking schedule
10 days to a week ahead (the earlier the better)	*Make phone calls* to place orders and set appointments. Arrange for delivery where possible, pickup time where it is not. If you plan to visit the florist or other supplier, do this early as well. Record *responses* to invitations so you have an accurate guest list. Send reminders as needed (telephoned or in-person invitations, people who were "going to let you know"). Extend invitations to make up for regrets.	*Telephone* sources about equipment you want to rent or borrow, arranging for delivery or pickup. *Prepare* in advance any menu items that can be frozen without loss of flavor of appearance— bread dough, pie crust, some casseroles.
About 5 days ahead	Take care of any major *house or equipment cleaning jobs.*	Do any necessary *polishing of equipment* for cooking and serving. *Shop* for nonperishable foods and staples; nonfood items; foods that are, or can be, frozen.
2 days ahead	Check on *deliveries,* if only to confirm. Do the *general housecleaning* (special attention to "guest" rooms). Polish *barware,* wash *glasses.*	Do the *balance of the shopping* (perishables). Fish and seafood, however, should only be purchased the day they are to be served (or cooked and frozen). Check to make sure that you have all the necessary *ingredients and foods* for menu and bar. *Pick up* any necessities that will not be delivered. Gather together all *equipment* to be sure it is complete.

PARTY COUNTDOWN	*Basic party preparations*	*Food & cooking schedule*
		Do any *advance food preparation* that is feasible (can be frozen or refrigerated for the intervening time).
		Polish *silver,* wash *glassware* (including bar glasses).
Day before	Check and accessorize *"guest" rooms.*	*If you plan to bake* bread or rolls, or a cake, this can be done a day ahead.
	Set up bar, moving into it any equipment still in the kitchen (hold refrigerated foods until party day).	*The same is true* for desserts that must "set" in the refrigerator, such as gelatins, some puddings, and molded salads. Pies are better done on the day of the party.
	Set the table except for final touches (best to wait with flowers, perhaps also candles, depending on the weather).	
	Do any necessary *furniture rearranging,* whatever *decoration* will stay "fresh."	
Early on the day	*Add flowers* (centerpiece, nosegays, corsages) to table, candles if they were postponed.	Take any feasible *preliminary recipe steps* (spreads, sauces, vegetable preparation, whipped cream; begin thawing of frozen foods; etc.).
	Prepare floral decorations elsewhere in house.	Prepare *salad* and refrigerate.
Hours (probably 2 to 4) before serving time	Check *bar setup:* ice supply, chilling facilities, cocktail napkins and coasters; set out snacks to be eaten with drinks.	Post a *list of foods* to be served so nothing gets forgotten.
	Make certain that *ashtrays,* lighters, perhaps cigarettes are in convenient places (unless you	The timing assumes a *main dish* (meat, poultry, stew, casserole) that will take several hours of preparation and cooking time.

PARTY COUNTDOWN	Basic party preparations	Food & cooking schedule
	wish to discourage smoking, as you well may).	*Vegetables,* potatoes, salad are either prepared or ready to be cooked. If rice is being served instead of potatoes, its cooking time will fit well within the allotted period.
	Take a final look at the *table,* to be sure it looks exactly as you intended.	
	Reserve time while food is cooking or "on hold" *to get yourself ready* in as relaxed a fashion as possible.	*Bread or rolls* need only be warmed, whether they were baked ahead or purchased.
		Dessert, too, will be on hand, whether baked or refrigerated.
		The first course can be prepared during this period (heated, say, if it is soup) or earlier (feasible with most appetizers).
Just before serving	If you will be serving mixed *cocktails* such as martinis, mix up a batch large enough for a first round.	Put *rolls or bread* into a slow oven to warm.
	If you *don't know* exactly what people will be drinking, have ice, glasses, liquor, and mixers lined up, and be ready with a hospitable "What's your pleasure?"	Plan to place the *first course* a half hour, say, into the before-dinner drinks period. Or, if you will be serving it in the living room with drinks, you can bring it in right away.

Keeping a party log

You will undoubtedly be making mental notes during the preparatory stages of your party and as the event itself unfolds. While these observations are fresh in your mind, why not put them down on paper? It will be useful for you to recall such things the next time you entertain:

About your "chore schedule"
- Did you allow too little time for any jobs? Forget one or two completely?
- Could you have used some outside kitchen help?

- Were you satisfied with your guests' reactions?
- Did you underestimate the time people would take over drinks before dinner?
- Might you have prepared far less of any food? Served fewer courses with no loss?

About the food you served

- Did the flowers last, or would you select something hardier another time?
- Was there too much on the table (was it "cluttered")?
- Were the candles the right size?

About your table

- Was the wine with dinner somewhat superfluous after all those before-dinner drinks? Should you have found some graceful way to "close" the bar?
- Would more glasses have been a good idea? Did you have clean ones for repeats without frantic in-between washing?

About the bar

- Did you provide adequately for guests' wraps so that there was no confusion, as people were leaving, about which coat was whose?
- Should sand or salt for the front walk have been added to your shopping list? Would an extra mat in the front hall have been a good idea?
- Is there anyone you will think twice about inviting again?

About your guests

These, of course, are hypothetical examples, intended to suggest the kind of afterthoughts a party can inspire. If you have a perfect memory, it won't need jogging, but if you're a mere mortal, a party log can be an immense help.

Maintaining an emergency larder

If you entertain often, or have friends who are inclined to turn up without warning, prepare yourself by stocking up on ingredients for favorite recipes and staples that you can convert speedily into a meal or snack, quick bread, or dessert. Such a larder, with its versatile inventory of basic needs, will also simplify planned parties.

Put in a supply, too, of "nibbling" foods—nuts, crackers, cheese spreads, the makings of a dip. These are handy to serve with an impromptu drink, or if cocktail appetizers run short.

The list that follows is broken down into pantry foods (cans, jars, bottles, packages) with an extended shelf life and foods that will keep under refrigeration, even after opening, for a comparatively long time. Freezers vary too widely—in capacity and reliability—to make many frozen food recommendations practical.

Conventional "bar foods" and garnishes are included, but not liquor. You may not want to keep a lot of liquor around, preferring to purchase for a party at the time. If you do keep quite an extensive array, only space might be a problem; except for opened bottles of wine, alcoholic beverages will never spoil.

Where large can or package sizes are practical—the foods that can be stored almost indefinitely or are usually consumed rapidly once opened—they can be economical buys, provided of course that you can spare the space to store them.

Pantry-shelf foods (in packages, cans, bottles, or jars)

Note: We leave it to your good sense to notice and observe the admonition "Refrigerate after opening" on any can or jar.

applesauce
baking powder, baking soda
bouillon cubes or instant broth
bread crumbs, croutons, cubes for stuffing
breakfast cereals
canned broths (beef, chicken)
cocoa, chocolate
coconut
coffee (including instant, perhaps espresso)
cornstarch
crackers
dried beans, peas, lentils, etc.
fish and seafood (tuna, salmon, sardines, shrimp, crabmeat, etc.)
flavorings (including liquors: brandy, rum, sherry); extracts (vanilla, lemon, etc.)
flours and meals
food coloring
fruit, fruit juices and drinks
gelatin
grated cheese
herbs and spices
honey
jams, jellies, preserves
meat extract
milk (condensed, evaporated, powdered)
mixes (cakes, muffins, pancakes, pastry; salad dressings; gelatin desserts and puddings; sauces, gravies, soups; seasonings for meats, poultry, chili, etc.)
molasses
mushrooms
nut-cereal snack mixes
nuts, whole, including unshelled; nut meats (longest-lasting in cans or jars)
pastas

pickles, olives, capers, cocktail onions and cherries
potato chips, cheese and corn snacks
processed meats (deviled ham, corned beef, roast beef, chopped chicken, liver pâtés)
raisins
relishes, mustard, ketchup
rice
salad oil, olive oil
sauces (barbecue, spaghetti, soy, Worcestershire, Tabasco)
seeds (caraway, poppy, sesame)
shortenings
soups
sugars (granulated, confectioner's, brown)
syrups
tapioca
tea
tomatoes (stewed tomatoes, tomato paste and puree, whole Italian tomatoes, etc.)
vinegars

Though potatoes, dried onions, and garlic do not properly classify as pantry-shelf foods, they are staples in the same sense as those listed, and should be kept on hand. Many of the foods that are listed—herbs and spices, baking powder and soda, nuts purchased in bags—lose freshness rapidly and so should be bought in prudent quantities. Many people, by preference, will put such condiments as mustard, ketchup, relishes, and pickles directly into the refrigerator, since they are often served chilled.

Refrigerated foods

dairy foods (milk and cream; cheeses, including cottage and cream cheese; sour cream and yogurt; butter and/or margarine)
dessert topping
eggs
horseradish
lemons and limes; celery
prepared pie crusts

Such foods as those immediately above cannot, of course, be kept indefinitely. The point is that they are almost indispensable in any kind of cooking and you should never, within reason, let yourself run out of those that are most basic.

Freezer storage (store-bought foods)

breads (spare standard loaves; party rye, French, or Italian bread; muffins, etc.)
fruits and vegetables (bulk bags are handiest)
fruit juice concentrates
ice cream and sherbets

One homemade basic that should be mentioned is soup stocks. Quantities are ordinarily large, too large to be used immediately. Divided into recipe portions and frozen in air-tight containers, they keep well for quite a long time—up to about 3 months. (Portioning is recommended because it simplifies getting only what you need for a quick soup base or for use in a recipe.)

Though amounts will be limited by your freezer's capacity, it is useful to know the storage conditions and approximate time periods for meat, fish and shellfish, and poultry. Besides being infinitely useful, such foods can frequently be bought more economically in quantity. First, a few general principles that apply to all:

• Quick freezing is important; cells break down when freezing is too slow, causing loss of juices.
• Use appropriate materials for packaging and get out as much air as possible. This helps prevent dehydration, with its damaging effect on flavor and texture.
• Don't thaw foods for too long a time. All should be cooked while they are still ice-cold; some can usually be cooked with no thawing at all (hamburger portions, chicken and turkey parts, fish fillets, chops).

Storing meat, fish, shellfish, and poultry in a home freezer

Raw meats (pork, beef, lamb, veal)
 Roasts: Trim fat; pad sharp or protruding bones. Pork will keep 6 months to a year; beef 6 months; lamb or veal, up to 9 months.
 Chops, steaks: Trim fat. Wrap in meal or recipe portions. Storage times same as roasts. Thin cuts can be cooked frozen.
 Meats cut (as for stew) or ground: Package in recipe quantities or portions. Will keep up to 4 months. Thaw cut meat sufficiently to separate; ground-meat portions can be cooked frozen.

Smoked meats and fresh sausage
 Ham and bacon: Trim fat from ham. Overwrap packaged bacon. Keeps for 1 to 2 months. Thaw before cooking.
 Fresh sausage: Whether bulk or in casings, freeze in meal- or recipe-size quantities. Keeps up to 2 months. Thaw before cooking.

Raw fish and shellfish
 Whole fish, fillets, or steaks: Clean as for cooking; leave wet. Individually wrap pieces; pack meal-size amounts in a bag or freezer container. Will keep from 3 to 6 months. Thaw slightly, or not at all, for cooking.
 Shrimp, clams, oysters, lobster: Clean raw shrimp (you need not shell unless you wish to); shuck clams or oysters; cook lobster and remove meat. Freeze shrimp, loosely packed, in containers; clams and oysters in juice with salt-water added to cover (a teaspoon of salt to a cup of water); lobster meat in containers.

Chicken, turkey, other poultry
   Whole: Rinse and freeze without stuffing; freeze giblets separately. Bird will keep 6 months; giblets, 2. Thaw until manageable.
   Parts: Rinse, sort if necessary. Wrap individually. Will keep up to 6 months. Thaw sufficiently to separate.

Cooked meats and poultry: Freeze roast, braised or stewed meat and poultry sliced, cubed, or chopped, adding gravy or broth to help preserve flavor. Keeps up to 3 months. Thaw and serve, or use in recipes.

Storing prepared foods in a home freezer

Casseroles, combination dishes: Undercook slightly or freeze before final baking, in containers or in baking dishes lined with heavy-duty foil. When storing food prepared in a baking dish, remove from dish and overwrap with foil. Keeps up to 3 months. Unwrap casserole mixture and place in dish, then thaw in refrigerator before warming to ensure even heating.
Breads, cakes, pies: Make as usual, cool before freezing. Freeze cakes unfrosted, or frost and freeze before covering with freezer wrap. Pies may be frozen unbaked. (Do not freeze custard or meringue pies.) These foods will keep for 3 to 6 months. Thaw before unwrapping to prevent condensation of moisture on food as it thaws. Unbaked pies need not be thawed, even those in ovenproof glass plates; just place in preheated oven.

The Demands of Formal and Special Occasions

As long as parties stay small and comparatively casual, like those described on pages 136 to 159, the job of "getting it all together" is not too exacting. Make a few phone calls, select and shop for your menu, round up the necessary equipment and, with the addition of fresh flowers and some supplements to the bar, your party is well in hand. It is when the guest list grows larger, and the event more formal, more social, more special, that planning takes on its real importance. The parties and menus on pages 203 to 214 are all in this demanding category. What follows will introduce you briefly to occasions of this more complex kind. After the review, we suggest that you run your eye over the menus and try to picture yourself doing what is involved in the meal and the other party preparations. When you do, we think you will appreciate the value of a step-by-step Party Countdown and understand why we have recommended that you set one up for yourself.

Formal dinners and lunches

You will notice, as you glance at our menus for formal dinners and lunches, that they are all designed for a guest list of eight. If your facilities can accommodate more people for a formal sit-down meal, there is certainly no objection to larger parties. Eight is the recommended maximum—the largest number most people can gracefully cook for and serve without household help.

A point that may be confusing: Should the term be "lunch" or "luncheon"? The two are often used interchangeably and either is correct. But unless the event is quite social, or an official or business occasion, "luncheon" can sound faintly pretentious.

Though many of the traditional niceties still apply to a formal meal, to dinner especially, we are blessedly free of most of the rigidities. Time was when only silver candelabra were permissible, and bowls of flowers. Not only was there specified china, flatware, and stemware for each of the many courses, but there was wine with each—and a waiter for every six guests. Tablecloths could be white damask only.

Servants being (for almost everyone) out of the question, what remains of formality is largely a matter of the menu and its service, plus some conventions covering the behavior of both hosts and guests. For example, punctuality is not just good manners; the meal is not served until all guests have arrived. Guests stand and chat, in deference to the hostess, until she is seated. The serving of pre-dinner cocktails is generally kept to a period of about half an hour, so dinner foods needn't suffer the effects of "holding."

No *formal dinner* today, not even the most official, has more than six courses; most are confined to four. Most often eliminated are the once mandatory fish course and either the appetizer or the soup, custom having conceded that one or the other is enough. Sometimes both of these remain and there is no salad course. Typically, formal four-course menus consist of one of these combinations of foods:

A. Appetizer or soup   B. Appetizer
   Meat and vegetables   Soup
   Salad   Meat and vegetables
   Dessert   Dessert

Beverages during the meal are only water and wine. Wines are served at the host or hostess's discretion. The usual number is two, one with the meal and a dessert wine with the last course; sometimes sherry will appear with the soup. Champagne, if you want to throw caution and cost accounting to the winds, can be served throughout a meal. Demitasses (French for "small cups") are served at its close, with liqueurs if you wish, away from the table.

Formal lunches/luncheons, in all but a few respects, are closely akin to formal dinners. The accepted lunch hour is one o'clock; the guests don't linger after the meal for much longer than half an hour. Three courses are customary and ample; if wine is served, a decision that is totally optional, one wine is sufficient; mats or table runners may take the place of a cloth. Coffee should be hot and preferably demitasse; liqueurs are not usual, but that is up to you.

For comments about degrees of formality in invitation mode and style, see page 18. Details about table plans, settings, and service appear on pages 120 to 133 of Part II.

Holidays and other "red letter" days

These occasions have one notable characteristic in common: They are all big days—in the life of the nation or of the world, of some community or individual. Also, of course, because they loom so large in people's hearts (and sometimes, brightly lettered, on their calendars), celebrations of these holidays tend to have a ritual flavor and great human warmth. But there the similarities end; each has an observance ritual and customs of its own.

Our holiday menus pay homage, each in a very different way, to five holidays. These menus are designed in contrasting styles to illustrate how well tradition can be served by today's more flexible attitudes toward entertaining.

Holiday hospitality

Easter, a day of deep reverence for Christians, is appropriately observed with a breakfast-brunch, an informal and friendly kind of get-together. Thanksgiving loses none of its meaning when the family circle is widened and the time-honored dishes are served buffet-style. Christmas dinner is customarily at the table but it could, in the same expansive spirit, be a buffet; the choice depends on how you can best serve the number of people you want to welcome. For New Year's Eve, we feel the right note is struck by the supper, a delightful after-the-party custom that is just as lightly refreshing after a movie, concert, or afternoon on skis. Finally, to mark the Fourth of July, what better choice than that most carefree of holiday observances, the picnic you can carry wherever the action is!

Table and house decorations for such national holidays require very little ingenuity or research. Each of us has his or her homegrown traditions, from our own way of decorating eggs or trimming trees to a special recipe for stuffing. For Christmas, the stores are full of made-for-the-purpose china, glassware, tablecloths, and placemats, in designs dignified and jolly, that are generally not very costly and can be kept from year to year. If you "do" your house for the holidays, you need not add much to the existing array—perhaps only a centerpiece that echoes the theme, and some strategically placed flowers or flowering plants. If you will be sending invitations, as you will want to do for a large party, be sure to peruse the "designs of the day" featured by your stationer.

Big days in your life

The red letter days for individuals or families are weddings and anniversaries, birthdays, graduations and promotions, reunions, births, moves to a new house or a new town. These are joys people like to share, sometimes with just one other person or a small group of intimates but often with a roomful, even a houseful, of friends. You will find menus for a host of such sentimental occasions—a reception, an open house, a housewarming—on pages 199 to 210.

One difficulty you can face, when you try to combine a large crowd with a party of great personal importance, is retaining the warmth you want the event to have. If it is a housewarming, you might invite smaller groups at several different times; this makes it simpler, as well, to conduct leisurely tours of the house and give time and attention to questions. If it is a one-time event, however, such as a wedding reception or an anniversary party, you must manage as best you can.

You can begin to set the tone with your invitations, making clear how significant the party is, and to whom. Explain your relation to the guest or guests of honor, if that is applicable. Such details send a human message that people are quick to respond to; you will find your guests rising to the occasion and helping you to make it a success.

Much depends, of course, on your own manner and menu, your thoughtfulness about decor and service, your attention to guests' needs and wants. All these pay a compliment to the assembled company that will come back to you as appreciation and enjoyment. And nothing warms a room like enthusiasm!

Certain parties require special gestures. To housewarmings and anniversary parties, for example, guests usually bring gifts. They won't expect you to open them in the flurry of other activities, but have a place ready to put them on display. Another gesture, not necessary but nice, is a record book for guests to sign at parties where you are introducing new people. It will be treasured by the newcomers long after the party as a remembrance (and useful, too, if phone numbers and addresses have been provided by guests who sign).

Except for these little human touches and the hope for a somewhat warmer atmosphere, one big party can be very much like another. Whether you are a cocktail party devotee or not, we recommend that you read the section that follows. The suggestions in it will help you cater to any crowd, whether they are close friends, casual acquaintances, or total strangers.

Cocktail parties

Though they are not everyone's idea of a good time, one thing must be said in favor of cocktail parties: They make it possible to entertain many more people than most homes could accommodate for a meal.

When you are expecting a lot of people, free as much space as you can, rearranging furniture and perhaps even moving a few pieces to somewhere else in the house. Put away, too, any valuable possessions that might be broken; with so many people going in and out, accidents can easily happen. Wraps, especially in cold or otherwise bad weather, can be too much for a bedroom or closet. Rather than risk a soggy mess, rent a coatrack or two, and let wet coats drip dry on the shower rail.

Unless yours is a "no smoking" house, put plenty of ashtrays and matches or lighters around. Cigarettes are rarely supplied at parties any more, as guests generally prefer their own brands. Be sure the ashtrays are emptied regularly (a child who is old enough can do this for you); they are natural catchalls at cocktail parties.

Bar service

People won't expect you to serve every imaginable drink, but you should have a reasonable selection: gin and/or vodka, a whiskey or two (one of them Scotch), sherry, soft drinks, and sparkling water or tonic.

Bar placement is important; you want traffic to flow freely around it. If possible, set up a second bar in the dining room or den. For a very large party, a bartender could be a wise investment; you may know a student who could use the extra cash. Another way to manage a large number: mix the drinks in the kitchen and pass them around on trays (or have a party assistant do it for you). For parties given by one person with no help, an excellent approach is to mix the first drinks for guests, then let them serve themselves for refills.

Remember the constant refills, which call for clean glasses. If you're not sure you have enough glasses, rent some extras. At an informal party, plastic glasses will do, but rentals aren't very expensive and glass is far better. Have plenty of cocktail napkins—stacked on the bar or handed out with every drink, with extras for guests taking hors d'oeuvres from a tray. Coasters should be plentiful, too. (These can be disposable.)

Food

In planning a cocktail party, you have a wide range of choices where food is concerned. (For selections see pages 204, 229, 241 to 242.) You can serve a virtually full meal—enough, that is, for guests to consider it a meal if they like. If the meal is this substantial, your party is really a cocktail buffet. Or you can serve walking-around foods, tidbits of finger food that are satisfying with drinks but not filling. Phrase your invitation so that it is clear whether or not the food will be a buffet. This will avoid misunderstandings when the specified time overlaps the normal dinner hour—and it is definitely a kindness to people who will be traveling some distance.

Outdoor meals

Before we get to particulars, a word of reassurance to those of you whose outdoor facilities are limited to a tiny apartment terrace or an almost-as-small backyard: You don't have to have a huge yard, or a pool or patio, to give open-air parties. Your guest list may be smaller but your menu can take any direction you like, from family-style picnic to elegant buffet. In fact, with so little distance between kitchen and party, you may have an advantage where elegance is concerned. You need not worry, for one thing, about foods staying hot or cold "on the way." Should you require more ice cubes, simply empty another tray. If the lack of a "setting" bothers you, be your own exterior designer with masses of plants and greens.

At night, lighting becomes an important feature of any decor, for practical as well as aesthetic reasons. It should be soft but ample, and protected against passing breezes. On a table or similar surface, you might use recessed candles (wax and wick well below the rim of an iron or other pot) or hurricane lamps. Some lanterns give good light; those of perforated metal or pottery are charming but not very functional. Out on the grass, where there is a place to insert them, torches can be effective for both illumination and decoration. At an evening poolside party, never mind appearances; just light the area generously for safety's sake.

Food for an outdoor party

The menu will depend more on guest list and time of day than on such distinctions as "casual" or "elegant." During the day, children are likely to be among the participants, and they like plain food and plenty of it. When the party is "adults only," you can go a bit more gourmet. Our al fresco menus (pages 249 to 267) go to the suitable extremes—plain and fancy, day and night, with and without children.

If an event is planned in celebration of a special occasion, use real china and glassware—no paper or plastic. The china and serving equipment can be rustic—baskets, pottery, earthenware—but it should be "the genuine article." One exception: Use plastic glasses at parties near a pool. Even when children are not present, liquor often is, and that makes real glasses risky.

Invitations to home outdoor parties

Except for very large or conspicuously social events, telephoning is perfectly acceptable. Just be very explicit about the nature of the party. Specify among other things: whether the event planned will be casual or otherwise (asking guests, for example, to bring a change of clothes to a swim party if lunch or dinner will be served indoors instead of at the pool); exactly what time; do or do not bring the children. Give guests a clue about clothes so they won't be embarrassed by wearing the wrong thing. Many hostesses like caftans or long skirts for summer entertaining; guests need not go to exactly these lengths, but they will want to select something appropriate. For a pool or beach party, let people know if you would like them to bring their own towels, perhaps beach towels or bath sheets because you don't have enough mats for everyone to lie on. Suggest bringing a light wrap or sweater if you think the weather might turn chilly.

Any party in the yard is likely to be plagued by insects. In addition to insect repellent, consider using insect strips or one of those devices that burns "incense" to keep flying creatures away. It is sensible to spray the area some hours before the party—long enough ahead for the smell to dissipate.

Protection of another kind—against rain or very hot sun—can be secured in advance from a rental agency. Possibilities are table umbrellas (these you might be able to borrow), tents, marquees, canopies, and awnings. You could specify a rain date but it is preferable to get the garage or carport clean enough to offer protection from inclement weather.

Invite only adaptable people when there is the possibility that your guests may have to "rough it" at a beach party or picnic.

Parties away from home

The picnic is far and away the most popular portable meal; tailgate picnics, barbecues, and beach parties may be trendier, but they are just picnics by other names. When you see advertisements for picnic gear, with tidy containers tucked into an impressive wicker carrier, don't be tempted unless you have discretionary funds to burn. At a picnic, it isn't the containers that matter; it's the food. Styrofoam containers are light, cheap, and efficient insulators; plastic bags, from food-storage to trash-can size, are leakproof and can carry wet towels and swimsuits back home. (Don't ever, incidentally, rely on ice for *chilling* to serve as ice for *drinks*. Keep the two carefully separate.)

Whether you make do or buy new, be sure you are equipped to carry any foods you plan to take along, in the right shape at the right temperature. If there will be hot dishes, is it best to heat them on the spot or pack them in an insulated container? Red wine has an advantage, if it is appropriate to the meal; it needs neither chilling nor warming.

Take things to sit or lie on, and to serve as a table; old sheets, blankets, or tablecloths will do, on the ground or to cover a picnic table and benches. (A folding card table, legs still tucked underneath, makes a fine picnic table.)

Equipment needs to be listed, collected, and cleaned. List foods in detail; it is all too easy to forget something you have made well ahead. You will have your own inventory of needs, but these are some often overlooked necessities: can and bottle openers; salt, pepper, and sugar (somehow mustard and ketchup are easier to remember); plastic bags for toting away garbage; fuel for portable grill; extra utensils, plates, cups or mugs, and napkins.

Do as much food and other preparation ahead as you can. If the meal is portable, know exactly how you plan to pack it and have the equipment rounded up and ready. Even when the party is to be held at home, advance preparation is advisable. It will make the occasion much more fun for you. When it is a pool or beach party, you want some time to swim, and you need enough freedom from distractions to keep an eye on other swimmers, particularly children, unless someone volunteers to do this for you.

When some of the swimmers are children, don't assume that they will be "just fine" because some are old enough to watch the young ones—*or* that parents will look out for their own. Establish your own water rules and explain them to the children, even paddlers and waders. Be firm about infractions; if you say "out of the water," make it stick.

Leave the site as clean as you possibly can; be sure all fires are out—no smoldering embers, nothing buried in the sand to give a barefoot passerby a painful burn.

Parties that make their own patterns

These are events that don't quite fit any of the conventional molds: *brunches,* a cross between breakfast and lunch born because Sunday is, for many people, the only leisurely day in the week; *buffets,* ideal when the celebration mandates the invitation of more guests than your dining facilities can accommodate at table; *teas and coffees,* a glorification of the custom of "serving a little something" when neighbors come to call; and *children's parties.*

Brunches

To many, especially those who like to sleep late, these informal combinations of breakfast and lunch blend the best of both. The appointed hour is 11 A.M. (Specified on the invitation, the early hour implies a fairly small party and asks for punctuality; an open-ended phrase, such as "after eleven," suggests a larger gathering and continuous food service through midday with acceptable arrival any time within, say, an hour of the stated time.) The menu, too, generally includes something typical of breakfast and lunch. The starter might be tomato juice, perhaps as a Bloody Mary; bullshots (beef bouillon and vodka for the uninitiated) are also favorite brunch beginners. Cereals and salads are both rarities, but main dishes often include (from breakfast) scrambled eggs with bacon, ham, sausages, or kippers; and (from lunch) creamed chicken or seafood on toast. Desserts are breakfast sweets: waffles, pancakes, sweet rolls, doughnuts, coffee cake, Danish pastry.

Buffet-style entertaining

Buffet service is favored with any sizeable group; even guests in a group small enough to seat at a single table often help themselves to at least a dish or two. Service is informal, even with a maid or other helper to clear away plates and glasses and replenish servers.

The canny host or hostess will, at any buffet, steer clear of foods that demand last-minute attention or elaborate service. Instead of both turkey and ham, for example, select a meat that can be kitchen-carved, or a meal-in-a-dish, such as a robust soup, stew, or casserole, that guests can serve themselves. It is wise to choose foods that can be kept at the appropriate temperature for second helpings, and acquire warming or chilling equipment to make it doubly certain.

An unusual holiday mantelpiece, adorned
with ropes of princess pine and wreaths
of birch branches and English holly.

"Greens" of many hues dress up a room
for any occasion.

A well-stocked party bar.

A wide variety of
available gear makes
parties away from
home easy to take
along.

Virtually any beverage can be served with the main course—water, wine, beer, iced tea. Coffee is usually postponed until dessert, but it need not be. The main-course beverage can be served any way that is convenient: filled cups or glasses lined up on the buffet, or passed on a tray to seated guests, or poured for them when they are seated.

Dessert service is just as flexible. A maid or helper can clear away used plates and glasses, then put dessert on the buffet or pass it. With no help, as is most often the case, the hostess must manage this herself, perhaps with an assist from a volunteer. It is probably best for her to ask guests to serve themselves, and for the host or hostess to take care of clearing. Coffee (a fresh pot if it's the second time around) can either be on the buffet with the dessert, or passed when guests have returned to their seats.

Our buffet menus (pages 203, 207, 240 to 249) lend themselves to self-service, complete or partial as you wish. If this serving style is new to you, examine the equipment options in Part II; some of the new equipment is most ingenious. Check the section on drinks as well, whether your bar will be a big item or a small one.

Teas and coffees

At their simplest—one friend, or a few, invited to share a warming cup—tea and coffee parties are much alike. Coffee is customarily a morning break and tea an afternoon pickup, but not always. "Dessert and coffee," perhaps because it is almost effortless when properly planned, has become a favorite form of after-dinner socializing; tea is sometimes savored the Irish way, in the evening. Whether it is tea or coffee, for two or twenty, one or more sweets accompany the beverage; for large groups, an assortment of tiny sandwiches is added.

Americans still look to coffee for the daily sustenance the English get from tea. Only the coffee parties of the South, New Orleans in particular, retain any formality to speak of. Coffee and sweets can both be made more eventful by giving them a continental flair and flavor. Iced coffee, too, can be done in a grand manner—see page 236 for some suggestions.

Tea lends itself to entertaining, even informal parties retaining a ceremonial charm. A delightful way to honor a guest or enchant a circle of friends, tea parties are conducted according to prescribed procedure.

- A cloth-covered table (dining or other long table, elongated if it extends; a tea-size cloth in white or a delicate color, traditionally linen, often embroidered or appliqued).
- Tea service on an uncovered tray at one end: a pot of tea; boiling water (preferably over a flame) for weakening tea; sugar (granules or cubes, with spoon or tongs); a pitcher of milk (not cream); thin slices of lemon.
- Coffee service on a tray (also bare) at the opposite end: pot of coffee (preferably on a warmer); sugar; milk or cream.
- Acting as hostesses at each end two friends who have been enlisted (in advance) to pour so that the hostess can attend to her other duties, such as introducing guests to one another.

Sideboard buffet.

Tea tray in the Japanese style.

- In between the tea and coffee trays, platters of small sandwiches and sweets.
- Also small plates for guests (who will serve themselves), along with the necessary napkins (one can be placed on each plate in the stack, if space is limited or you just like the idea).

Invitations to coffee or tea parties may be telephoned if the list is small and the event casual; they should be written, perhaps on fold-over informals, for a larger, more social occasion, such as a party in honor of a visiting celebrity or other special guest.

There are almost as many theories about the making of good tea as there are people with pots. About some things, however, there seems to be general agreement: the pot should be made of a material that holds heat; the pot should be hot when teamaking begins; the water for tea should be not just boiling but freshly boiled (that is the reason for the flame under the water meant for weakening). Some say tea bags are all right; some insist only loose tea will do. One school of thought holds that the tea should be very strong in the pot, and always weakened at least a little with water at the tea table, to cut the flavor somewhat. Experiment until you find a method that pleases you, and be adventurous about trying teas you have never tasted. You may come to understand, if you are not already a tea lover, why it inspires such devotion in the people of England and the Far East.

"Good" coffee, and the "best" way to brew it, is really a matter of personal preference. Whether you favor a mild or robust blend, an old-fashioned percolator or the sleekest electric filter system, serve coffee hot and make sure to keep it hot for those coffee-loving guests who are sure to come back for more.

For tea and coffee menus, simple and elaborate, hot and cold, see pages 224 to 239.

Parties are steps in the socializing of youngsters and it is important to take into account how much camaraderie they can handle at any given age. Until a child is at least three, festivities are best confined to eating ice cream and birthday cake and opening presents. Children who attend any sort of preschool grow accustomed to the company, and the competition, of others their own age; they will soon be comfortable sharing the fun and the spotlight. Other children may need a year of regular school attendance to achieve a similar degree of social composure.

Parties for the very young, then, should start small and never get too big. The number of guests will increase but it is better if they are all friends, not strangers. Food, too, should be familiar and portions not too large—except for dessert, which children this age see as the main course. Children revel in bright colors and parties with themes; games tied to the themes seem to encourage participation. Neither the games nor the party

Children's parties

47

Creative setting for a children's party.

should go on too long; when children tire, as they do quickly, irritability sets in—and they haven't yet learned to cope with it.

Very early in their school years, children begin to develop a veneer of sophistication. This may be surface worldliness, but they take it seriously and hate to be patronized. While they are younger than they like to think, you must still control events, preferably without seeming to. Accomplish this by planning what they will eat and what they will do at the party. Then let go, and observe from a safe distance while they make their own good time.

Tastes will be broader at this age, but foods should still be ones that young people take to. Have a little fun with the menu and the decor, getting advice about both from your offspring. They will know what is or is not too "babyish" for their friends.

When they become teenagers, your children should be in on all of the planning—timing, occasion, menu, and activities—perhaps even location. Exert what influence you can in advance but be prepared, on the day of the party, to see matters taken completely out of your hands. You should be accustomed, by this time, to loud music. If you are not, don't nag; just make yourself scarce. The menu should be simple and designed to permit a lot of fix-it-yourself.

Part II

⇓ ⇓ ⇓

Getting Organized

Special dishes for serving and entertaining (left to right): large oven-proof casserole, footed compote, au gratin dish, asparagus platter, terra cotta soufflé, corn-on-the-cob dish, napkin ring with salt and pepper shakers, terra cotta quiche mold, scallop shell, crescent salad plate, artichoke plate, plate for beef fondue.

Cooking and Serving Equipment

The working tools in an "entertainer's" kitchen may be few but versatile, or a highly specialized collection. It all depends on the tastes and style of the resident chef. Memorable parties can be turned out of a small kitchen (in size and/or facilities) when the host or hostess has mastered the preparation and serving of a few classic dishes—and the art of sitting back and letting the guests enjoy the food and each other.

On the other hand, when both chef and guests like to experience new tastes, cuisines, and culinary creations, the food itself becomes part of the entertainment, and the kitchen must be ready to accommodate all kinds of activity, even watching or participating by your guests. A well-equipped kitchen is a necessity, too, in homes where entertainment is frequent and fairly formal. Whoever cooks for such occasions, whether home talent or hired, requires a full complement of hardware.

In this chapter you will find an overview of numerous items of cooking and serving equipment. You will probably find that you already own much, if not all, the items necessary for your style of entertaining. You may want to supplement your existing equipment by purchasing or borrowing (for special occasions).

BASICS FOR COOKING

First up is a quick rundown of kitchen equipment, some of which you may already have for regular, everyday meals. Except for preparing very large quantities, these basic utensils will probably see you through all but the most complex recipes and party menus. (Suggestions for quantity food preparation are given on page 63.)

Stove-top cookware

This includes all utensils that can go directly over gas or electric ranges. Sizes given are either full capacity in quarts (and sometimes liters), or top diameter, rim-to-rim, in inches (and sometimes centimeters) for shallow items such as skillets, griddles, etc. Metric sizes specified in liters (L), milliliters (mL) and centimeters (cm) are close approximations, not exact equivalents, of customary sizes. Equipment will be labeled with actual sizes in either system or in both.

3 saucepans: 1, 2, and 4 qt. (1, 2, and 4 L) with lids
1 Dutch oven: 5 or 6 qt. (5 or 6 L)
1 double boiler: 1½ or 2 qt. (1.5 or 2 L)
2 skillets: 8 and 10 in. (20 and 25 cm) with lids

53

Professional quality stock or stew pot.

Ovenware

Utensils for both baking and roasting are made in a wide range of sizes, usually given as inside dimensions or full capacity, sometimes both. A choice of size in the larger items such as cookie sheets and roasting pans might depend on your oven's dimensions.

This will be a basic assortment:

1 casserole with cover: 1½ or 2 qt. (1½ or 2 L)
2 layer cake pans: 8 or 9 in. (20 or 23 cm)
1 loaf pan: 9 × 5 × 3 in. (23 × 13 × 8 cm)
2 cookie sheets: 14 × 10 in. or larger (36 × 25 cm)
1 tube cake pan, Bundt type: 9 or 12 cup (2.1 or 2.8 L)
1 muffin pan: 12 cups, 2½ × 1¼ in. (6 × 3 cm)
1 roasting or baking pan with rack: 14 × 10 in. or larger (36 × 25 cm), 2 in. (5 cm) deep
1 or 2 pie pans: 8 or 9 in. (20 or 23 cm)
1 baking pan or dish: 13 × 9 × 2 in. (33 × 23 × 5 cm)

Mixing, measuring, and cooking tools

The list below includes all the accessories needed to put a meal together, but you might want more than one of some items, to avoid washing between steps in a recipe.

Spatulas and turners: 1 long and 1 short spatula for spreading and icing, 1 turner for eggs, etc., 1 rubber spatula for bowl scraping.

Spoons: 2 metal (1 slotted or perforated), 1 wooden for stirring (can be left in mixture without getting hot).

Forks: Large, two-tined fork for lifting, turning, carving.

Mixing bowls: A set of 3, 4, or more for mixing, tossing, and combining and for food storage in refrigerator (preferably with lids).

Grater: 4-sided from fine to coarse, stainless steel to avoid rusting.

Colander, wire strainer: 1 of each for draining and straining.

Rolling pin: 10 in. barrel with ball-bearing action.

Cutting and carving boards: Small and large of hardwood, Plexiglass, or glass-ceramic.

Knives: A good set—1 paring, 1 utility, 1 carving, 1 slicer, 1 serrated bread knife, and 1 chef's knife. For peeling, a swivel-bladed slotted peeler (vegetable peeler).

Juicer: Electric juicer or glass, plastic, or metal hand reamer.

Egg beater and whisk: Electric mixer or rotary beater and an 11 in. long wire whisk for many whipping and smoothing jobs.

Graduated set of measures for dry ingredients; 3 pitcher cups for liquids, holding 1 cup, 2 cups, and 1 quart; at least 1 set of graduated measuring spoons.

Miscellaneous tools: Can opener, bottle opener, corkscrew, timer, cooling racks for cakes, shears, tongs, knife sharpener, apple corer, skewers for trussing and stuffing poultry, roast meat thermometer, funnel, soup ladle, ice cream scoop, tea kettle.

Appliances

The basic group usually includes toaster or toaster/oven, blender, portable mixer, and coffeemaker. Some also consider a slow cooker and electric frypan among the basics.

ADD-ONS FOR MORE ADVENTUROUS COOKING

To the basics you can add cookware and gadgets galore that will equip you to handle almost any recipe in the "gourmet" category. But don't feel you must run out and buy every possibility listed. It takes even dedicated cooks years to accumulate such a collection. It's more fun to buy and learn to use things one at a time, whether it's a butter curler or a food processor.

Stove-top cookware

You can buy duplicates of the basic saucepans, pots, and skillets, or go to larger sizes. A cookware collection of special shapes, sizes, and constructions, however, is more versatile. It allows you to match a recipe with its traditional utensil, and even serve in it; to cook for two or twenty; and to control heat by choice of material as well as by a turn of the stove dial. Here is a list of possibilities to consider:

**Sauté pans,
round or oval**

These flat-bottomed, straight-sided, heavy pans are deeper than skillets so splattering is reduced when food is being sautéd. A chef often will shake the pan, and the high sides keep food from sliding out. Pans should be large enough for food to brown quickly and without crowding; an oval is a good shape for long cutlets and fish fillets. Dutch ovens can be used if they are heavy enough for food to brown nicely; in fact, some pans are called Dutch-sauté and serve many purposes.

A useful choice: 1 or 2 sauté pans in 10 or 12 in. (25 or 30 cm) size with lids.

Crêpe pan

One with a 6 or 7 in. (15 or 18 cm) bottom diameter can double as an individual omelet pan. For larger omelets, an 8 or 10 in. (20 or 25 cm) pan (top diameter) will do nicely. Both crêpe and omelet pans have sloping sides to make lifting and turning easy. Pans need not be heavy for these quick-cooking foods, but should have good heat distribution.

Pressure cooker

A 4 qt. (4 L) size is useful for tenderizing tough cuts of meat, as well as speedy cooking of root vegetables, stews, beans, etc.

Saucepans

In addition to basic sizes, a 1½ pt. (750 mL), plus a 3 or 3½ qt. (3 or 3.5 L) with a double boiler insert, a perforated steamer insert, and a lid will greatly expand your sauce and vegetable preparation options.

Stock pot or kettle

Six to 8 qt. (6 to 8 L) pot with lid for boiling bones for stock, cooking large amounts of sauces, stews, preserves, etc. With a perforated steamer insert, it can be used for vegetables, puddings, shellfish, blanching vegetables for freezing.

Deep fat fryer

This can be simply a wire or perforated basket that fits into a deep saucepan, a complete 2-piece set, or an electric fryer/cooker. For safe frying, the pan should be deeper than it is wide, yet broad enough to take a fair amount of food. If you think that a deep fat fryer is strictly for fast-food addicts, try beignets and homemade croquettes.

Griddle

Square or rectangular, large enough to fit over one or two stove-top units. Electric griddles with heat control can be used at keep-warm setting for buffet foods.

About 18 in. (46 cm) long and 8 in. (20 cm) wide, with a rack and lid, for gently simmering a whole fish and removing it intact.

Fish poacher

Ovenware

For this, you can check through favorite cookbooks and food pages of magazines to see what special pans and dishes you might need on occasion. Some choices to think about:

Soufflé dishes are generally 1½ or 2 qt. (1.5 or 2 L).

Soufflé dishes

You may want several sizes and shapes—shallow and deep; square, round, or oval; with or without lids. Since food is usually served right from casseroles, they should be attractive. Some can be set in a cradle or basket to protect the table, or you can use a trivet.

Casseroles

This includes all somewhat shallow dishes or pans, without covers, designed to provide a large area for top-browning or crust, whether for a cake, cobbler, baked pasta dish, or crumb-topped creamed combination. Beyond the 13 × 9 × 2 in. suggested, there are smaller and larger rectangular ones, plus some very decorative round and oval dishes.

Baking dishes

Really a baking dish, but oval or round and made of a material that can go under a broiler as well as into the oven, usually porcelain-on-iron, stainless steel, copper, or ceramic. They come in many sizes, from individual ones about 8 in. (20 cm) long to large ones 11 in. (28 cm) long.

Au gratin dishes

This can be used for baking cookies, meringues, and hot hors d'oeuvres as well as sponge cakes. Size is generally 15½ × 10½ × 1 in. (39 × 27 × 3 cm).

Jelly roll or sponge cake pan

Has removable sides for gentle handling of delicate desserts such as cheese cakes, mousses, charlottes, or tortes that would break if turned out. The most common and useful size is 9 × 3 in. (23 × 8 cm).

Spring form pan

A heavy, loaf-shaped pan or dish with a cover for the long, slow baking of ground meat mixtures or pâtés.

Pâté terrine

This is simply a pie dish or pan with fluted sides, made of ceramic rather than glass or metal.

Quiche pan or dish

These come in sizes from miniature to 8, 9, 10, and 11 in. (20, 23, 25, and 28 cm) in diameter. Made of metal, the larger ones have a loose bottom so that it, and the finished tart, can be pushed up and out of the ring that forms the sides, then placed on a serving plate. Used for French apple (or other fruit) tarts, quiches, tart shells.

Tart pans

French bread and Pain de Mie pans	These enclose or restrict bread dough to form it into loaves of traditional shapes.
Flan pan or ring	Similar to a tart pan but may have a second (alternate) bottom with a circular raised area in the center. When a cake baked in such a pan is turned out, it will have a center depression that can be filled with fruit, custard, cream, etc. A flan ring (or rectangle) is set on a baking sheet to form and hold a pastry shell while it bakes, as a tart pan does.
Miscellaneous pans, dishes, and molds	Add any that fit favorite recipes, such as popover, brioche, or cornstick pans, custard cups and ramekins, bean pots, clay roasters, special cake pans for holidays and weddings.

Mixing, measuring, and cooking tools

To tempt the advanced or adventurous cook, stores are overflowing with gadgets and tools. Acquisition of many of these can lead to overflowing drawers and cupboards at home, so be selective. A condition sometimes called "gourmania" has inspired such silliness as a gadget that presses hard-boiled eggs into cubes, another that scrambles a raw egg inside its shell with an electrified needle. Fortunately, many tools are useful (some almost indispensable), well designed, well made, and even fun to use. This is a sampling:

Scales in customary and metric measures	You might need two if you weigh foods often, one that weighs up to 10 lbs. (4.5 kg) by ounces and grams for recipe amounts, another that goes up to 25 lbs. (11.4 kg) for meat, poultry, and produce.
Thermometers	In addition to the basic meat roasting thermometer, you might want one for candy-making, deep fat frying, yeast and yogurt, and an instant-reading thermometer for checking roasts in regular and microwave ovens, or monitoring any mixture for proper cooking or serving temperature, as when reheating food.
Scoops	For shaping ice cream balls, making meatballs, serving salad mixtures. Also a melon baller with a large scoop at one end and a small scoop at the other end.
Cookie cutters	And perhaps a cookie press, biscuit and doughnut cutters, tiny assorted cutters for pastry cut-outs and fancy canapés. A croissant cutter is a barrel-shaped wheel that is rolled over a strip of dough, cutting it into triangles which can be rolled up to form crescents. A pastry wheel cuts strips for a lattice-top pie in a zigzag pattern. A pizza wheel can be used also for straight cutting of pastry, noodle, and pasta dough as well as baked pizza.

Boning, pineapple and melon (a longer version of the curved, serrated grapefruit knife, also nice to have), clam and oyster opening knife, cleaver, butcher knife (to cut large pieces of meat into desired cuts), one or two more chef's and paring knives. Don't forget a lemon zester; one with a slot peels a strip of rind for drinks, etc., one with five tiny holes at the end cuts lemon or orange rind into fine, long shreds for garnishing and sauces.

Knives to consider adding to the basic set

Wood or metal mallet that can break up tough meat fibers and cartilage with the notched, pointed side, flatten slices of veal, chicken breast, or beef for sautéing (or stuffing and rolling) with the smooth side.

Meat pounder, tenderizer

A metal or plastic cup with a tight lid is handy for shaking a flour and water mixture used to thicken liquids. Sifters are rarely used for flour these days, but are convenient for confectioner's sugar. Dredgers are large cups with tight-fitting perforated tops for shaking flour or granulated or confectioner's sugar onto food or a work surface.

Shakers, sifters, and dredgers

An ingenious merry-go-round that does a good job of removing the excess water that can ruin a salad. The vegetables or greens go into an inner, perforated basket after washing, the lid with rotating handle spins the basket, and water drains quickly into the outer bowl.

Salad or vegetable spinner

This purees and strains seeds from cooked apples or tomatoes, serves as a sieve for any soft food. Its rotating paddle, attached to a handle, makes pureeing fast and easy. For a finer puree, there is a drum sieve with a fine mesh screen stretched across the bottom of a circular frame, usually wood. This also can be used to sift flour over a pastry or bread board. A conical sieve that purees in the fashion of a food mill is called "chinois"—a wooden, cone-shaped pestle (pusher) is rotated around the sieve to force food out through the holes in the cone. These come with a stand or a hook on the rim to fit over a bowl. Even if you own an electric food processor, a food mill or sieve is a necessity for removing skin and seeds from cooked fruits and vegetables.

Food mill

A pepper mill belongs in every kitchen; some have two grinders, one for white peppercorns, another for black. (Purists prefer white pepper in light-colored and white sauces, soufflés, and soups.) A nutmeg grater is also a good, "fresh" idea.

Graters and mills

A pastry cloth, or a plastic sheet with a series of circles to guide in shaping and sizing; special rolling pins for different doughs (tarts, strudel, pasta, etc.); pastry blender with wires or blades to blend flour and fat; pie weights (little metal nuggets) to keep unfilled pie shells from puffing as they bake; pastry bag and tubes for decorating cakes and piping out potatoes, cream puff batter, whipped cream; pastry brush for basting and glazing, with bristles of tampico (nylon can melt), or goose feathers for a gentle brushing of tender pastry; a pastry board scraper with a wide blade (5 or 6 in.) to clean the surface and scoop up dough.

Pastry aids

59

Miscellaneous tools

Vegetable brush; trussing needle (to be used with twine); garlic press; ice crusher; fish scaler; larding needle; molds for gelatin, cakes, ice cream, puddings, butter, ice sculptures; strawberry huller; mortar and pestle for grinding herbs and spices in small amounts.

Appliances for the adventurous

It is well-argued that great cooking long preceded electricity. In fairness, however, there were no shortages of time or assistants when Escoffier and Brillat-Savarin held court. Appliances have in fact made the preparation of the greatest creations of the culinary masters possible in home kitchens within a reasonable amount of time and without extraordinary effort.

Food preparation machines

Here you have one or more possibilities to choose from. Large mixers equipped with special attachments can handle batters and dough, whip egg whites and cream and, depending on the attachments you buy, grind, shred, and slice vegetables; puree and blend; stuff sausages and grind grains. Some even open cans, make ice cream, and grind coffee beans. The one-bowl appliance known as a food processor does a superior job of chopping and mincing, blending, pureeing, grating and cutting vegetables and some fruits. You can, of course, use separate appliances for almost every job, from juicing to grinding to slicing to blending to mixing and beating. In the range of appliances on the market, there is something for every taste and purse.

Coffeemakers

These are part of the "gourmet" appliance group, filter-drip coffee and espresso being considered by many the only really full-flavored brews. If you are serving sophisticated guests, you may even want to try such coffee combinations as café brûlot or cappuccino. There are many equipment variations, all applying basically the same brewing principles but differing in the extent to which they function "automatically."

Pasta makers

These can be hand-operated or electric. Some both mix and extrude the dough, with cutters or dies forming traditional pasta shapes and sizes. Other machines roll, and cut or shape, dough that you have made in a mixer or food processor, or by hand.

Rice cooker and steamer

These are simply electric pans that shut off automatically when the water has steamed away (timing is controlled by the amount of water you put in at the beginning), leaving food with a wonderfully fresh, undiluted flavor. They cook rice, vegetables, fruit, seafood and shellfish, steamed puddings, custard, and a variety of other foods. Several sizes are available.

Crêpe makers and omelet pans

These maintain a perfect temperature for such cooking, have a non-stick surface, and let you cook away from the range, even in the dining room where guests can choose their own fillings if you like.

For a grand finale, nothing beats homemade ice cream or sherbet. Some machines make 2 quarts or more, using ice cubes and ordinary table salt; freezing takes under an hour. The frozen mixture is then hardened in containers in the freezer, where it stays hard until serving time. *Ice cream maker*

Sandwich/waffle grills, griddles, warming trays, and table ranges all help to keep foods satisfyingly hot. Some sandwich grills are patterned to make attractive, interesting "company" sandwiches. *Electric table-top cookware*

This is becoming an everyday appliance, and can help out both before and during a party. Guests, if you like, can use it to heat their own mugs of soup, hot appetizers, or coffee. For a buffet meal, extra casseroles can be heated or reheated in minutes, second servings of vegetables reheated right in their serving dishes. Most microwave ovens today have a choice of power levels from slow, gentle heat to full, fast heat. In the rush of getting food ready for a party, a microwave oven can be a blessing: cooking sauces, melting butter and chocolate, thawing any ingredients that need it, and much more. *Microwave oven*

These countertop ovens are excellent for baking and roasting, doing these jobs up to one-third faster than conventional ovens. Such a unit can be a second oven, or you may want convection heating incorporated in your next regular or microwave oven; these options are available. *Convection oven*

Egg cooker/poacher, food dehydrator, yogurt maker, cookie gun, juicer, fruit and vegetable juice extractor, broiler/rotisserie, coffee mill, corn popper, electric knife, deep fryer/cooker, indoor barbecue, fondue pot, shish kebab broiler. *Some other appliances to consider*

"Specialties of the house"

Some of the best parties start with a host's or hostess's fondness for a particular cuisine or type of food. If you enjoy learning new skills and food ways, by all means make a party of it. What's the good of getting very good at something if you can't share it with appreciative friends? Following are some suggested directions to take, and ideas about tools to assist you. Don't hesitate to enlist a friend or relative as assistant-in-training. You may want, also, to augment your cookbook library or take some courses.

China, Japan, Korea, and other Oriental countries can teach us much about making scarce and costly ingredients go further and about beautiful presentation. Important equipment includes the round, deep, flared skillet called a wok, stir-frying tools, and knives and cleavers of various sizes to cut the food for cooking. An electric or stove-top skillet can handle a portion at a time if you want to try Oriental recipes before buying a "wardrobe" of authentic equipment. *Oriental cuisine*

Italian cuisine

This is no spaghetti-and-meatball cuisine, once you have dipped into a few good books. Compare regional specialties, too, to discover how suprisingly varied Italian meals can be. A pasta maker is fun, and fresh pasta is totally different in texture and flavor from the boxed kind. In Italy, vegetable cooking is the art of combining and sautéing or simmering familiar and unusual varieties. Herbs and aromatics such as onions and garlic can be quickly chopped on a board or in a bowl with a *mezzaluna,* a half-moon shaped blade with handles at each end, that you rock back and forth. A food processor almost earns its keep just by its efficient pulverizing of hard cheeses such as parmesan, romano, fontina. Fresh-grated cheese is superb: your veal parmigiana deserves no less.

Mexican and South American cuisine

South-of-the-border travelers and a few celebrated cookbooks have launched this cuisine, which ventures far beyond chili and taco parlors and what is known as Tex-Mex. Once it was clear that tortillas, from scratch, could be the basis for party dishes from dips to casseroles, tortilla presses, racks, and servers began appearing in kitchens from coast to coast. Paella pans—those big, round, shallow metal or iron casseroles made to show off that intriguing blend of fish and fowl, rice and spices—hold enough for eight or more guests to help themselves generously at the table.

Greek cuisine

From egg-lemon soup to baklava, Greek food is moving up fast on other ethnic foods. Not much special equipment is needed, but you will want plenty of baking dishes, individual as well as "group," for moussaka, baked lamb dishes, and spinach pie. Learning to handle phyllo dough, a staple for dozens of main dishes and desserts, is an experience that turns out far better than you expect as you try to build the first few layers.

Middle Eastern cuisine

As in the Orient, typical dishes are mixtures of meat or fish with, in this case, grains such as couscous, as well as rice. Meat can be slow-cooked, after long marinating, in a smoker-barbecue. The unleavened bread we know as pita is fun to make. Salads, sweet-sour in flavor, accompany the main dishes. Another specialty is couscous, a tiny pasta cooked over boiling broth. Yes, there's a pot to cook it in, called a *couscoussier.*

Classic French cuisine

Unlike countries in other parts of the world, France, indeed most of Europe, has generally had a rich and varied food supply, and therefore, cuisine. The infinite variations and the challenges the foods offer probably account, in part, for our love of French food. Many pieces of equipment have traditional uses, their designs, shapes, and materials contributing to the results. The straight sides of the soufflé dish, for example, help the airy mixture to rise high above the rim of the dish. Au gratin dishes are wider than they are deep to maximize the amount of delicious crumb and/or cheese topping. A brioche is just another bread unless baked in its traditional fluted tin. Whether yours is a classic specialty, a fling at nouvelle cuisine (using less butter, flour, and cream), or a hearty provincial main dish, you will find most recipes quite specific as to techniques and utensils. You don't need a "batterie de cuisine" to come very close to the great French authentics; the most helpful books give American equivalents for hard-to-find equipment. You may want however, as you explore new foods, to invest in some typically French items, if only an omelet pan and a quiche dish.

Notes on cooking in quantity

The job of entertaining a large group, perhaps 25 to 50 or more, is manageable in a number of ways, including having some or all of the food catered. If you want to "do it yourself," you can keep food to a minimum by having a cocktail, tea, or punch party with hors d'oeuvres, or cake, cookies, and pastries. A late evening dessert buffet with coffee can be a great treat, especially if you enjoy making a variety of sinfully good things. This can be appropriate after a community meeting or sports event. Much of the food for these parties can be prepared at least several days ahead, longer if foods are freezable, as cake layers and cookies are, and many hors d'oeuvres.

When you want to serve a complete meal for a crowd, buffet service is probably the only feasible way. A possible alternative is a "chow line" set up in the kitchen, for a very informal chili, spaghetti, or franks and beans meal, or moving the meal outdoors where guests can visit a series of barbecue grills (some borrowed), and a condiment and salad table. In either case, it's well to recruit assistants and perhaps have some guests contribute dishes or pots of food.

An interesting and substantial indoor buffet for a crowd takes considerable planning in buying, cooking, and serving. It is easy to over- or under-estimate the amounts, hard to time successive batches of food to be cooked, or just to keep the buffet table fresh and full for the oncoming guests. Some tips that will help:

- Decide the menu well in advance and be sure you have duplicate casserole and other baking dishes for quick replacements, or the means of refilling empty servers on the buffet without risk of burns, spills, or splashes. (One person can't hold a two-handled pot of hot food, and ladle or spoon out its contents at the same time.)
- It pays to draw up a serving schedule and a map of the buffet table. They will help you organize yourself and others who may be assisting you with the party.
- Choose foods that will not change color or lose texture sitting on the table. Fish fillets, and delicate crepes and dumplings, for example, don't take well to waiting. Salad greens and raw vegetables hold up better than cooked green vegetables. Salad greens can be ready and waiting in a large plastic bag in the refrigerator, so only the dressing need be added at the last minute.

- Cook food in several batches rather than in one large pot or baking dish. While many recipes can be multiplied two, three, or more times, the quantity will throw the cooking times off and stirring such a large amount will break up the texture and spoil the appearance of many foods. For example, even if your oven could take a baking pan large enough to hold lasagna for 25, it would take much longer to cook than three separate pans in the same oven. Besides, you would want to bake them separately, as needed, if serving time during the party stretched over an hour or more. When you stir gallons of stew in one very large pot, the result can be uneven cooking and ragged pieces. You can, however, round up, cut, mix, and prepare ingredients in quantity, ready for final assembly and/or cooking, a batch at a time.
- To avoid bottlenecks at the buffet, try to eliminate from the menu any foods that require slicing, carving, spreading, draining, or difficult spearing for self-service. Every item should be easy to transfer onto a plate with a spoon or fork, and foods should not be so saucy that they run together. To avoid backtracking on a buffet line, be sure a dressing, sauce, or condiment follows the food it is meant to be served on or with.
- A 25- or 50-cup coffeemaker will be a tremendous help. Try to borrow or rent one if you don't want to buy one.
- What follows is a brief list of quantities you would need in order to serve about 25 portions of typical buffet foods (amounts consumed will vary, of course, depending on what else is served):

  Coffee: ¾ lb.
  Cream: 1 pt.
  Chicken to fry: 15–20 lbs.
  Chicken to cook in casseroles: 10–12 lbs.
  Ham, bone in, to bake: 11–13 lbs.
  Chopped meat for loaves: 7 lbs.
  Turkey, to roast: 20 lbs.
  Potatoes to be scalloped: 7 lbs.
  Lettuce, other greens for salads: 5 heads
  Dressing: 1 pt.
  Fruit salad: 5 qts.
  Chicken, potato, tuna salads: 4 qts.

Keep these guidelines in mind when planning a specific menu for a large party.

Shopping for kitchen equipment

The choices in cookware, ovenware, tools, and appliances are almost infinite. Materials may be metals, ceramics, glass, or plastic; each has its own characteristics and uses. The range of sizes, shapes, features, and functions is wide, and so, of course, is the price range. The decisions aren't easy and advice can't realistically be very specific. Even experienced chefs have their prejudices and often disagree with one another as to what's best in any category. There are, however, some basic areas of agreement.

These pots and pans should be flat-bottomed, and good conductors of heat; have durable, heat-resistant handles and knobs, snug-fitting covers where needed; be heavy enough to resist dents, warping, and tipping. Finishes, inside and out, should be easy to clean. These are some of the characteristics of materials in frequent use:

Aluminum: Good heat conductivity, and heat retention in heavier weights (specified as gauges, which indicate thickness; the smaller the number, the thicker the metal).

Copper: In this application, not used in contact with food, but as an outer layer. Excellent heat conduction, but little retention.

Iron, cast: Slow heat conduction but long retention. Requires "seasoning" to prevent rusting and sticking.

Porcelain-enameled iron and steel: Decorative and highly successful coverups of the deficiencies of iron and steel (tendency to rust and stain). Cooking performance depends on the thickness of the base metal; cast iron has greater heat retention than steel and is slower to heat. The porcelain-enamel exterior is a glass-like coating fused on at high temperatures; some care is required to prevent scratches and chips, particularly with porcelain-on-steel.

Stainless steel: Fast heating, but uneven conduction unless the steel is combined with a layer or layers of copper, aluminum, or carbon steel to spread the heat. The smooth, hard stainless steel exposed surfaces resist staining, pitting, and to some extent sticking. Stainless steel contains a minimum of 11 percent chromium, and may have traces of other metals to contribute hardness, capacity to take high temperatures, resistance to scratching and corrosion.

Non-stick finishes, which vary in both trade names and application processes, are most often applied to aluminum to overcome its disadvantages, such as staining and sticking, so that its good properties can be enjoyed.

Stove-top cookware

Many stove-top utensils can go into an oven if handles are of the same material as the cookware or another that is heat-resistant, such as another metal or a plastic that withstands normal baking temperatures (usually up to 375° or 400° F.). This is a convenience for dishes that call for stove-top browning or boiling before a baking period. Never assume that an oven-proof piece will take direct broiler heat; always check cookware and ovenware labels to be sure.

Ceramics, glass: These materials, except for special types of "flameproof" glass, porcelain, and pottery, are used mainly for oven baking and roasting. They include glass, clay, earthenware, stoneware, and porcelain (see definitions under *China,* page 71). Glass cannot take direct broiler heat; some stoneware and porcelain pieces can take it briefly, long enough to top-brown a dish.

Ovenware

Metal pans: Aluminum, porcelain enamel-on-steel, stainless steel, tinned steel, and carbon steel all turn up among the many shapes of ovenware, from tiny tart pans to big roasters. The design, weight, and finish of the pan affects the end product more than the actual material. A dark, dull, or matte finish absorbs oven heat; a shiny, bright one reflects it. Cast iron, a heat absorber, is valued for popovers, cornbread, and some similarly crusty baked foods. These oven-performance characteristics are the reason pie and bread pans are usually dull or dark on the outside; they are also the reason why recipes for cakes often tell you to lower the oven temperature 25 degrees when your pan has a dark enamel exterior (also for glass bakeware, because of its fast heat absorption).

Plastic: With the advent of microwave ovens, plastic cookware has become a significant option. Though many ovenware pieces made of glass and ceramic can be used in a microwave oven, plastic offers new shapes and sizes better adapted to the energy patterns and levels characteristic of these ovens. A ring mold, for example, bakes a better cake or meat loaf than a square or round dish simply because the waves can reach more area of the mixture, producing more even results. Muffin pans are circular rather than rectangular. Two-piece dishes let foods drain as they cook. Some of these plastic items might even legitimately be called "appliances" in that they make coffee, pop popcorn, and brown pizza in a way conventional utensils cannot. If you own a microwave oven, do look into the new plastic possibilities.

Mixing, measuring, and cooking tools

Shopping for these items is fairly easy, and often fun. Display racks inform as well as sell, and packages explain uses. You might prefer glass mixing bowls to metal as quieter when you are using a beater, or the reverse because metal is lighter. A few tips: A stainless steel grater won't rust as tinplate might. Markings on measuring cups and spoons should be readable and durable. Knives should have strong blades secured through the full length of the handle with rivets (ads often say "full tang"), smooth finishing, good balance in the hand, forged blades of high-carbon steel (ordinary carbon steel takes a keener edge but is quick to stain and rust, making high-carbon a good compromise). For garlic, take the time to find a press that is self-cleaning, with prongs that push out the remnants. Pepper mills are another item where quality pays; look for a smooth-working, adjustable mechanism.

Appliances

Prudent purchasing calls for advance research in consumer magazines, among friends, and in stores. You will want to comparison-shop brands, prices, and features—all important factors in any decision. Insist on seeing and reviewing the instruction book before making any major purchase. Such a manual will cut through all the advertising jargon and give you a clear and accountable statement of what you can, and cannot, expect an appliance to do.

Serving equipment and accessories

Gift and gourmet shops are filled with enticements, items designed to help you entertain not just competently but with flair. Chances are you already have, or can improvise, the basic serving dishes, platters, baskets, bowls, and oven-to-table cookware. There are some novel ideas and inventions, however, that might fill some special need or give you a fresh approach to your own dining or buffet table.

Hot food servers

Besides the wood, metal, and basketry racks to hold hot dishes, look for insulated caddies of plastic, in merry modern colors, that keep a casserole hot for hours or sizzling platters of metal that you preheat and then rest on wooden planks. Among the many electric warmers, there are glass hot trays (some with a hotter spot for coffee), a three-compartment buffet server with warming drawer beneath, bun warmers, one- and two-element table ranges (we used to call them "hot plates"). Kitchen electrics that can do dining room duty include the slow cooker, frypan, and griddle. *Some cautions:* A circuit probably can't power more than one heating appliance at a time. Cords should be taped to the floor so guests won't trip over them—a danger you won't risk if the buffet table is against the wall. If you need to use an extension cord, be sure it is made for appliances up to 1650 watts. Chafing dishes of silver, copper, or stainless steel are available with alcohol burners or canned fuel. Candle warmers can't be expected to cook as a chafing dish can, but will keep food warm; use only heavy ceramic or metal dishes over a candle or you are likely to get a scorch spot. There are several ways to keep food warm in the kitchen until it is time to serve it: set an oven to 200° F.; put food in an insulated picnic chest; wrap dishes in double layers of aluminum foil; partially fill a large roasting pan with water, put it over low heat on top of the stove and set food pans in it.

Avocado serving dish.

Artichoke plates.

Cold fish and seafood
service.

68   Attractive party platter.

*Unusual
party platter.*

Finger foods such as raw vegetables or shrimp can be served directly on crushed ice in a bowl. You can buy ice packs, or make your own by filling a plastic pouch with water (leave some air space for expansion) and heat-sealing it; freeze the filled pouch and use it underneath platters, placing it first in a glass pie plate. Ice molds are made in a variety of shapes (birds, fish, etc.) to decorate and chill food platters, or you can freeze water in an ordinary ring mold. To decorate an ice ring, layer fruits such as cherries or citrus slices and water, an inch at a time, freezing each layer before adding the next. Rings can be used on a tray of fresh fruits, vegetables, or shrimp, or floated in a punch bowl. To keep food cool in the kitchen, use a picnic chest, set pans in a container of ice cubes, or freeze a shallow panful of ice on which you can stand a plate or dish of food such as molded salad. Wine coolers and ice buckets come in a variety of colors and kinds, often with matching plastic or glass barware. — *Cold food servers*

These can be of wood, glass, ceramic, even plastic; for large tossed green salads, a punch bowl may do the trick. Generous-size servers with a number of compartments let you set up a salad bar with a choice of toss-ins and dressings so guests may help themselves. At sit-down dinners, salad can be served on plates that match your china, or in clear glass or even wooden bowls if that would be easier. When salad is served as a separate course, you can match your china or not, as you please. — *Salad bowls and servers*

Casseroles, of course, qualify, but consider also such unusual individual servers as onion soup pots, scallop shells for baked seafood appetizers or main dishes, individual cheese or dessert soufflé dishes, round or oval bakers for deep-dish meat, chicken, or dessert pies. Also worth mentioning here are the broiler-to-table skewers of various lengths for shish kebabs of all sorts. Materials are variously metal, wood, and bamboo. — *Oven-to-table servers*

Pitchers for water and cold drinks can be glass, silver, pewter, ceramic, even plastic for informal occasions. Carafes for hot beverages are most often made of heat-proof glass, but coffee and tea pots of silver, pewter, or china are always in good taste. If you have a coffee service, by all means use — *Beverage servers*

69

Ironstone. Sometimes confused with porcelain, ironstone is in fact a hard white earthenware constituted of several kinds of iron ore with admixtures of silica and clay. Introduced at Staffordshire in 1813 by the British potter Charles James Mason, it was very similar to a stone china first shown by Spode in 1805. Valued for its pure whiteness and simplicity of design, ironstone is an adaptable, attractive, and long-wearing dinnerware choice.

Stoneware. Regarded as the forerunner of porcelain, vitrified stoneware containing feldspar was made in China before the 7th century A.D. A heavy, nonporous earthenware that is hard, and always fired in a high-temperature kiln, stoneware does not require a glaze. When one is used, it must be of a special type to withstand the extreme heat.

Bone china. First introduced in England in 1748 by Thomas Frye of Bow, who applied for a patent for the use of bone ash in a near-porcelain combination that produced a new pure white in the ware. This white, powdery substance was later used, with china clay and stone, to form a hybrid bone-ash paste. Covered with a lead glaze, this became the standard English bone china body and remains in use today.

Porcelain. The most admired and collected of all ceramics, porcelain is characteristically hard, white, and translucent. Made of kaolin (a fine, white clay), quartz, and feldspar and fired at high temperatures, it can be unadorned or elaborate, formal or casual, but it is always a proud possession.

Firing and glazing

Because of their bearing on colors and decorations—the range, the surface impression, the durability—it is useful to know something of the three methods of glazing. Each has its merits, preference among them depending on the effect desired.

Under-glaze firing. Traditional blue-and-white Japanese china is an example. The design is handpainted or transferred directly to the bisque (clay after firing), which is then glazed and fired at about 800° F. Color has a soft, "absorbed" look because the pigment goes into the pores of the bisque and is then protected, and slightly dimmed, by the glaze.

In-glaze firing. A relatively new technique developed in Japan in which a special glaze (used in this technique only) is applied to the bisque; the piece is then fired a second time. When it has cooled, the decoration is put on. The in-glaze pigments are made to seep into the pores of the glaze during the second firing, always at temperatures of 1000° F. or above; this produces a smooth surface with a design imperceptible to the touch.

Over-glaze firing. Here the bisque piece is fired first with a simple glaze; the decoration is applied (by handpainting or decal transfer), and the piece is fired again, at about 800° F. This method permits greater color variety and intensity than either of the other two; it is the only one in which gold or platinum decorations are possible. Over-glaze decorations can be felt with the fingertips and are more vulnerable than others, which accounts for the need to hand-wash such wares.

Friendly atmosphere for lunch.

Dramatic place setting.

The preceding explanations necessarily oversimplify the procedures. They also omit such details as the many techniques for decorating china—interesting, but not nearly as pertinent to a practical understanding of china as some sense of firing and glazing, and their effect on strength and durabilty.

Selecting china

There seems to be no way to phrase "selecting china" without its having a sound of finality, of something you do once and forever. If that is your impression, it couldn't be further from the truth. Tastes change, lifestyles change, incomes change. What you loved yesterday you may detest today. Where you once followed rules scrupulously, you may now make your own.

Even the rules cannot be relied on to remain rigidly in force. At formal meals, where it was once decreed that all china, for all courses, must match, you are now free to vary it from course to course. No mismatches allowed as yet within courses, but that may be coming. (For antique demitasse collections, often all different, it has already arrived.) Finger bowls have all but disappeared and butter plates are not far behind them. Considering the number of plates that once had to be part of a formal set of china (bread-and-butter, salad, breakfast, luncheon, dinner, and service), it is no wonder that common sense has intruded and the most exacting of experts now advise using only the china, glasses, and utensils required for the comfort of your guests and the look of your table.

Start where you are. Knowing that nothing stays the same, the best approach is to base your choices on your present circumstances, and allow yourself some latitude to make alterations as those circumstances change. This means buying a limited number of place settings (four to eight, depending on your finances and the number of people you entertain) in an open stock pattern, to be supplemented as the need arises. Confine matching serving pieces to a very few, perhaps platter and vegetable bowl, or you may prefer all servers to be different from the basic china, in which case you needn't buy *any* in your pattern. Keep your basic china to a "standard" color (today that can mean such livelier shades as brick or yellow along with still-fashionable and adaptable white or bone). This way you can add extra place pieces, such as salad or dessert plates, and servers (platters, bowls, sauce or gravy boats, condiment dishes) in other colors, designs, even materials.

Such gradual purchasing will be easier on your budget, partly because it spreads the investment over a longer period. Just as important, it permits you to pick up odd pieces that strike your eye. (Being strays, these pieces are often marked down to bargain prices.) You will find, too, that your original "set" doesn't grow tiresome as fast, if ever, because it can be varied endlessly.

The earlier descriptions of china types and of firing and glazing methods should give you an overall idea of comparative durability. Porce-

Use your heirlooms and your imagination.

Oriental elegance.

Colonial look.

Simplicity of Scandinavia.

Drama of color.

Splendor of gold.

lain, stoneware, and ironstone are all hardy enough for everyday use and appropriate for every kind of entertaining. China that is plain, or decorated by the under-glaze or in-glaze techniques, takes repeated trips through the dishwasher cycle better than china with over-glaze patterns or trims, which will fade with repeated machine washings. If you want to be sure your china is dishwasher-safe, check that feature with your supplier.

As you read the recommendations that follow, won't it be nice to know that you don't have to buy everything that is listed? Or that, if you do, they need not all be the same, safe color? How far you deviate in color, patterns, and materials is your decision. If you want your table to retain a sense of unity, keep the elements similar in character. Today, that need not mean monotony.

The list that follows includes all the possibilities, with comments that should help you make appropriate choices. Where it is recommended that a larger number be bought because a piece is subject to breakage (e.g., cups and saucers) or especially versatile (salad plates), the number should be up to twice as many as you have basic places: 8 if you have 4, 12 for 6, 16 for 8.

Basic china

(All possibilities are listed, with comments, where pertinent, to guide your decisions.)

Place pieces

Dinner plates	
Coffee cups and saucers	Best if they match; advisable to buy extras because of breakage and chipping.
Salad plates	A good place for contrast; can avoid need for dessert plates.
Bread-and-butter plates	Seen less and less often.
Soup/cereal bowls	Useful as well for side vegetables.
Luncheon plates	Sizes not being very different, salad plates will usually suffice here.
Dessert plates	Salad plates can be used; glass dessert plates, however, can be an interesting variation.
Buffet/service plates	Not necessary except for formal events; very handy, however, to have for buffet service and, on occasion, to use as sandwich platters.
Soup cups or mugs	Excellent for family and informal use.
Soup plates (rimmed soups)	Can be postponed until occasion calls for them.
Cream soups	Same as above.
Coffee mugs	Fine for family and informal use; will save wear on china cups.
Demitasse cups and saucers	Ideal item to choose in another design; postpone until needed, then look for attractive, inexpensive set.

*The best of everything by candlelight—
bone china, fine crystal, lovely silver.*

Ambience through accessories.

Ultra modern flair.

Country kitchen lunch.

Others

In addition to these four basics, flatware is made today with handles of other materials: bone, porcelain, stoneware, plastic, even bamboo. Often quite contemporary in design, these can be charming on a casual table. However, they can present a care problem: the handles are glued to the blades, and repeated washings at high temperatures can cause the two to separate. For this reason, it is best not to put any such "combinations" in a dishwasher.

Not properly flatware in any formal sense, but fine for picnics and children's parties, are plastic knives, forks, and spoons. They vary considerably in quality, some being made to be tossed out at the end of the party, others usable at least several times if you wish. You won't find many plastic special serving utensils. The knives cannot do any strenuous cutting, and few of the plastic utensils can take prolonged heat, but those few objections aside, they are bright, cheerful, and fine for many purposes.

Buying flatware

Going back, at this point, to standard cutlery, the choice of materials and design is up to you. Except that for certain formal occasions materials probably shouldn't be mixed, any flatware is appropriate for any occasion. And even the "no mixing" admonition could certainly be ignored if your only cake server was silver, and everything else stainless.

Design choices are broad in every category; once you have found your dream design, be certain that it is sold in open stock. You can then "start small" with just the basic place settings—as few as four at the beginning—and add settings and special pieces as you have both the money and the need. Look, both at the start and as you are considering additions, for the excellent sales on flatware from famous-name manufacturers. As you watch the ads, however, be aware of the differences in offerings. "Place setting" does not always, or even often, mean the same thing. Offerings vary from the basic four pieces (dinner knife, dinner fork, salad fork, teaspoon) to as many as five, six, occasionally seven. The supplements, in approximately this order, are a soup spoon, seafood fork, iced tea spoon.

Quite often the special offers will feature a so-called hostess (or completer) set of servers, again variously four, five, or six pieces. These, generally speaking, will include some or all of the following: butter serving knife, cold meat or buffet fork, gravy ladle, sugar spoon (or "shell," as it is sometimes called), tablespoon and pierced tablespoon, occasionally a cake/pie server. They are all useful, and for more purposes than their names imply; if you decide you would like to add a few to your flatware collection, wait for reduced prices. They need not, incidentally, be bought as a set, though sets can be a bargain. Such standard servers are available in open stock.

Though you can get by with utensils that can be purchased as place settings, certain of them are more versatile than others. It is worth your while to have more of these, even twice as many as you have place settings, because of this adaptability. (The alternative, at a meal of many courses, is washing cutlery between courses, something to be avoided if possible.)

Color and charm.

There is usually a special utensil to be found for each purpose (dessert spoon, fish knife, fruit knife, etc.), but unless you are an almost professional partygiver, the investment isn't warranted.

Among the highly-usefuls are: salad or other small forks and small knives (both come in more than one size) for first course and dessert, fruit, cheese, and so on; teaspoons (for coffee or tea, desserts—ice cream, puddings); serving spoons (three or four, both standard and slotted); ladles (useful for sauces as well as gravies).

Generally speaking, the following would accommodate parties of up to eight for virtually any kind of meal.

Starred (*) pieces are desirable, not fundamentally necessary.

***Basic flatware
(eating utensils)***

8 dinner forks	*8 cream soup spoons
8 soup spoons	*8 demitasse spoons
12 to 16 of the following:	*8 iced beverage spoons
salad forks	*8 cocktail forks
teaspoons	*8 grapefruit/melon spoons
knives (8 large, 8 small)	*8 steak knives

83

Servers

Serving spoons (3 or 4, both standard and slotted)
Cold meat/buffet fork
Sugar shell
Butter server
Sauce and gravy ladles (2 or 3)
Cake or pie server
Cheese serving knife
Salad servers (in flatware, generally fork and spoon)

Glassware

Many people feel that fine glass and ordinary glassware shouldn't be mentioned in the same breath. There is, in their minds, no comparison between elegant crystal and stemware and the commercial glass found on the average bar or table. Unfortunately, in their admiration for the one, they overlook the merits of the other—and the origin of both in the glassmaker's art. To the artisans of many centuries and many parts of the world we owe the broad choice we have and the overall excellence of design.

Blown glass, in the original meaning, is mouth-blown, or shaped without a mold, an art still practiced here and abroad. Some present-day glassware is blown by machine into a mold and shaped by compressed air; examples are light bulbs and inexpensive thin glasses.

Crystal, the ultimate in glassware, is not to be confused with true crystal, which is a semi-precious stone. Nor is it correct to call all fine stemware "crystal," as some people do. Crystal, in this usage, is fine glassware that has lead as one of its basic components; the lead content affects its weight and the tone of the tinkling sound it makes when tapped. Crystal can be "worked," the designs varying from elaborate shaping to decorations of great intricacy. Some of the finest modern crystal, of course, is almost austerely simple.

Cut glass. Here facets are cut in heavy glass or crystal by means of an abrasive wheel, in an attempt to simulate the brilliance of diamonds.

Engraved glass. The process used to produce this glass employs an abrasive wheel, in this instance to engrave (cut) shallow designs into thin crystal and low-cost glassware.

Etched glass. The cutting medium here is acid, which etches a decoration into the glass, producing a design with a frosty look.

Pressed glass. This is made by pressing molten glass into a mold and is typified by a heavy raised or indented pattern. The best known form: the Boston and Sandwich glassware of the last century.

Glass is best bought for the purpose

Nothing that is about to be said is meant to belittle fine glassware and crystal. They are things of priceless beauty, much to be desired and a great good fortune to have. But they are fragile and they are expensive to replace, if indeed the pattern has not been discontinued by the time you go in search of replacements.

Buy delicate crystal and stemware if you wish and can afford to. But be prepared to treasure it, in every sense of the word, and bring it out only on what are "state" occasions for you. For the rough-and-tumble of day-to-day use, and for every kind of party except the most formal, buy glasses for as little as you can at the quality level you desire, and in shapes that are pleasing to your eye (and hand, for that is a consideration) and suited to their purpose.

In this section we will deal with glassware for table use, including some that can double for table and bar. For a full-scale review of barware (where you will see some of the same shapes again), we recommend a look at the *Bar glassware section.*

For table service it is advisable to have at least a dozen of each glass type or its alternative, where one is given. That means, because of breakage, buying at least 16 to begin with; even when you are buying the simplest barware, you will be happiest if everything continues to match if any accidents happen. The glasses are listed in order of appearance—that is, of the probability of a particular beverage being served at a meal. The described shapes and capacities are only approximations; you will encounter many design variations and some differences in capacity.

Basic glass type	Alternatives or other ideas
Water glass (informal): straight-sided tumbler; for family meals; at breakfast or away from the table for guests	
Water goblet (stemmed): for formal meals	The capacity is about 10 ounces, not too different from a generous size all-purpose wine glass, which some people use as a goblet.
Juice glass	Holds, as a rule, from 3 to 6 ounces. A single old-fashioned glass can be used instead, or a tumbler-shape cocktail glass.
Iced drink glass	Between the bar and the table, you might have as many as three kinds of glasses of roughly this type: straight sides (though a goblet shape exists as well), capacity of about 12 ounces. A highball holds 10 to 12, a cooler up to 16. Many homes make do with a compromise—just highballs, or just iced drink glasses—for all three purposes.

TOP ROW: *cocktail (4 oz.), cocktail (4 oz.), sour (6 oz.), Collins (14 oz.), highball (12 oz.), old-fashioned (9 oz.).* MIDDLE ROW: *saucer champagne (6 oz.), white wine (7 oz.), balloon red wine (9 oz.), Rhine or Moselle wine (6 oz.), tulip champagne (9 oz.).* BOTTOM ROW: *liqueur (1 oz.), liqueur (2 oz.), liqueur (1 oz.), pousse-café (1 oz.), Irish coffee (6 oz.), brandy snifter (10 oz.).*

Wine glasses:

Sherry (traditionally stemmed, the bowl rounded or pointed; 2 to 3 ounces)

Red wine (bowl; 8 to 10 ounces)
White wine (smaller bowl than red, straighter sides, 5 to 8 ounces)
All-purpose wine (see right)

The trend today is away from special purpose and small sizes in wine glasses. A great and growing favorite, and acceptable for both red and white wines, is the all-purpose wine glass; its bubble-shaped bowl holds from 6 to 9 ounces, sometimes considerably more.

Champagne (saucer, about 6 ounces; or tulip, about 8 ounces)

A white wine glass is often used for champagne, a saucer champagne glass for frozen daiquiris.

Though glasses for these purposes are not literally used at table, they are often an intrinsic part of a meal, certainly of its planning, and warrant being considered with table glassware.

Cocktails, liqueurs, brandy

Basic glass type	*Alternatives or other ideas*
Cocktail glasses may be the conventional stemmed type, or a tumbler shape; capacity in either case is about 3 to 4½ ounces.	These, as a rule, are used for cocktails served "straight up." When such cocktails as martinis are served over ice or "on the rocks," the choice is usually the smaller-size ("single") old-fashioned glass.
Liqueur glasses, also called "ponies" or cordial glasses, are tiny (1 to 2 ounces) and usually stemmed.	
Brandy glasses, by tradition, are the balloon-shaped snifters, sometimes referred to as "inhalers," made in a range of sizes from quite small to ostentatiously large.	Brandy may be served in a liqueur glass or small tumbler-type cocktail glass.

87

The growing list of glass servers

Probably because glass shows food off so beautifully, more and more serving pieces are being made of that material. Besides the familiar salad bowl, so flattering to mixed greens with scarlet bits of tomato, you will see on the shelves of fine stores and on well-appointed tables: cheese and sandwich plates and platters; dessert sets (combination bowl and service plate); "icers" for shrimp and other seafood cocktails or other appetizers that are best served ice-cold; domed cake and cheese servers; ovenproof casseroles with basket-like cradles, often of silverplate, that serve as carriers and make a dramatic presentation of your one-dish specialty.

Glass has been prized, as long as anyone can remember, for ice creams and sherbets and variations on the two such as parfaits and chilled puddings. There are special servers for parfaits, for displaying the contrasting flavors and colors, and for sherbets. Stemming no doubt from the renewed trend to ice cream parlors, you can now get replicas of the heavy glass soda and sundae servers that recall everyone's childhood. A charming special server for a not-quite-dessert (children won't appreciate this until they grow up) is the Irish coffee glass, sold in sets at a quite reasonable price.

Color in glass

If you like tinted stems, or gold rims, or color in any other form, such embellishment is certainly suitable. Color is a strong feature of much museum-quality glass, some of it irreplaceable and priceless. Be careful, only, that the colors do not do battle with your china or other elements of your table setting. A way to satisfy a craving for colored glass might be to limit it to liqueur glasses, which are used away from the table. But remember, many liqueurs have lovely colors of their own you will not want to obscure.

Plastic "glassware"

For certain purposes, notably at children's meals and parties and at outdoor, particularly poolside, events, plastic glassware is incomparable. Some very cheap plastics are obviously meant to be disposed of at a party's end; others, while still far from expensive, can be washed a limited number of times before they reach the end of their usefulness. Designs improve every day, some plastic "glasses" being such faithful facsimiles of quality glass that you wouldn't be ashamed to bring them out at a big, informal gathering such as a cocktail party. Don't forget, also, that, as mugs do for coffee cups and saucers, plastic glasses cut down the wear and tear on your more fragile and costly-to-replace tableware.

Table linens

When you consider that the linens on your table must complement your food and china and also coordinate with other colors in the room and in your centerpiece, it might seem that you would need dozens of cloths, mats, and napkins—and a professional decorator to put each scheme together. Not at all. What you need to do is trust your own color sense—and to collect a linen wardrobe carefully.

These can be expensive, but you only need one, or two at the most. It is best if these basic cloths are plain white or another solid neutral or, if you prefer, pastel. Then you can play with contrasts in china and foods, and in mats (often used as added protection under plates) and napkins, available in an extraordinary choice of materials and colors, often for not much money.

Tablecloths

Cloths for rectangular or square tables are easy to make if you are adept with a sewing machine. The sizes, whether you are buying or sewing, should be the length and width of your table, plus an 18 to 20 inch overhang on each side. If your table is the kind that "grows" from a basic to a medium and a long length, you may want cloths to accommodate all three, each with its appropriate overhang.

Round cloths may be either "knee" or floor length. Round sizes seem a bit harder to calculate but, for knee length at least, there is a fairly simple way to get at them. For a knee drape, merely add 36 inches to the table diameter. Thus a 36-inch table would need a 72-inch cloth, a 48-inch table an 84-inch cloth, etc., up to a 72-inch table (the largest standard size), which would take a 108-inch cloth. Floor-length cloths don't work out quite so neatly, the additions to table diameters running from 54 to 64 inches. Cloth sizes in this case are better spelled out.

Table size	Cloth size (to reach the floor)
36-inch round	90-inch diameter
48-inch round	100-inch diameter
54-inch round	110-inch diameter
60-inch round	120-inch diameter
72-inch round	136-inch diameter

The sides of buffet or bar tables that can be seen must be covered to the floor. In other words, if the table is against the wall, the wall (invisible) side need only have an overhang of 8 to 10 inches; the weight of the food and equipment will keep the cloth firmly anchored down. When all four sides will be visible, assuming the tabletop is the usual 28–29 inches from the floor, you need a tablecloth (or other finished fabric rectangle, such as a sheet) that is:

the *length* of the table plus 28–29 inches at *each end;*
the *width* of the table plus 28–29 inches at *each side.*

Besides using a sheet, there is another way you might achieve the necessary size without buying a big cloth (perhaps to use only once): use two smaller cloths, the first with an overhang at the front, then the second, layered over the first, with the overhang at the back.

Although a table covering need not be a conventional cloth, it is advisable to have at least one that can "go formal," which a bed sheet could not. If a material is very thin or flimsy, a table protector or underlayer of flannel would be advisable. Unless you don't mind paying for professional laundering, (which some damasks, laces, and fine linens require), confine your cloths to those that can be thrown into your washer and, ideally, into the dryer as well. Most bright solids and prints today are reliably colorfast (sheets unquestionably) by home methods—provided, of course, that you follow the care instructions on the labels. Take care, in considering patterned cloths, that a print is not one you will tire of or that will conflict unflatteringly with foods. It might be better to confine brilliant color splashes to inexpensive napkins, in which case anything goes.

There is another economical possibility when you feel an urge for color and hesitate to spend much for a one-time use: Rent small square cloths in bright shades to layer over your quieter colors. Renting linens, as a rule, is not too sensible; there is too great a risk of stains, burns, and other damage. These colorful squares, however, are generally made of sturdy materials. And they also protect your own linens, making the "layered look" quite a practical fashion. It is hardly a new one, though. People for years have been layering cutwork or lace cloths, even netting, over solid-color undercloths.

For informal use within the family or among friends, you might think about vinyl-coated cloths. They can be wiped clean after meals, an unbeatable asset with children. The vinyl surface makes such cloths excellent for outdoor use. Just be sure yours are heavy enough so that they won't blow away.

Napkins

The approach here is similar to the recommendation for tablecloths: Have some conventional napkins in classic white or pale neutral for meals that demand dignity; indulge in colors and patterns for any informal meal from breakfast to dinner. For formal dinners, tradition calls for dinner napkins, 20 to 24 inches square; they are a perfect choice for any evening meal in which you are after an impression of elegance. Such oversized napkins (an 18-inch square is the size most frequently used) are not limited to formal duty, however, or even to dinners. King-sized napkins, somewhat bolder in color and design, have become highly popular at buffets and brunches, where the generous proportions are a great convenience to guests balancing foods precariously in their laps. At such events, allow two napkins per guest—one for protection and the other for conventional use.

The 18-inch square can be used for lunch or dinner; a true luncheon napkin is actually 14 to 16 inches square and can double as a breakfast napkin.

That is really all there is to say about "rules" governing napkins. Today the sky is really the limit. Match napkins to your cloth if you like, or to each other. And be on the watch for the "sets" in which each napkin is a dazzling

Napkins can be folded flat in many interesting ways, or opened up in goblets for a blossom-like look.

different shade. Another popular mismatch is bandannas, in the familiar design but no longer the traditional red or blue; these "sets," again all different colors, are a rainbow of variations on that country theme.

When you buy napkins, or get them ready for a party, plan on more than one to a person. Besides the dual-purpose pair suggested for buffets and brunches, napkins get wet or stained or soiled and must be replaced, which calls for a supply of spares. Napkins are also useful for lining a basket of bread and rolls, for wrapping a bottle of wine, and for carrying a clean supply of cutlery to a buffet table. It will cost very little to have two or three dozen, in a palette of colors, to mix and match according to whim, occasion, and season.

Cocktail napkins, instead of or in addition to coasters, are a nicety that guests, and your furniture, will appreciate. Folded, they do a better job of absorbing condensation from glasses. In some shops and direct-mail catalogs, you may see a variation on these that is part coaster and part napkin: a fabric round with a slit in the top layer to take the base of wine and other stemmed glasses.

Cocktail napkins of paper, beautifully designed as many of them are, have become perfectly acceptable in any social situation. Have stacks of these; they are meant to be disposable, so guests feel free to pick up a clean one with every drink. Other paper napkins, except those meant for children's and holiday parties, are still outcasts (no pun intended) at most social functions. Use them at will at home, even for informal dinners with friends or relatives, but stay firmly with fabric, even if it's only madras or gingham, whenever you entertain.

Placemats

No matter how dressy and elegant a mat may look, its nature is informal; placemats do not belong at a formal or otherwise "dressed-up" dinner. With that single proviso, however, placemats are the least defined of table linens. Many of them are far from "linen" in the fabric sense, being made of mirrors, acrylic, straw, bamboo, mother-of-pearl. Those that are fabric are a long way from the plain cotton rectangles with which the mat mania began. Cottons are quilted, or interesting products of China, India, or Japan; sumptuous satins, moirés, and brocades have made an appearance. Striking, too, are the woven mats, and the braided ones, looking like miniatures of old-fashioned rugs.

Runners

This is a word that may surprise you, runners having been relegated in people's minds, like doilies, to grandma's day, or earlier. They are still a rarity, but here and there, runners are being revived. Perhaps "rejuvenated" would be a better word, because these are runners that grandma wouldn't recognize: Japanese obis, the traditional kimono sashes; brilliant Scandinavian stripes; heavy upholstery linens in wonderful colors. If you sew, runners are a cinch to make. They should be about 20 inches wide, sufficient to accommodate a place setting, and long enough to run the length of the table with an 18 to 20 inch overhang at each end, the same as for a tablecloth. A clever, and not difficult, way to accommodate six people:

Make a runner for the table length, then make two that will span the width plus overhangs and lay these across the longer one. Dishes and serving pieces, or an elongated and fairly heavy centerpiece, will weight the top runners sufficiently to keep them in place. Or you can attach self-fastening tabs to top and bottom runners so that the three stabilize each other.

Though the charm of table linens needs no justification, the original intent of table coverings was to protect the table (and, much further back, the knees of the diners from drafts). With the advent of tables that have protective finishes, plastic-laminate major among them, coverings have become optional. As such changes will, this led to something of a style: tables bare except for china and flatware. A bit stark for the tastes of some, the bare look, enhanced by soft lighting, can show off a table and its setting in a most unusual, and often effective, way.

The bare-table look

Advisable accessories

Although these items are incidentals, no table is completely set without some of them, and others can add greatly to your guests' convenience and your piece of mind. Several have been mentioned here and there, in other connections, but good advice bears repeating.

- Table protection should be provided for well in advance of a party; hot foods and certain liquids (even water, on some sensitive woods) can do instant and irreparable harm to a table's surface. An excellent guard against all such mishaps is a padded, waterproof cover that spans the entire table. You lay this under your cloth, as you do the flannel under-cloths that stabilize a top cloth you fear may be too light to stay in place. For partial coverage in crucial spots, if your server doesn't have its own cradle, you can use trivets—of wood, metal, cork, quilting, among other materials. Mats, particularly those that are extra-thick or made of a tough material, give some protection at each place. If a dish will be very hot, however, it's better to bank on a service plate.
- Ornamental, and also useful, when wine is being served, is a tile for the bottle (or a chiller, if it is white or rosé) and a coaster for each glass. Consider using carafes, a simple and splendid idea catching on across the country.
- In centerpiece style, appearances are not the only consideration. What-ever you choose, be it a bowl of floating flowers or figurines on a mirror, keep it low, and small enough that it does not overpower or crowd the other elements on the table.
- If you will be adding candles, *their* height is also important. The key is not hindering visibility or conversation, which means wicks well below or well above eye level. And light them. Though it is often forgotten, candles are meant to be sources of light; time was when they were the *only* source. This is the reason candles are omitted at lunchtime, when natural light is considered sufficient.

Caring for your "company" equipment

It's not that we use our tableware, linens, kitchen cookware, and serving pieces just for company, though some of them see comparatively little duty. But somehow, we seem to inspect more carefully when a party is in the offing. Spots, dull film, and tarnish must come off eventually, so why not now, we say. Many materials today carry their own care labels, and cleaning products come with directions, so little general information is needed here. But here are some tips you may find helpful:

- If possible, use your dishwasher a few days ahead to wash all the china, glasses, and flatware you will be needing; then set these items aside so they won't have to be washed or counted on party day. Cover with tents of plastic film.
- Stainless steel flatware brightens up with silver polish just as silverware does. The fine abrasive removes water spots and helps to smooth any pitting. Rinse stainless well in hot suds and then clear hot water; towel dry.
- When polishing silver accessories such as candlesticks, coffee pots, sugar and creamer—any hollow ware—polish surfaces that do not come in contact with food with an anti-tarnish polish or rub them with an anti-tarnish cloth.
- Brass and copper items, if seriously tarnished and perhaps even corroded, may need two cleanings. First, apply a paste of salt and vinegar or lemon juice to remove the worst accumulation, then follow with a cream cleaner to brighten and shine. This saves on the more expensive cleaner.
- Glass pitchers, carafes, vases, and other items that are apt to get cloudy or filmy usually clear up with a soaking. Fill them with hot water and a teaspoonful or two of automatic dishwasher detergent; let soak about an hour, then rinse. If the outside is spotted or dull, soak the entire piece in the sink in a warm suds and ammonia solution. About ½ cup of ammonia to a sinkful should do.

Wine coaster.

- Table linens that have been stored away may well be wrinkled, perhaps dusty; some spots that weren't apparent before may show up on closer inspection (they darken in storage). Rewash linens rather than try to iron out wrinkles, and pull them from the dryer barely dry (or, if they are heavy linen or cotton, when still quite damp). If your linen inspection discloses any spots, use a pretreater before washing. When ironing large pieces, work next to a table or bed so they won't drag on the floor and can be laid smoothly in folds as you iron. A coating of spray starch, at least in the center of a large tablecloth, will give it extra smoothness, a bit of body, and some resistance to staining and spots.
- Wooden salad bowls and servers do need a quick, hot bath in suds on occasion. When a film of oil collects in the pores, it attracts dust and may take on a rancid odor. Don't be afraid to wash wood well; just do so quickly, then dry well (of course never soak). Even bread baskets need an occasional swishing in suds.

Rented, borrowed, and caterer's equipment

Interesting and attractive as present-day equipment is, unless you are fairly certain you will use what you buy, it is not worth the investment or the strain on your storage space. By all means be on the alert for tools and special dishes and pans that will help you to broaden your skills or that just perfectly suit a recipe you want to try. But, for a large party of a kind you have never given before and may never give again, don't run out and buy everything on your list of necessities. Much of what you require can be rented or borrowed, or obtained along with a caterer's other services. One general word of caution about rental services and caterers: Contact such suppliers early for whatever you need. At busy seasons, you might well be disappointed if you wait too long.

China, flatware, and glasses can all be rented, though they may not always be up to the standard you set for your permanent possessions. Before placing an order, see if you can cut down the quantity: by eliminating a course, by serving vegetables or rice on the main-dish plate instead of in separate servers, by being less ambitious about your liquor service. Make an accurate list, piece by piece, of what you rent and check off each one when it is time for the equipment to go back. Be careful about mix-ups, especially of flatware. At a glance, one fork or spoon looks pretty much like another, particularly when yours and theirs have been lumped together.

It is risky to borrow anything valuable from friends, worse if it is fragile as well. Even if you offer to pay for anything damaged or lost, you may notice a certain chill in your friendship, a result surely not worth the small saving. If you decide to take the risk, take care to list what you borrow, use it as carefully as possible, and return it in good, clean shape.

You should not need to rent cloths unless you are using several tables or one that is unusually large. Avoid it if you can; linens are all too easily stained. On the other hand, a rented cloth layered over your "good" one does keep *it* from harm. A napkin wardrobe is so inexpensive that renting is absurd. Acquire a supply gradually, half in conservative shades and half as bright as you like, and you should always be adequately prepared.

If a friend has a handsome damask or cutwork cloth and you don't, it can be tempting to ask if she will lend it for a formal occasion. We strongly advise that you not put her on the spot. Far better to do a quick hemming job on a few yards of good linen (in a pinch you can even leave the selvages; no one will ever know).

It is for the "big party" items such as huge platters and bowls, chafing dishes, coffee urns, serving trays, and punch bowls that you will want to turn to a renter. These may be worthwhile buys for frequent entertainers, but for most people they are "sometime things," and best treated as that. Be prepared for very heavy and nondescript china, and "silver" that is not. Unless you are a hopeless perfectionist, you will be happy to secure what you need without buying, and let it go at that.

Serving pieces are not as delicate as other tableware and so not hazardous to borrow. In this case, you could even ask around; almost anyone will lend big platters and trays.

What caterers can supply

Just as caterers can do as much or as little as you require, so they can bring along whatever it takes to handle your needs, including people. Precise services vary from one caterer to another, but generally speaking they will only supply the food, cooking it in their kitchens or yours, *or* both prepare and serve it; most can help you as well with liquor and beverages, table-setting equipment, even tables and chairs. When a caterer does the whole party, her own crew cleans up—a benefit not to be taken lightly.

Caterers are easier to find in large cities than in smaller ones, but harder to judge, since there are so many. In any town, it is best to try to get a personal recommendation from someone with first-hand experience. When you talk to caterers, be precise about the occasion you are planning and thorough in your questions about the services available and their costs. Misunderstandings can cause awkwardness at your party, a price no one wants to pay.

Other rental equipment you might need

Tables and chairs are good possibilities, both to be had from party rental services. Rented tables are the only practical solution for multiple-table service, unless you have, or have access to, a supply of card tables with plywood or other covers to enhance their seating capacity. Another natural for renting: a long rectangular table for bar or buffet service.

When your need is for chairs, friends may be able to help you out. Many people have folding chairs they would be willing to lend. For a large number of chairs, or something more dignified, it's back to the rental agency.

If the chairs are for an outdoor party, borrowing again becomes feasible. No one worries much about yard and patio chairs, which are prized more for their toughness than their charm. Such other summer needs as umbrellas, awnings, canopies and the like can be rented from most party agencies. If you are considering any such protective device, ask about shape and dimensions, also means of support. Before getting something too large or cumbersome, reconsider your party's location. If it were to be in a sheltered corner, for example, rather than out in the open, something smaller might suffice.

When Drinks Will Be Served

T he necessary knowledge about bars begins with liquors and wines and their service. It ends on a practical party note, with suggestions about bar setups that will work in different amounts of space and for larger and smaller numbers of people. Wine is so popular today that it is not unusual for it to be the only alcoholic beverage served at parties. Remember that beer, mineral water, and soft drinks are also favored by many party guests. To add variety to the non-alcoholic beverages you offer your guests, you will find suggestions for drinks like iced coffee and lemon-iced tea in Part III.

The wide world of spirits

Taking them alphabetically, the most widely enjoyed spirits are brandy, gin, rum, vodka, and whiskey. All of these so-called "hard" liquors are made by a combination of fermentation and distillation; wine and beer are made by fermentation only.

Also spirits or liquors, but sweet (as those named above are not), are liqueurs. These are potent spirits to which sweetening, flavorings, and sometimes coloring are added before bottling. The word "cordial" is often used interchangeably with "liqueur," but there is a technical difference between the two. Fine liqueurs are made by the distillation method (flavoring is added to a spirit that, after a waiting period, is redistilled and sweetened); cordials are produced by an infusion process (flavorings such as fruits and herbs are steeped in the spirit until the flavors are absorbed, then the solids are strained out). Lower-quality liqueurs are made by a third manufacturing method, the essence process, in which essential oils and sweetening are simply added and the liquor bottled with no further processing.

To better understand what you are buying, it is useful to know the meanings of a few trade terms.

Aging is not required by all liquors, but those that need it are not suitable for drinking until they have aged a given number of years. Longer aging improves the quality of some liquors. Aging is done before bottling, since liquors do not appreciably mellow or mature in the bottle as some wines do.

Neat and *straight* are used synonymously to mean liquid exactly as it comes from the bottle—nothing added, not even ice. "Straight," however, also has a technical meaning, signifying a liquor that has not been blended.

Proof pertains to alcoholic content. In this country, for all practical purposes, a proof number is double the liquor's percentage of alcohol. A gin that is 90 proof, for example, is 45 percent alcohol.

Individual spirits and their service

Brandy is a broad term for liquors distilled from, among other things, beets, grains, sugar cane, fruits, and berries; the latter often carry the fruit or berry name: e.g., peach brandy and blackberry brandy. Brandy is aged before bottling. The most celebrated brandies are cognac and armagnac, both proud products of France. With brandies as with restaurants, stars indicate quality. Initials signify particular quality characteristics: C=Cognac, E=Especial, F=Fine, O=Old, P=Pale, S=Superior, X=Extra. "V" before an initial stands for "Very." Thus, VSOP, one of the best-known initial groups and most expensive.

Brandy is served with soda or water as a highball, or on the rocks. Fruit brandies appear in some cocktails. But the classic use is after-dinner, with or following coffee, neat or half-and-half with a liqueur. Brandy-liqueur combinations are served in liqueur glasses. For straight brandy, a liqueur glass is correct, but a snifter or inhaler is traditional—and much more fun. For one thing, they permit "warming": cupping one's hands around the bowl so the heat of the hands will bring out the aroma. No more than about two ounces per serving, however, no matter which glass you use.

Gin, being almost pure neutral spirits, can be made from many substances, but is usually produced from grain. It gets its name from the French *genévrier*, or juniper, whose berries give gin its distinctive taste.

Gin is the basis for two favorite drinks: the martini, for which dry gins are best, and the gin and tonic, for which any gin will do, since the flavor is very nearly lost in the mixer.

Rum is distilled from fermented molasses or other sugar cane products. Rum drinkers usually choose one of three types: very pale rum, light in taste as well as

Rum is a favorite for punches and cocktails, some of the better-known names being planter's punch, mai tai, daiquiri, and piña colada. Some like it hot, as grog

color; golden rum, somewhat heavier and darker; or dark rum, heaviest of all and strongest in taste.

(the updated version, which is spiced, sweetened, and laced with lemon) or as hot buttered rum.

Vodka, at its best, is made from grains. White, crystal clear, and somewhat "fiery" or biting on the tongue, it has no distinctive flavor or aroma and so leaves less "breath" than other hard liquors. Vodka does not need aging.

The service of vodka is similar to that of gin, this liquor being used, like gin, in martinis and tonic drinks. Vodka is favored in its own right, however, in many celebrated drinks, among them the Bloody Mary, screwdriver, gimlet, and stinger. Europeans often down it ice-cold and "neat" from shot glasses.

Whiskies are a story in themselves, with their many varieties and distinctive tastes. Colorless when they come from the still, whiskies acquire color in aging and finishing. They are aged in casks or barrels, often of a very special character that affects both taste and color; color may be heightened with small amounts of caramel and other substances. What goes into blended whiskies is a carefully kept secret among distillers because blending influences a brand's characteristics. Bourbon is never a blend; it is always the product of a single distillation. "Bottled in bond," another familiar phrase, doesn't signify quality, as many people assume, but simply that a whiskey is government-inspected, four years old, and 100 proof. A quick way to recognize such whiskies: seals on their bottle tops are green; all others are red.

Most whiskey drinkers have an undeviating loyalty to one type or another and will "accept no substitutes." To the home partygiver, this means having both Scotch and a choice with other attributes. Whiskey served straight in a shot glass should have a chaser of water on the side. Use an old-fashioned glass for on-the-rocks, mists, or "ice and a little water," the whiskey styles many people like as pre-dinner drinks. For whiskey and water or soda, or whiskey with a soft drink such as ginger ale, either a straight-sided tumbler or a highball glass will do. So popular are these simple styles of serving that it is easy to forget the many mixed drinks based on one whiskey type or another. Among the classics: Manhattan and Rob Roy cocktails; old-fashioneds and sours; milk punches; boiler-makers; and that most hospitable of Southerners, the mint julep.

Liqueurs and cordials

Though, as explained earlier, there is a technical difference in the processes by which these liquors are made (cordials being fine liqueurs produced by infusion, other liqueurs by distillation), for party purposes the two are interchangeable. They are served after dinner, preferably away from the table, either with or right after coffee. It should be remembered that these pretty liquors are powerful—few less than 30 percent alcohol (60 proof) and some as high as 160 proof. Thus the use of the tiny stemmed liqueur glass, holding only about an ounce, and never more than two—and even then filled no more than two-thirds full.

Because liqueur and cordial colors are as varied and distinctive as their flavors, an assortment, in decanters or the original bottles, is in itself a handsome display. The names, too, are exotic and elegant: Benedictine, Cointreau, Chartreuse, Grand Marnier, Amaretto, creme de menthe, creme de cacao, Galliano, Drambuie, Sambuca, Kahlua. Served straight as a rule, many liqueurs make phenomenal mixed drinks and certain ones do wonders for desserts. Grand Marnier soufflé is a notable example; others are liqueurs used as flavorings for cut-up fresh fruits and as sauces for ice cream and pudding.

Aperitifs

Though these appetizer drinks are far from displacing the more familiar pre-dinner drinks, they, like the simple glass of white wine, are changing the before-dinner drinking habits of many Americans. Long fancied in European countries for this purpose, their names speak of their origins: Dubonnet, Lillet, Campari, Cynar, Punt e Mes, Pernod, Ricard, ouzo. Long before these were ever heard of, however (in this country at least), the classic aperitifs were, as they still are, dry sherry and sweet and dry vermouth.

The red-and-white, sweet-and-dry choice offered by the vermouths is a clue to the variations among aperitifs, important to understand because people's preferences generally lean toward one characteristic flavor or the other. Essentially, aperitifs are sweet (red vermouth being sweeter than white) or bitter (Campari is an example). Which characteristic predominates depends on the blend of herbs and spices, roots and barks, quinine, wine, or brandy from which an aperitif is compounded. (Vermouth and sherry are exceptions, both being forms of wine, herb flavored and fortified respectively; see *Wines* below.) Quinine gives Campari its distinctive bitterness, as it does Cynar and Punt e Mes, the latter two both made from artichokes. Certain aperitifs are based on aniseed—Pernod and Ricard from France, ouzo from Greece.

Lest it be assumed that these are as innocent and harmless as the glass of white wine, the fact is quite the opposite. Far from mild, aperitifs are stronger than brandy, and need dilution with water or soda before serving.

Wines

Whole books having been written on this subject, and whole lives devoted to its study, what follows will not be an attempt to deal with wines in all their complexity. For the needs of most people, it is necessary to know only the general wine classifications, their purposes and their service, plus the meanings of a few frequently used terms. There is a growing trend toward offering guests wine, beer, and soft drinks, thus eliminating the need to set up a bar stocked with many different kinds of liquors.

Basically, wines are sweet or dry—or, less simplistically, definitely more one than the other. Markedly sweet wines are correctly served only with or immediately after dessert. All others can be classified as "table wines," those that go best with main courses.

Before discussing wines in particular, it might be well to explain two terms often used in connection with them: *Aging* is important to wines, but there is no desirable standard length of time or method, each wine having its own "prime point" and requirements. Among other considerations, wine is the only alcoholic beverage that ages in the bottle (unless aging has been intentionally halted before bottling). Age alone does not signify that a wine is a fine one, and the date on the label will not make a good wine of a poor one. *Vintage*, in wines, does not mean old. It simply means wine from a year in which weather was favorable for the production of superior wine grapes. Unless you plan to make a research project of wine buying, it is best to find, and be guided by, a trustworthy dealer as to good and bad years.

Dessert wines. These very sweet wines are served before, rather than with, coffee; only liqueurs are powerful enough to compete successfully with coffee's strong taste. Generally confined to dinner service, dessert wines are sometimes served in the afternoon with cake or cookies. Some, though by no means all, such wines are *fortified,* which brings their alcohol content to about 20 percent. (A small amount of spirit, usually brandy, is added; sherries are fortified wines.) Besides sweet sherry, well-known dessert wines include port, tokay, muscatel, sweet sauterne, sparkling burgundy, and champagne. Service, except for burgundy and champagne, is usually in a small glass—wine, sherry, or even liqueur types.

The significance of "dry" and "sweet." A dry wine is one that has been fermented until all the grape sugar has been converted to alcohol. Sweet cannot be defined so flatly, the problem being "how sweet is sweet" in any except the intensely sweet dessert wines. A wine will be "on the sweet side," by varying degrees, if fermentation is stopped before all the sugar is turned to alcohol. The amount of remaining sugar may be so small only an expert can detect it, but the tiniest bit is enough to justify its being too "sweet" to be called a dry. The wisest course is to try a few wines (mainly whites; red tend to be on the dry side) until you find one or two that you like. Again, your liquor dealer can advise you.

Champagnes come sweet and dry; sweet ones are best with desserts. The choicest champagnes are the driest; words to look for are, in order of dryness: *natural,* the driest; *brut, sec,* and *demi-sec.* If none of these appears on a label, the champagne is sweet. A champagne should be served well-chilled, and opened just before serving (see *Opening wines*).

(In the dry-sweet connection, a word about the fortifying of wines, mentioned above: its purpose is to stop fermentation before all the sugar turns to alcohol, and also to act as a preservative to prevent souring after the bottle is opened, and to add strength and flavor.)

Table wines. Here we meet another false assumption: that "table wines" are "humble" wines for everyday meals, comparable to the "house wines" in undistinguished restaurants. Table wines, quite simply, are so classified to distinguish them as wines that go well with main courses from wines that do not. Nowadays, in wine service with meals very nearly anything goes: red or white, as you choose, with the foods you are serving (no more absolutes about "red with meat, white with fish and poultry," unless that is what you like); several wines with the main course, or just one; glasses meant for the red or the white, or an all-purpose glass for either. And of course wines may be imported or domestic, our domestic wines having become world class.

Red wines more often than not tend to be dry, and heavier than most whites. They are generally served at roughly 65° F. Red wines are excellent with red meats, dark-meat fowl such as duck and goose, and pasta and strong cheeses, but can be served with chicken, veal, or fish.

White wines range in color from pale gold through amber to faintly green. More delicate in flavor, by and large, than the reds, they are highly compatible with lighter foods—seafood and such white meats as veal, chicken, and turkey, as well as egg dishes and other lightly seasoned entrées. White wines should be chilled, which should not be interpreted as "ice-cold."

Rosé wines, those pretty pinks that fall between the reds and the whites, find few fans among wine connoisseurs but they are refreshing to see and taste, in the summer months especially, when cool lightness in any form is welcome. A bit too light to keep company with beef—and, some say, too heavy for seafood—rosés are delightful with white meats and poultry and with summer's light salads and sandwiches.

Sparkling wines, another form that experts do not take too seriously, are themselves unpretentious. They can be served any time, with or without food. Be they red, white, or pink, the sparklers should always be nicely chilled.

All of these wines find their way into punches and coolers: red wine in the Swedish glögg and the Spanish sangría; burgundy in mulled wine; whites or a sparkling wine in summer coolers. A white-wine form of sangria is popular in Latin American countries and becoming popular here.

Bringing wine to its proper temperature. Proper temperature, even for red wines, is never warm. "Room temperature," the recommendation for reds, does not mean the actual temperature of a comfortably warm dining room, but 60 to 65° F. If a red wine has been stored in a cool place, it should be allowed to stand in a warmer room for several hours. If, on the other hand, its temperature must be reduced rapidly, it may be cooled briefly in a refrigerator.

In the matter of cooling or chilling, you may hear that "cool" and "chilled" have sharply different meanings. While it is true that rosés are served cool, and whites, along with champagne and other sparkling wines (red or white), are supposed to be chilled, not to worry. Chilled is colder than cool (about 45 as compared to about 55° F.), but a wine that is too cold will soon warm up after serving; one that is not quite cold enough will chill quickly in a bucket or wine cooler of ice.

The cool-to-chilled wines can spend varying times in the refrigerator, even very briefly, in an emergency, in the freezer. They should never, however, be allowed to freeze. Time in the cooler will produce results faster if salt is added to the ice; twirling the bottle will speed the process, too, by bringing the warm center contents of the bottle in contact with its cold sides. Wine coolers or chillers (the new, simpler kind, not the champagne bucket on a stand) can be kept on the table so refills will be reliably cool (or chilled). If a wine bottle is dripping from melting ice or condensation, wrap it in a napkin for pouring. That is the traditional napkin's only purpose, so using it on a dry bottle would be pointless and a bit ostentatious.

Decanting. Decanting is essentially pouring wine (but not sparkling wine) from its bottle into another container, leaving any sediment behind. You may choose to decant because the wine was bought in bulk or because you own a beautiful decanter you enjoy using and displaying. Decanting keeps traces of sediment or bits of crumbled cork from getting into the glasses when the wine is poured. (Sediment is a problem mainly with old red wines; white wines produce no sediment.) Decanting is seldom necessary. Sediment will stay undisturbed in the bottom of a carefully handled bottle, all of it remaining in the final few ounces, which are not served.

Wines to be served cool are generally brought to the table in their original bottles. If they should happen to be decanted, the decanter should also be chilled. Wine decanters are, by convention, placed on the table without their stoppers.

There is an informal kind of decanter that is basically nothing but a server. These decanters are charming and convenient but have nothing whatever to do with the filtering of sediment. Such a decanter, if it is to contain white or rosé wine, should, as a practical matter, be chilled.

Wine glasses. Red and white wines have their traditional glasses, but an all-purpose glass is incomparably the more sensible buy. These are much

Informal wine carafes.

like other wine glasses—stemmed and fairly straight-sided—but they have much greater capacity: six ounces and up, quite far up, as a matter of fact. They can be used for any table wine, red or white, still or sparkling, though champagne still deserves the compliment of one of the special glass shapes made expressly for its service (preferably the "tulip" shape, from which less carbonation will escape). Since wine glasses of adequate quality are so often sold in inexpensive sets that work out to very little per glass, many people buy a dozen or two ordinary glasses for everyday and casual purposes, and keep in reserve a quantity of the more specialized types, perhaps in a better quality, for more formal or special occasions. Glasses of any quality are subject to breakage and—at buffets if not at table—the need for a clean supply to accommodate refills, so it is best to purchase in dozens when you buy, unless matching is of no importance to you.

Opening wines. Red wines should be opened about an hour before serving; most need time to "breathe," though some—beaujolais, for example—do not. Whites are generally opened just before guests are seated, sparkling wines not until just before the wine is to be served. If a metal foil covers the cork, cut it off neatly so there is a smooth edge below the lip. Wipe the cork, then insert the corkscrew or cork puller very gently to avoid knocking crumbs from the cork. Ease the cork out—don't jerk it. Before pouring, give the bottle top another wipe to remove any stray bits of cork.

Champagne is a little tougher to open. For one thing, the cork is held by wire to secure it against the built-up pressure in the bottle. The wire need not be cut. Find a little loop in it, pull the loop up, and the whole wire cage will come off. Then, grasping the neck of the bottle firmly with both hands—and aiming it away from all nearby targets—slowly ease the cork out with your thumbs. A loud pop may be a thrill to some, but experts try for a muffled pop, knowing from experience that an explosive sound too often means a fountain of foam. Have an ice-cold teaspoon on hand in case a bottle should start spurting. Insert its handle into the neck of the offending bottle, and the deluge will stop.

Pouring wine. Along with omitting the napkin unless the bottle is dripping wet, there are a few guidelines worth knowing about pouring. Holding the bottle around its middle, fill each glass to the proper level (not more than half to two-thirds full so the bouquet has room to rise) and, after each pour, give the bottle a bit of a twist to keep the last drop from falling onto the cloth. Wait until guests are seated before pouring the first glass; after that, wine can be poured for (or with) each succeeding course.

Wine storage. Wine to be kept for any length of time should be stored in a dark, cool place not subject to wide variations in temperature; 55° F. is considered ideal. It should not be allowed to chill below 40° F. or, conversely, be stored next to heating pipes or any other source of excessive warmth.

Store bottles with cork stoppers on their sides to keep the cork moist. If you do not, the cork will dry in due course, the seal will be broken, and the wine will spoil. They can be stored upright, though, if you will be using them within a month or so. Bottles with screw tops or plastic stoppers need no special precautions—except, of course, avoidance of extreme heat or cold. Jug wines, some of which have screw-on or plastic tops and some corks, can all be stored upright—for evidence, glance at any liquor store's refrigerated supply.

Beer and ale

Beer and ale drinkers, like whiskey loyalists, have their favorites, but they are less rigid about them. This releases you from any need to search for a particular brand or brands and makes it possible to buy the beverage you select in the most economical form. This may be economy-size bottles or cases; choices are obviously broader by the case since very few brands are bottled in extra-large sizes.

Choices as to type and container are quite simple: beer or ale, imported or domestic, regular or light, cans or bottles (imports and premium beers and ales are generally bottled). The strong, dark beer called stout, though something of a rarity on American bar lists, is another possibility. What is important is that your selection, whatever it turns out to

Attractive garnishes for a variety of drinks: celery rib, cucumber peel, whole cloves, horse's neck, half-slice of fresh lemon, orange peel rose, scallion brush, fresh mint springs, cinnamon stick, cherry tomato, stemmed strawberries, stemmed maraschino cherries, cocktail onion and olives, slices of fresh lime.

be, be served icy-cold. Don't put chilled cans or bottles on the bar; keep them in the refrigerator or in a container of crushed ice or cubes until it is time to open them.

There is a school of thought that insists no beer or any variation thereon should ever be served *too* cold, the theory being that a temperature of 45 to 50° F. brings out its flavor best. While this is unquestionably true of some imported beers and ales, you are the best judge of how you like your domestics.

Beer by the keg, perhaps the greatest economy of all for large quantities, has been left to last because it poses a different chilling problem. Order it chilled if you can, but be sure you know beforehand how you will *keep* it cool; if advance chilling is not possible, you must also figure out how to chill it in the first place. Burying in crushed ice is the best solution for reaching or maintaining the proper degree of "chill"; most distributors will provide a tub big enough for both keg and ice. If serving will be prolonged, two kegs—one being chilled while the other is in use—are best. If a single keg must be chilled and used at the same time, maneuvering it can be quite a job. A filled keg, very heavy to begin with, becomes even harder to handle when it's slipping around in melting ice. Tapping a keg, too, is quite a trick; if you have never tapped one, ask your supplier to explain how it's done.

The proper "party" way to serve these beverages is in steins or pilsner glasses or straight-sided tumblers. If, at a very casual event, people prefer drinking right from the can or even bottle, guests, like customers, are always right. Glasses, if they are used, should be sparkling clean and preferably chilled.

These include the flavored types (ginger ale, colas, citrus soft drinks) and those that are unflavored (tonic water, club soda, and sparkling waters—the latter two being much the same as to taste and purpose). Citrus-flavored tonics are available, if you or some of your guests like this quite different taste. All of these are useful for "straight" drinking and, in one situation or another, as mixers. They can be bought in 6-packs or economy-size glass or plastic bottles, as you think most convenient or easiest to chill. Cases are a possibility if a party is very large.

Soft drinks and mixers

Like beer, these canned or bottled beverages should be kept refrigerated but you can chill a supply, if you want or need to, in any big, clean, preferably plastic (plastic-lined) container that will hold both the beverages and an adequate quantity of ice cubes. Never count on ice used for this sort of chilling as emergency ice cubes for drinks—keep the two carefully separate so they cannot be confused by anyone, including your guests.

Bar glassware: choosing the right shapes and sizes

All glasses for bar use fall into two main categories, tumblers (any glass without either stem or handle) and stemware. This is very close to useless information, however, in view of the fact that either type often suits a particular purpose (cocktail glasses may be either tumbler or stemmed, for example). The best way to understand glassware is in terms of types meant for specific purposes. You will also be able to grasp immediately how well they might serve another pupose, or how a quite different glass might be appropriate to theirs.

Pilsner and stein

Glasses expressly for beer are the pilsner, which holds about 10 ounces; and the stein or mug, with a capacity ranging from about 8 to 16 ounces. Beer may also be served correctly in a straight-sided tumbler (see *Water goblet and tumbler*); the average water glass holds 7 to 10 ounces.

Glassware types and their purposes

Snifter	Brandy is traditionally served "neat" in what is called a snifter (or inhaler) composed of a balloon-shaped bowl on a squat stem. Its value lies in the round bowl, narrower at the rim, which holds in the aroma of the liquor—to brandy fanciers, the key to its charm. Capacities range from about 6 to 25 ounces. A liqueur glass is also appropriate for straight brandy (see *liqueur glass*). Even if served in a huge balloon, no more than about 2 ounces of brandy should be poured at one time.
Stemmed and tumbler-type cocktail glasses	Cocktail glasses, whether stemmed or tumbler-type, will hold about 3 to 4½ ounces, though only about 2 ounces of that capacity should be filled at each pouring. Cocktails "on the rocks," such as martinis, should be served in a single-size old-fashioned glass (see *Old-fashioned*).
Typical cooler	Coolers or Collins glasses are the tall glasses meant for "long" drinks, often packed with ice. Capacities are generous—up to, in one popular size, 16 ounces. In a pinch, a highball or iced-tea glass will suffice.
Straight-sided and stemmed high-ball glass	Highball glasses, like so many others, may correctly be straight-sided or stemmed. A point to remember about tumbler types as you consider buying them: be sure they are sufficiently bottom-heavy so they won't tip. A highball glass will usually hold from 10 to

	12 ounces. Good for drinks made with soda, water, tonic, or comparable mixers.
Iced-tea goblet and tumbler	An iced-tea glass, in either of the basic shapes, holds a bit more than a highball—about 12 ounces is the usual size.
Liqueur glass	Liqueur or cordial glasses (also called "ponies") are a tiny 1 to 2 ounces in capacity, perhaps because of the powerhouses these sweet and pretty liquors really are. Among the loveliest liqueur serving styles, and one for which there is a special glass, is a drink called a pousse-café, a sort of parfait concoction in which different liqueurs are floated on top of one another.
Old-fashioned glass, single and double	Old-fashioned glasses are straight-sided and "built low to the ground." They come in two sizes: the smaller, or single, holding about 8 ounces, the larger, or double, about 16. These are fine for any drink served on the rocks, and are sometimes used for sours, though there is a special glass (see *Sour glass* below) for that kind of drink.
Glass punch cup	Punch cups made of glass, and handled, range from 4 to 5 ounces in capacity. Fill these two-thirds full.
Shot glass	Shot glasses are for drinking whiskey and high-proof imported vodkas "neat," the custom of many devotees of these drinks. Candi-

Shot glass (continued)	dates for this treatment are vodkas from Poland, Russia, Finland, and Sweden. Neat vodka should be served ice-cold. Shot glasses range in size from 1 to 3 ounces, 1½-ounce being most popular.
Sour glass, stemmed and Delmonico	Sour glasses that are stemmed hold about 4½ ounces, the Delmonico, or straight-sided version, about 5. Though Bloody Marys generally go in old-fashioned glasses (always when several ice cubes are desired), a sour glass is sometimes used.
Water goblet and tumbler	Water is served, on formal occasions, in stemmed goblets; at any and all other times, a water tumbler will do. Tumblers are handy, too, for casual servings of beer. Total capacity tends to be about 10 ounces or slightly more.

Wine glasses

Glass choices here are best understood in terms of the four types into which wines can be divided at the simplest level: pre-dinner or aperitif wine (dry sherry); the table wines served with main courses; dessert wines; and champagne, in a class by itself as suitable for serving all through a meal. Dry sherry has another, increasingly rare, mealtime use: it is sometimes served with clear soups, or soups in which sherry is an ingredient, such as turtle or snapper.

Traditional "pointed" sherry glass and one with more rounded bowl	For the service of sherry, the "pointed" shape is traditional but a more rounded shape, not unlike a diminutive red wine, is equally acceptable. Capacities range from about 2 to 3 ounces in the traditional glass, to 4 in the more rounded shape. The glass remains the same whether sherry is dry or sweet, and regardless of when it is served.

Red, white, all-purpose, and "balloon" wine glass

Rules for table wines have relaxed considerably in recent years, and the options continue to increase, generally in the direction of greater capacity and versatility.

The classic red wine is relatively tulip shaped, with a capacity of 6 to 9 ounces.

The traditional white wine is slimmer, straighter, and smaller —about 4 to 6 ounces.

The all-purpose wine glass is fast stealing the table scene, adapting itself to reds and whites, rosés and sparkling wines—and to uncomplicated and economical buying, being "cheaper by the dozen" and often sold that way. A bubble-shaped hybrid of the red and white wine glass contours, it holds 6 to 9 ounces and upward.

So-called "balloon" glasses are primarily for red wines, such as burgundy, to be consumed in lusty quantities. They are generous containers, too, for the light wines such as rosé, still or sparkling, and for sparkling burgundy and Asti spumante.

Glasses for dessert wines

Dessert wines can be served as a rule, in a white wine glass; sherry (sweet in the case of dessert) has its own special-purpose glass. Among the familiar names are port (served at room temperature) and sweet sauternes (these, like sweet sherry, should be chilled). Once a fixture of formal meals, dessert wines now appear less and less frequently.

Saucer, tulip, and flute champagne glass	Champagne glasses may be saucer-shaped (the most familiar, used also for champagne cocktails and frozen daiquiris) or tulip- or flute-shaped. Capacity is generally about 6 ounces. A white wine glass is also a suitable server for champagne.
Rhine/Moselle glass	For certain special wines, there are specialized glasses, always striking in design and often decorated or made of colored glass as well. Not necessary to any basic wine-glass inventory, they are incomparable, in appearance and function, for their purpose and, on the rare occasions when they come proudly off the shelf, add immeasurably to the drama of the event.

A point is made, by many experts, of precisely how full any glass should be in its particular situation: half, three-quarter, to the top, and so on. Except for the very powerful liqueurs and brandy, for example, where small quantities are obviously prudent, this depends on your preference. If two authorities can't agree as to whether a cocktail glass should be half-filled or filled to the rim, why should you listen to either?

Calculating quantities

What amounts are necessary—of liquors, mixers, even ice—will depend to a great extent on the drinking habits (or capacities) of your friends, and whether you are a precise measurer or a freehand and somewhat generous pourer. There are general guidelines, however, for all of these necessities that will help you to work up a basic liquor list, subject to amending—as to quantities, or particular liquor types—as you see fit. Liquors are generally used roughly in these amounts: 1½ ounces in cocktails (allowing for varying ratios, as in, for example, martinis); 1½ to 2 ounces in mixed drinks, and neat or on-the-rocks servings; 1 to 1½ ounces of liqueurs and aperitifs (a bit more of some, such as dry sherry or vermouth); and 4 ounces of wine (the amount going up proportionately with the size of the glass).

In the days when most hard liquors were sold in quarts, an even 32 ounces, calculation was simple: 32 ounces would yield an even sixteen 2-ounce drinks, about 20 to 21 if they were 1½-ounce. Now that liters (at 33.8 ounces) have virtually replaced quarts, calculations might seem more complicated but actually are not. A liter gives you about one more 2-ounce drink, perhaps two more 1½-ounce drinks. (Fifths still line liquor store shelves, and remain what they have always been: 25.6 ounces. For entertaining, it is almost always more practical to buy the larger sizes, since the price difference isn't significant and the convenience is, along with the reassurance of knowing you are amply supplied. An even better buy, in all these ways, is the 1.75 liter bottle, close to a half gallon, now a standard size for most basic liquors.)

Liqueurs and aperitifs, coming as they do from countries that have always used the metric system of measurement, are bottled in liter or part-liter (milliliter) sizes. Because these liquors are infrequently used and a selection is recommended, liqueurs and cordials, and aperitifs as well, are generally bought in smaller sizes than the whiskies, gins, rums, and vodkas. (An exception is brandy, most favored of the after-dinner drinks and served highball-style as well. A good-sized bottle of an excellent cognac may be the only post-dinner choice in many households, and a fine one it is. Vermouths, too, are versatile, acting as aperitifs and as components of cocktails, which justifies buying the liter-size bottle.)

The popularity of wines has led to a wide choice of brands and types, and of bottle sizes as well. Quantities are indicated in liters or milliliters (thousandths of a liter), and two sizes in wide distribution are the 750 mL size (¾ of a liter, close to a standard fifth) and 1.5 liters, exactly twice the 750 mL size. Both imports and domestics can be bought in a comparable range of sizes, in all the routinely used table wine types—whites, reds, and rosés. Champagne has its own bottle sizes, ranging from the small splits to magnums (two quarts) and beyond.

Economical purchasing of liquors and wines varies according to the quantity, and sometimes quality, required for a particular party. For a party, the economy possibilities are larger bottle sizes; cases; discount buying. A fourth is house brands, often cheaper than name brands (but not necessarily as good; buy better brands for neat or other drinks where quality counts, and a lack of it is obvious). Since each state has its own laws about liquor sales—where it may be sold, and on what basis—it is best to investigate the sources in your community until you find one whose prices seem most reasonable to you. In some areas, liquor is available at semi-wholesale prices (slightly above wholesale) to retail purchasers. Ask about returns of unopened bottles; this feature, common in consignment buying, can often be arranged. Bear in mind that a spare supply can be useful for future entertaining, and bottled liquors, tightly capped, can be kept virtually forever.

The following guidelines may be useful when stocking your party bar. To be sure you have plenty of supplies on hand, substitute quart or liter-size bottles for fifths. The calculations for wine are based on serving a single glass of red or white during the meal. When purchasing club soda, mineral water, ginger ale, or other mixers, buy a quart for every three guests.

	Number of People	Number of 1½ Ounce Drinks	Quantity Needed
Cocktails	6	12–18	2 fifths
	8	16–24	2 fifths
	12	24–36	3 fifths
	20	40–60	5 fifths

	Number of People	Number of 4 Ounce Servings	Quantity Needed
Wine and Champagne	6	12	2 fifths
	8	16	3 fifths
	12	24	4 fifths
	20	40	7 fifths

	Number of People	Number of 1 or 1½ Ounce Servings	Quantity Needed
Brandy and Liqueurs	6	6–12	1 fifth
	8	8–16	1 fifth
	12	12–24	1 fifth
	20	20–40	2 fifths

Liquor types for a basic bar

The all-purpose list that follows may very well not include all the liquor types that you favor. Some are well-liked in certain areas and less so in others; tequila for margaritas is an example. Also, no such list can take into account a drink that becomes a rising star, as the piña colada has quite recently done. The list below includes the appropriate liquors for those two drinks, but the popularity list changes every day. By the time any book is printed new stars may well be on the horizon.

The liquors listed are all candidates for entertaining but not all of them, of course, for any one party. The actual choices and quantities will depend on the occasion and number of guests, and on how large a drink selection you plan to offer. If you have the "advisables" on hand, or most of them, you will never be at a loss for bar service at a small dinner party or for incidental drinking. You may feel that some of the "advisables" belong on the "optional" list or vice versa. This is to be expected, since liquor, like food, is very much a matter of taste.

Advisable	Optional or occasional
"General drinking" (mixed drinks, highballs, neat, cocktails)	
Whiskies	
Scotch	2 Scotches, one light and one
Bourbon and/or	heavy
Blended whiskey	Rye
	Irish whiskey
Gin	Tequila
Vodka (low-proof, for mixed and tonic drinks)	Vodka (high-proof imports for martinis and neat drinking)
Rum (light)	Rum (dark)
Pre-dinner	
Vermouths (sweet and dry)	Larger supply if used, on occasion, both as an aperitif and as an ingredient (dry in martinis; sweet in Manhattans, Rob Roys, etc.)
Sherry (dry)	Additional sherries (medium-dry, sweet)
Aperitifs (one of the sweets, such as Lillet, Dubonnet, Byrrh; one of the bitters, such as Campari or Punt e Mes)	

A basic bar supply

115

After-dinner

Brandies

Cognac

Liqueurs and cordials*

A selection of 3 or 4 "familiars": Benedictine, B & B, Cointreau, Drambuie, Galliano, Grand Marnier, Kahlua

Fruit brandies (Kirsch, framboise, Calvados, mirabelle, etc.)

Other popular choices to try from time to time: Amaretto, anisette, Chartreuse, Midori, Triple Sec, creme de cacao, creme de cassis, creme de menthe, Irish cream

*It can be interesting to experiment with liqueurs as dessert ingredients or sauces for ice cream and pudding.

Wines

Dry white

Dry red

Rosés

Port or Madeira

Sparkling wines, such as Asti spumante

Champagne

Beer is best considered separately because it is consumed differently from other liquors. Beers and ales, with comparatively few exceptions, are sold in what might be called "individual containers." Even a 16-ounce can, which could theoretically provide two or three servings, might as a matter of courtesy be given to a guest and the extra servings become refills.

From an economy standpoint, beer (including ales), imported and domestic, can be bought in six-packs of cans or bottles (eight-packs of smaller-than-standard bottles); the most popular beers come in several can and bottle sizes. Beer-by-the-pack is probably as economical a way as any to buy beer for a small-to-average party, and certainly the handiest. Cases will affect a further economy. For a very large and prolonged event, consider purchasing beer by the keg.

Just as with the sale of liquors, laws covering the sale of beer vary from state to state. Sometimes it is sold in supermarkets, sometimes by liquor dealers or distributors. The best approach to purchasing is to check into local sources and find the one with the best prices and service—such as pre-chilling, which is sometimes possible and can be most convenient. Also, as with unopened bottles of liquors, unopened cans or bottles can sometimes be returned for refund. This might lose you any discount advantage, however. In either case, liquor or beer, such a refund arrangement may be more trouble than it is worth. Neither will ever "go bad," and both will eventually be useful.

When buying such mixers as quinine (tonic) water, club soda, ginger-ale, or sparkling mineral water, allow about a quart-size bottle (or the equivalent) for every three persons. Soft drinks, regular or diet, can be bought in cans or glass bottles; these are easier to chill than the large 1- and 2-liter plastic bottles, but in every other way the "giant" sizes offer advantages. Take care, when you bury cans or bottles in ice to chill them, to mix up beer and soft drinks, or stack them in alternating layers, so that you can always get at whichever one you want.

Have separate ice supplies for chilling and for drinking and don't be tempted to use the former for the latter. (Ice used for chilling isn't clean.) For drinking purposes, allow about a pound of cubes per person, a little less for a short party or very few drinks, a bit more for prolonged drinking or on a very hot day. As for chilling, ice cubes melt faster than blocks; best is a combination of the two. There is no harm in a certain amount of ice water; it can even be beneficial, because water comes into such direct contact with the sides of the cans or bottles. Maintain a good ratio of water to ice, however; never let it get down to anywhere near water alone.

The well-equipped bar

Basic bar tools, if they are good ones, can be lifetime investments; as with kitchen implements, it is actually a saving to buy quality. The list of what you need depends, as with every other kind of supply, on your style of entertaining—kinds of occasions, number of people, selection of drinks. The items listed are all traditional equipment—for one kind of bar situation or another.

- measure (jigger glass, or two-ended measure with jigger on one end, the smaller pony on the other)
- cocktail shaker (metal shaker for drinks that require that sort of mixing, sturdy mixing glass for those that should only be stirred)
- long spoon or glass stirring rod
- wire strainer
- set of measuring spoons
- corkscrew or cork puller
- bottle/can opener
- small paring knife
- small cutting board
- muddler (for crushing sugar cubes, mint leaves, etc.)
- lime squeezer
- lemon stripper
- ice container and tongs
- coasters and cocktail napkins
- straws and toothpicks or cocktail picks
- ice pick or breaker (for block ice)
- paper towels and sponges

Electrics that can be handy

- blender or food processor
- juicer
- ice crusher

Bar "groceries" (garnishes, characteristic touches)

- green cocktail olives (pitted, or specially stuffed, as with almonds or anchovies)
- maraschino cherries
- pearl onions
- fresh oranges, lemons, limes (for ingredients, slices, wedges, strips)
- bottled lemon juice
- bottled lime juice (e.g., for gimlet)
- tomato juice (or vegetable juice, clam-and-tomato, etc.)
- Worcestershire sauce
- Tabasco
- special or occasional garnishes, stirrers, etc.: fresh celery, cucumber, scallions, mint, cherry tomatoes, stemmed strawberries, whole cloves, cinnamon sticks
- sugar (granulated and cubes)*
- salt and pepper*

Setting up a suitable bar

For comparatively small situations, such as before- and after-dinner drinks for up to a dozen people, no special bar set-up will be required. You need only provide a place for supplies (liquors, ice bucket, mixers) and an adequate "mixing" surface. The two can be the same or not; if not, they should be easily accessible to one another. One household keeps the makings, including glasses, on an étagère and uses a large cocktail table, an arm's length away, as a work surface. Homes with built-in bars are especially well prepared. Folding tray-tables are a convenient resting place for supplies, but rarely large enough for mixing.

Drinks for a small group can also be mixed in the kitchen. If you are serving only one kind of drink nothing could be simpler. But even if you are "taking orders" for drinks of several kinds, kitchen mixing is still feasible for a limited number. Whereas drinks mixed "on the spot" can be handed around individually, those mixed in the kitchen are best passed on a tray.

It is for large parties, upwards of a dozen to as many as fifty people, that special bar arrangements become unavoidable. What you must decide then is whether a bartender is advisable or the bar can be self-service.

A bartender, professional or competent amateur, is invaluable for groups of 20 or more. One tended bar, properly positioned, can handle as

---

*For dipping rims of glasses in salt (margaritas) or sugar (Sidecar, some coolers and liqueurs), use coarse salt and superfine sugar. Technique is simple, and the same for both: Moisten rim about ¼ inch down with lemon, dip in saucer of salt or sugar, shake off excess.

many as 50 people rapidly and smoothly. If you were to settle for self-service to accommodate groups of that size, you would need to set up at least two bars. When the only space you can spare for a bar is either cramped or enclosed, a bartender becomes just about indispensable if traffic is not to bottle up uncomfortably.

The bar itself, in either case, should be 5 to 6 feet long and not more than 2 to 2½ feet wide. A bar any wider is difficult to reach across—for the bartender if there is one, for the guests if there is not. A bartender needs room *behind* the bar to move efficiently, guests need room in *front;* for a big crowd, a circulating space 10 by 10 feet is desirable. Be sure, too, that you can get at the bar easily to replenish ice or other supplies.

Try to keep self-service bars separate from one another. The two will act as magnets, attracting people to different areas and avoiding long lines or traffic jams in either. When a buffet table is involved, the principle is the same: encourage a smooth and speedy traffic flow by making it necessary for people to move away from the bar to the food, and vice versa. If the distance between the two is great enough, you will find this happening almost automatically.

Keep either bar or buffet table away from places where some other activity will inevitably be taking place: doorways and entry halls, coat closets, etc.

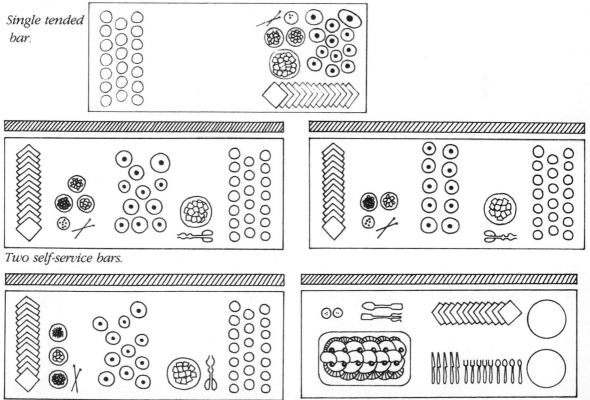

Single tended bar.

Two self-service bars.

Self-service bar and self-service buffet table.

Perfecting Your Party Setting

Table capacities

1. For a seated dinner: The best way to grasp the number of people that can be comfortably seated at tables of various standard sizes and shapes is to see them "in action." These drawings, to scale, will help you to picture the indicated numbers of guests at the specified tables. The progression goes, as actual tables do, from 36" square to 96" by 36" (straight tables) and from 24" to 72" (round). Seating capacities of oval tables are like those of rectangular tables having similar dimensions.

Square and rectangular   *Round*

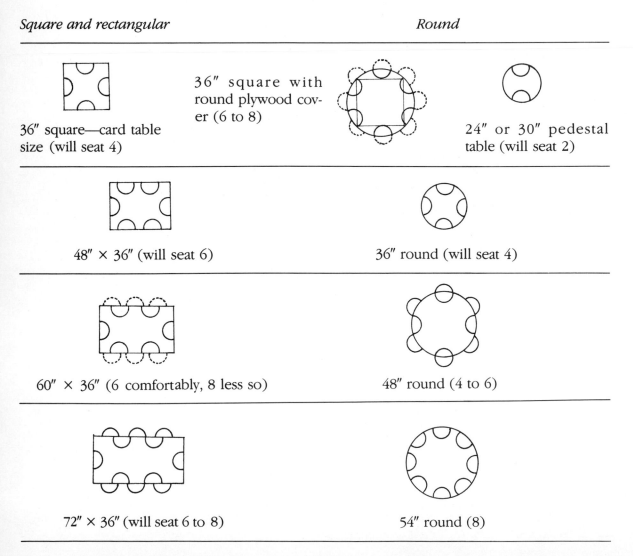

36" square—card table size (will seat 4)

36" square with round plywood cover (6 to 8)

24" or 30" pedestal table (will seat 2)

48" × 36" (will seat 6)

36" round (will seat 4)

60" × 36" (6 comfortably, 8 less so)

48" round (4 to 6)

72" × 36" (will seat 6 to 8)

54" round (8)

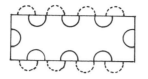

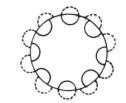

96″ × 36″ (8 comfortably, 10 less so)   60″ round (8 comfortably, 10 less so)

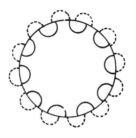

72″ round (10 comfort-
ably, 12 less so)

2. For buffet service: Any of the tables shown in the preceding chart can, of course, be enlisted for buffet service. In the small-to-medium range (up to about 60″ long, about 54″ in diameter), supposing a simple, one-dish entrée (indeed, nothing more lavish makes sense on a comparatively small table), the charted tables can accommodate roughly the same number of buffet guests as seated guests, perhaps an additional one or two. As tables grow larger—longer in the case of rectangular shapes, wider when it comes to round—buffet capacities increase significantly, progressing to a maximum, in the case of the largest, of some 12 to 18 or 20 people.

There are other table sizes, of course, than the range charted, especially among rectangular shapes. But rectangular tables, no matter what their dimensions, tend to be longer than they are wide, and rarely too wide to be reached comfortably across. Thus they are suited for either single access (table against a wall, guests filing by on only one side) or double access (table away from the walls, guests moving along both sides).

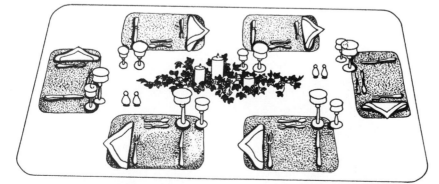

Place settings for seated dining after buffet service.

Round tables are a different matter, their length and width (diameters in both directions) being exactly the same. Very large round tables can handle a great many people, but only in a double access mode, with guests' needs arranged around the table's edge so that they never have to reach farther than, at most, halfway across its span—30″ or 36″ rather than 60″ or 72″. An exception is a round table of the drop-leaf type, which can successfully be placed against a wall if only one leaf is lifted, leaving the opposite side flat.

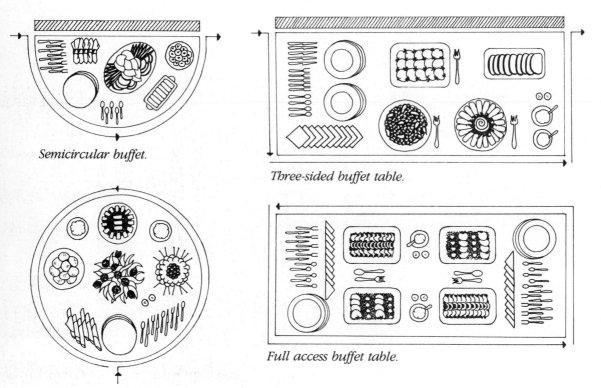

Semicircular buffet.

Three-sided buffet table.

Full access circular buffet.

Full access buffet table.

Table settings

Seated meals. With some understanding of the number of guests individual tables will accommodate (one of them, surely, exactly or very much like your own), the next step is the individual settings for these guests. What follows shows the essentials for a range of sit-down meals from breakfast through dinner, formal and informal. It is wise to have a mental picture of what *must* be on your table before going on to its decoration and accessorizing.

Informal breakfast.

Informal lunch.

Informal dinner.

Simplified formal place setting.

Formal place setting where appetizer is to be served.

Formal place setting where soup is first course.

Elaborate formal place setting.

Table-setting principles

Although table-setting rules are more rigorous for formal meals—largely because they involve many more, and often unfamiliar, elements—the basic principles do not vary a great deal from one meal to another. This is because, as is true of so many traditional procedures, the reason for the rules remains the same: to make a meal go smoothly, comfortably, and without confusion for the guests. If everything has its familiar place, people know how to proceed without either embarrassment or awkwardness.

The first element to be positioned is the plate. Plates are distributed symmetrically around the table, establishing the number and location of the settings. They may be service or place plates (usual only at comparatively formal meals), or breakfast, luncheon, or dinner plates at more casual meals.

Flatware is placed in a precise relation to the central plate: forks to its left, knives (and spoons, if any at the start of the meal) to its right. Placement is from the *outside in*—utensils are placed in order of their use, beginning with the one at the far left or far right. At a very formal meal, for example, the fork on the far left might be a fish fork (something of a rarity today but still seen on occasion); dinner fork and salad fork, in that order, would follow. If the salad were to be served before the entrée, the dinner-salad order of forks would be reversed.

Knives, with their blades always facing the plate, are generally no more than two: an appetizer knife (farthest out as first used) and a meat, or dinner, knife. A salad knife, in its proper order of use, is a possibility when cheese will accompany the salad—or simply as a thoughtful gesture should guests need its help in cutting such things as hearts of lettuce or other big, stubborn, or slippery salad ingredients.

Spoons, to the right of the knives, might be one or more of the following: a soup spoon (formal or informal meals), coffee spoon (teaspoon) when the beverage will be served as part of an informal meal (quite often this goes on the saucer), dessert spoon in a similarly informal situation. The only fork that is ever properly placed on the right is a seafood fork—far right, of course, this being the first course.

Elements surrounding the setting

Bread and butter plates and butter knives have all but disappeared from everyday tables. If used, they should go to the center plate's left, just above the forks. Even without them, butter (or margarine) should be presented with some style: butter in ¼ in. slices, perhaps on ice to keep the slices firm; margarine (the soft kind) in one of the ceramic or metal containers that enclose the entire tub.

Salt and pepper can be whatever suits your personal style: individual sets of shakers, small pepper mill or shaker with salt dish and spoon, mills for just the pepper, or for both peppercorns and coarse salt. Whichever you decide upon, have one "set" for every two guests.

Wine and water glasses for formal meals are arranged above the knives (and spoons, if any) on the right: water goblet first, wine glasses in diminishing order of size in a straight row to the goblet's right, or staggered (each one just a bit behind the other) in a slanting row down toward the right. This general row arrangement is functionally sound for any meal where there is to be both water (whether in goblet or tumbler) and wine—out of the way and still handy to get at. To see how this would work with a fairly extensive collection of wines, look at the illustration on page 123.

Dessert silver, on formal occasions, is not inserted into the order of use that applies to other flatware. It should either be put horizontally in place above the center plate at the start of the meal, or brought in at dessert time—fork balanced on the left edge and spoon on the right edge of the dessert plate. The guest then puts the silver down to the plate's left and right so the dessert may be placed on the plate.

Sugar and creamer sets need not be individual, or even one for each pair of guests, but should be plentiful enough to be within easy reach of everyone. A sugar shell is a nice touch for spooning granulated sugar; if sugar is in cubes, supply sugar tongs.

Coffee cups and saucers, or coffee mugs, are suitable table appointments when coffee will be served as part of an informal meal. Though demitasse coffee is ordinarily served in another room, on rare occasions it will appear at table. Its service should await the finish of the meal; it may be poured in the kitchen and passed on a tray, or poured by the hostess and passed from her place to individual diners. However its service is managed, the place of the demitasse cup and saucer is to the right of the dessert plate.

Ashtrays and cigarettes, perhaps attractive matches or small lighters as well, are entirely optional. More and more partygivers are omitting them. Some are motivated by a distaste for smoking in general, or at table in particular. Others place ashtrays on the table, but don't supply cigarettes, feeling that most guests prefer their own brands.

Fingerbowls have so nearly disappeared that it seems pointless to mention them. Should you, for any reason, wish to include them, they are most conveniently brought with the dessert plate and silver: on a doily or smaller plate on the dessert plate. Each guest rearranges the entire "assembly" to make way for the dessert, placing the finger bowl on its plate or doily up to the left.

Napkins

Napkins are the first of the table-setting components that can be chosen with a certain decorative latitude—in folding and placement for formal meals; in color, pattern, folding, and accessorizing for more casual ones.

As is illustrated by the drawings on page 123, napkins for formal meals may be on the service plate at the meal's beginning or, if that place will be taken by the appetizer (or soup), to the left of whatever forks are laid for

the meal. Folding possibilities are quite limited by formality. The usual style is to fold the napkin square into quarters, producing a smaller square; the sides are then folded under, each about one-third, turning the small square into a rectangle. If the napkin is initialed or monogrammed, or has a decorative corner motif, it should be folded so that this decorative element shows when the napkin is put in its position on the plate or table. Another method involves folding the square in half diagonally, then tucking under the two long points.

When meals are informal, all kinds of fun can be had with napkins—starting, of course, with almost complete freedom of choice. For intricate folding, napkins need to be fairly large (about 18″ square) and of a material that can be manipulated, creased, and pleated and then relied on to hold the contrived shape. This virtually eliminates fine and soft fabrics and synthetics, which lack the necessary body. Smaller breakfast or luncheon napkins, and paper napkins, which are folded squares when you buy them (already decorative if you select bright colors or patterns), need only be folded into rectangles (right and left sides folded under) or diagonally into triangles. Instead of making any special attempt at folding, you may prefer to use napkin rings that complement your table setting—ceramic, bamboo, wood, metal, plastic, to name just a few choices. Ribbon, wound once or twice around and tied in a big bow, makes a fine do-it-yourself napkin ring—and offers a natural chance to introduce more color contrast.

Think of your general decor, too, if you decide to try your hand at folding. Possibilities include a stand-up cone, into which greens can be tucked; an Oriental fan, which looks very pretty on a plate; and the more rounded lotus leaf shape. For buffets, you can fold the napkins into pocketed containers for silver: fold a big napkin square in half, fold one of the top (open) edges down to the fold, then fold the napkin, face down, back on itself in four quarter-folds. Turn it face up, and the bottom has become a flatware pocket.

Place and menu cards

Place and menu cards originated as accessories for formal or state functions, written or printed in black on white or buff stock. To a great extent, menu cards today are relegated solely to such occasions. Place cards, on the other hand, are used whenever they can simplify seating at

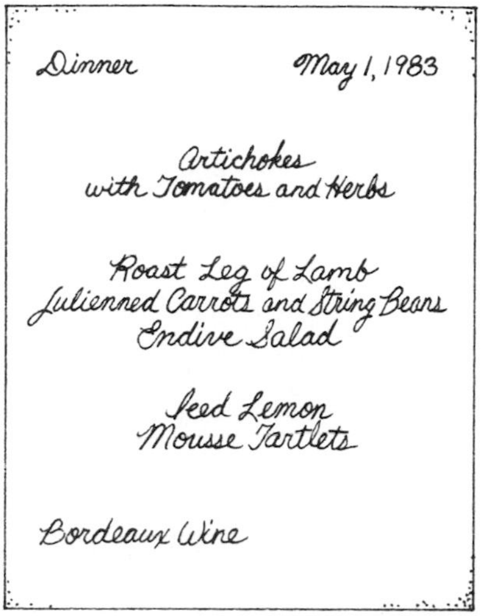

Dinner   *May 1, 1983*

*Artichokes
with Tomatoes and Herbs*

*Roast Leg of Lamb
Julienned Carrots and String Beans
Endive Salad*

*Iced Lemon
Mousse Tartlets*

Bordeaux Wine

fairly big events. Many authorities say they are advisable for guest lists of more than eight, though hostesses often value them at a party of any size simply to avoid confusion and to assure that their seating plan is followed.

Rare though they may be, menu cards can be a charming way to mark a very special occasion or to show pride in one's own cooking. The illustration shows a typical menu card, handwritten, with the meal name and date at the top and the courses, spaced well apart, filling the balance of the page. If the occasion celebrates a birthday or anniversary, the meal description should make that clear. Some menu cards give wine names and dates, if they are sufficiently special. A card for each two guests, placed between their settings, is sufficient; if the card is to be a memento of the event, one for each guest is better. The card itself should be about 5 by 7 inches or a bit smaller; the style can be as dignified or as relaxed as the occasion. If the foods are French or Italian or of some other foreign cuisine, it can be fun to name them in their native tongue. You can write, print, or type menu cards, using a form available from stationers, or using any good quality cards or notepaper.

If place and menu cards are to appear at the same party, it is best that they match, even to being written in the same hand. You can buy place cards from any good stationer, or you can make your own of card stock. If you want "tent-style" cards that can stand alone, choose a stock that is not

Emily   *John*

*Distinctive
candle arrangement.*

too stiff to be folded. Before folding, such cards are about 3 to 4 inches long by 2 inches wide, and can be folded in half lengthwise. Place cards that will remain flat need the support of special holders (available in gift shops) if you want them upright. Before deciding which way you want to go, look at the commercially available place cards. For special occasions, such as holidays or children's parties, you will often find very clever and colorful designs, not too expensive and more festive than most amateurs could manage.

Place cards need not convey much information. The handwritten name alone is enough if the cards are to be placed on the table. First names are acceptable if all the guests know one another sufficiently well; add last names if two guests have the same first name. Do the same for those with the same surname; both a John and a James Smith, for example, could not find their way if both cards just said "Mr. Smith." Flat cards without holders can go on the place plate; standing cards, whether tented or in holders, just above it.

If the party is very large, and you want to distribute place cards to guests as they arrive, each card should show the guest's name and the table number, plus a seat number if you want to follow that fixed a plan. (Remember, then, to number the places at each table.) Arrange the cards (enclosed, preferably, in small envelopes) on a small table at the door, in alphabetical order. Use more than one table, if necessary, to spread the cards out so that they are easy for guests, or a helper if you have one, to find.

Candles

Usually thought of as part of centerpiece arrangements (or, in clusters or decorative holders, as the centerpiece itself), candles deserve a separate mention as a unique decorative element with special properties that demand consideration.

First and foremost, candles should never be left unlighted on a table, or even on a sideboard if it is in buffet use. Further back than most people today can remember, they were a source of light. It is in deference to that original function that custom continues to call for candles to be lighted.

Candles are things of beauty. The color range is almost limitless, and every year candle manufacturers introduce new ones, often keyed to changes in decorative tastes. Shapes and sizes are almost as varied: short and stocky, tall and slim, and every height and contour in between. Candles may be a single color, or a marbleized effect. Surfaces are sometimes smooth, at other times ridged. Choices are limited only by preference—except for candles to light formal occasions. Tall, tapered candles, either white or off-white, are prescribed for formal table decor.

One height limitation is imposed on all occasions, not by tradition, but by consideration for guests. On a table where guests will be seated, have your candles a height that will place the lighted wicks either well *below* or well *above* eye level. Even more so than flowers at a distracting level, a flickering candle can be downright disturbing.

Fresh flowers in autumn.

Silk flowers for the year 'round.

Holders can be as simple as the little cups that hold votive candles or as elaborate as many-branched silver candelabra. Between the two, a versatile approach to arranging is provided by sets of individual holders, each a different height, to be grouped as suits your fancy, or the arrangement of your table.

When centerpieces are mentioned, the first word that springs to mind, naturally, is "flowers." Certainly fresh flowers bring a vibrant breath of the outdoors to an indoor party and are a complement in living color to the rest of the decor. Flower variety is such that, whatever your theme or scheme, blooms can be found to enhance it.

Centerpieces in focus

Fresh flowers need not always be a centered burst of blossoms. Individual arrangements at each guest's place—nosegays; corsages; boutonnieres; tiny bud vases, each with a single bloom—have their own kind of appeal, including the gift of being picked up and worn, or taken home after the party.

The word "artificial," applied to flowers, has to many people an unpleasant sound, until they see the superb flowers that are made of soft, shimmering fabrics. Called *silk flowers or foliage,* many of these are actually made of synthetics with a look of silk. Far less expensive than flowers of genuine silk, they range widely over a superb color palette, and are simplicity itself to arrange. Though they will not last forever, even with tender care, fabric flowers do stay beautiful over many a party season.

Dried flowers, too, make arrangements of distinction, though not everyone takes to their very special effect. Colors tend to be earthy, ranging from russet browns to palest beiges. Not surprisingly, they look their best in "countrified" containers—baskets, crocks, pottery at its most

129

Colorful autumn branches.

primitive—and at casual meals with similarly down-to-earth appointments on the table. They last reasonably well, but eventually grow dim and dusty. Since they cannot be successfully cleaned, they must be replaced periodically.

Green plants and leafy branches can also be used as centerpieces. Not as colorful as flowers, greenery is still lively and, in terms of color, adaptable to most schemes. Because of their height, flowering or leafy branches can be used more satisfactorily in arrangements elsewhere in the house. Leafless branches have a statuesque beauty, a bit stark for the tastes of many but, in the proper circumstances, graceful and impressive. Some "branches," such as eucalyptus, are preserved to make them long-lasting with no loss of their original charm. Eucalyptus processed in this way is sometimes left its natural green, but often given other tints such as gold, russet, or deep red, none of the shades beyond the limits of what might seem natural colors.

Fresh fruits and vegetables are second only to flowers as contributors of life and color to the look of the table. Select, from what is in season, the best and the brightest vegetables (free of blemishes), aiming for the strongest possible color contrasts: peppers green and red, eggplant for its deep purple, carrots for a streak of orange. In a fruit basket (though there is no reason not to mix the two), imagine pears, apples, oranges, cherries, blueberries, grapes, bananas, limes. When fruit is in high season, the centerpiece might also be the dessert.

Baskets are natural containers for fruit and produce, but a wooden bowl, crystal compote, or china tureen would all work just as well and handsomely. Be certain that any container for fruits and vegetables is broad and fairly low, and heavy enough not to be tipped by the weight at its edges.

Artificial forms of fruits and vegetables, at their best, are remarkable facsimiles of the real thing and they will, with care, last just about forever. Made of such materials as alabaster and marble, and generally imported, they make arrangements that look good enough to eat.

Any room in your home is a candidate for floral or other arrangements, including the kitchen and bathrooms. The only stipulation, where fresh flowers or live plants are concerned, is that they not be anywhere near a heat source. For the sake of your furniture, you may want to put extra protection against water spills under each container.

Arrangements elsewhere in the house

Such "green thumb" decorating need not always mean costly purchases of fresh flowers. Consider repotting or just rearranging the plants that you have, or supplementing them with a new plant or two. Plants cost money, but they will live to freshen your home another day, as cut flowers will not. Another idea that gives you the best of both worlds is flower vials, not unlike test tubes, that are embedded in the soil around a plant and filled with water; then, through a hole in their tight-fitting rubber caps, the stem of a single flower is inserted.

Unusual vegetable centerpiece.

Part III

⇟ ⇟ ⇟

Party Menu Cookbook

Crêpes

Makes 9 (6-inch) crêpes

½ cup flour
½ tablespoon sugar
¾ cup milk

2 medium-sized eggs
1 tablespoon butter, melted

In a medium-sized bowl combine flour, sugar, milk, and eggs and beat until smooth. Stir in butter and refrigerate for at least 1 hour. Heat a small skillet, 6 to 7 inches in diameter. For each crêpe, brush the skillet lightly with butter, pour in about 2 tablespoons batter, and rotate pan until batter covers the bottom. Cook the crêpe until browned, then turn and brown the other side.

NOTE: Crepe batter may be made the night before and refrigerated until morning. If you make the crêpes the night before, cool them completely, stack with 2 pieces of waxed paper between each crêpe, and wrap the stack in a plastic wrap. Refrigerate until you are ready to use them. The extra crêpes may be wrapped in this manner, frozen, and saved for another brunch or dessert.

Sweetened Whipped Cream

Serves 1

¼ cup heavy cream
2 teaspoons confectioners' sugar

In a small bowl combine the cream and sugar, and refrigerate to chill. Beat until stiff.

Time Out for Lunch

Instant Bouillon with Tomato and Chives

Fluffy Egg Casserole

Cookies

Coffee or Tea

This lovely luncheon is a fine idea for a crisp autumn or winter weekend noon. Sleep late, if the idea appeals to you, then rise and prepare this lunch in a leisurely fashion to fortify yourself against the elements you will face later on in your day. It will be less difficult to brave rain (or snow) if you have been warmed from within. Have this lunch, pick up your umbrella, and go to the library this week, just as you had planned before the weather took its dismal turn.

Just as suitable for a late afternoon or early evening meal, this menu can be prepared when you return home in the rain or snow. And it can be easily doubled if you bring home a friend.

Fluffy egg casserole.

Instant Bouillon with Tomato and Chives

Serves 2

1 (10-ounce) can beef bouillon
¾ soup can water
¼ cup dry sherry
2 thin slices lemon

2 tablespoons chopped tomato, flesh only
Chopped chives

In a saucepan, heat the bouillon and water. Stir in the sherry. To serve, put a lemon slice in the bottom of a soup cup or mug and pour in the bouillon. Garnish with the chopped tomato and chives.

Fluffy Egg Casserole

Serves 1

2 eggs, separated
⅛ teaspoon cream of tartar
1 tablespoon milk
Salt and white pepper to taste

FILLING:

1 small tomato, peeled
¼ teaspoon grated onion
2 teaspoons dry sherry or dry vermouth
⅛ teaspoon dried basil, *or* ¼ teaspoon chopped fresh basil
½ small avocado, peeled and cut into ½-inch pieces

Preheat oven to 375°F. In a medium-sized bowl, beat the egg whites with the cream of tartar until they are stiff, and set aside. Beat the egg yolks in a small bowl until they are thick and lemon colored. Stir in the milk, salt and pepper. Gently fold the egg-yolk mixture into the egg whites until well combined. Pour into a buttered 1¾- or 2-cup casserole. Bake for 15 minutes, or until puffed and golden.

While eggs are baking, make the filling. Mash half the tomato in a small saucepan. Add the onion, sherry, basil, and a dash of salt and pepper. Bring to a boil, then simmer for 5 minutes. Coarsely chop the remaining tomato and add to the sauce with the avocado. To serve, gently spoon the filling into the center of the baked eggs.

NOTES: This recipe doubles nicely to serve 2.

To peel the tomato, place it in a small heat-proof bowl and pour boiling water over it to cover. After 2 minutes remove the tomato with a fork. With a paring knife, carefully pull off the skin.

The remaining avocado may be used to make Avocado Dressing (page 144).

Dining in Style

Pâté and Toast Points
Currant-glazed Lamb Chop
Confetti Pilaf   *Vegetable Salad with Avocado Dressing*
Fresh Fruits with Cream or *Fruit Ambrosia*
Coffee or Tea

This is a dinner menu for all seasons. Broiling, a healthful method for cooking meats year-round, is especially good in the late spring and through the summer, for although the heat will be on in the kitchen, the process is a relatively quick one, and the broiler does not require preheating. The pâté and the salad dressing should be made at least an hour before serving so the flavors in each have time to "marry." Vegetables for the salad, and fruits for the dessert, can be prepared ahead of time as well. Dessert can be simple or elegant, dictated by your mood (and appetite). For fresh fruits with cream, simply slice a ripe peach, sprinkle on some fresh berries, top with a little sugar if you like, and pour on the cream.

Fresh fruits with cream.

Pâté and Toast Points

Serves 1 or 2

1 (4-ounce) can liver pâté
1 teaspoon brandy
½ teaspoon minced onion

2 slices white bread
Black olives *or* chopped onion for
   garnish

In a small bowl, combine the pâté, brandy, and onion. Cover with plastic wrap and refrigerate until serving time (at least 1 hour). To serve, toast the bread and trim the crusts. Cut each slice into 4 triangles and spread with the pâté mixture. Top with chopped onion or a slice of black olive.

Currant-glazed Lamb Chop

Serves 1

2 tablespoons currant jelly
1 teaspoon water

1 lamb chop, about 1½ inches thick
   (2 if they are small)

In a small saucepan, melt currant jelly with water over low heat. Remove from heat when melted and set aside. Adjust the broiler shelf so that the lamb chop will be 2 to 3 inches from the heat. Broil on one side for 5 to 6 minutes (the chop should be nicely browned), then turn and broil on the other side for another 5 minutes. Brush chop with melted jelly, and broil for 1 minute longer. A 1½-inch chop should be cooked to the medium stage in about 12 minutes. For a "pinker" chop, cook for slightly less time on each side.

NOTE: Apricot preserves and apple jelly (melted with water in the same manner) are also good glazes for a lamb chop.

Confetti Pilaf

Serves 1

½ cup chopped onion
2 tablespoons chopped red pepper
2 tablespoons butter or margarine

1 cup chicken broth
⅓ cup rice
¼ cup frozen peas

In a small saucepan, sauté onion and red pepper in the butter. Add the chicken broth and rice. Bring to a boil, cover, and simmer for 5 minutes. Add the peas and continue simmering, covered, for 15 minutes, or until peas and rice are cooked and broth is absorbed.

NOTES: If you want to use cooked peas (leftover or canned), add them during the last 5 minutes of cooking.

To make chicken broth from bouillon, combine 1 cup water and 1 bouillon cube.

Vegetable Salad

Serves 1

Cauliflower (broken into florets)
Cherry tomatoes or tomato wedges
Celery slices
Zucchini slices

Cucumber slices
Carrot slices
Boston lettuce

Combine 3 or 4 of the above vegetable choices on lettuce leaves. Top with Avocado Dressing (recipe follows) or your favorite ready-made dressing. For extra zip, try adding orange sections, apple slices, black olives, or cheese cubes (Monterey Jack or Edam) to your salad.

Avocado Dressing

Serves 1

½ small ripe avocado
2 teaspoons lemon juice
¼ cup light cream
1 teaspoon chopped onion

¼ teaspoon salt
Dash of cayenne
1 small clove garlic

Peel avocado, remove the pit, and cut avocado in 1-inch slices. Place in a blender with the remaining ingredients and blend until smooth. Pour into a small container, cover with plastic wrap, and refrigerate for 1 hour, or until serving time.

Fruit Ambrosia

Serves 1

Combine any of the following fruits in an individual compote, dessert bowl, or saucer champagne glass. Be sure the fruits are well chilled.

Mandarin orange sections	Apple slices
Kumquats, peeled	Plum slices
Bing cherries, pitted	Peach slices
Green grapes	Strawberries
Banana slices	Blueberries

Sprinkle 1 or 2 teaspoons apricot brandy, apple brandy, cherry brandy, peach brandy, Triple Sec, kirsch, or rum over the fruit. Top with shredded coconut.

NOTE: To prepare for guests, combine cut fruits in a bowl and chill. Serve in individual compotes, adding the liqueur and coconut topping just before serving.

Company Lunch

Cream of Avocado Soup
Curried Chicken and Shrimp Salad
Hot Rolls with Herb Butter
Orange Sponge Cake Supreme
Tea or Coffee

This is a pleasant lunch to share with a friend, and you will have enough of everything to serve this meal to other members of your family later in the week (or later in the day) if you choose. If time is important to you, this way you know you'll be making the most of it when preparing these dishes. You might want to warm the salad for an evening meal; the leftover cake can be frozen for another meal, or sliced and wrapped before freezing so you can have (or serve) a little something sweet whenever you like. Buy the rolls at a good local bakery; herb butter, easily prepared, will elevate them to company fare. And of course, if you want to meet with the whole committee rather than with your co-chairperson, spend the morning cooking and count on compliments rather than leftovers.

Cream of Avocado Soup *Serves 6*

½ cup minced onion
2 tablespoons butter
2 tablespoons flour
3 cups chicken broth
1 tablespoon fresh lemon juice
1 tablespoon drained prepared horseradish
1 tablespoon tarragon vinegar

1 clove garlic, crushed
½ teaspoon salt
¼ teaspoon curry powder
¼ teaspoon dried tarragon
Freshly ground white pepper
1 ripe avocado
1 cup milk
1 cup light cream

In a large saucepan, sauté the onion in butter until transparent. Add the flour and stir until smooth. Stir in 1½ cups broth and cook, stirring constantly, until it boils and thickens. Add the lemon juice, horseradish, vinegar, garlic, salt, curry powder, tarragon, and pepper to taste. Simmer, covered, for 10 minutes. Puree the mixture in a food mill, blender, or food processor and return it to the pan. Peel the avocado with a stainless-steel knife to prevent darkening and puree it with the remaining 1½ cups broth. Add the puree to the pan and stir in the milk and cream. Cook, stirring, until the soup is heated through. Serve hot or cold in glass bowls.

NOTE: If you serve the soup cold, reserve the remaining four servings and serve hot at another meal in a day or so. If serving the soup hot, serve the rest of it cold another day.

Curried Chicken and Shrimp Salad *Serves 4 to 6*

½ cup mayonnaise
¾ cup sour cream
1 tablespoon Dijon mustard
1 teaspoon curry powder
1 clove garlic, finely chopped
1½ cups cold cooked rice
Dry white wine *or* water
¾ cup cold cooked chicken, in chunks

½ pound cold cooked shrimp, shelled and deveined
1 red pepper, cut into julienne strips
1 green pepper, cut into julienne strips
½ cup sliced leek, white part only
2 small endives, separated into leaves

In a bowl, combine the mayonnaise, sour cream, mustard, curry powder, and garlic and blend thoroughly. Add the rice, toss, and add a little white wine or water to thin the mixture, if necessary. Add the chicken, shrimp, peppers, and leek. Toss gently and adjust the seasonings. Transfer the salad to a bowl lined with endive leaves and serve.

NOTE: You will have 2 to 4 servings left over for another meal.

Orange-frosted spongecake.

Herb Butter

Makes ½ cup

¼ pound (1 stick) unsalted butter, softened

1 tablespoon finely chopped parsley

1 tablespoon finely chopped fresh basil

1 tablespoon finely chopped fresh chives

In a bowl, cream the butter by mashing it against the sides of the bowl with a wooden spoon until it is light and fluffy. Add the herbs, blending thoroughly.

You can keep Herb Butter in the refrigerator in a tightly covered container for up to 2 weeks. Or, shape the butter into a cylinder on a sheet of waxed paper, roll it up tightly, and freeze. Cut off what you need each time.

Orange Sponge Cake Supreme

Serves 4

1 cup sifted flour
1 teaspoon baking powder
¼ teaspoon salt
3 eggs
1 cup sugar

1 tablespoon grated orange peel
⅓ cup fresh orange juice
Orange Frosting Supreme (recipe
   follows)
Fresh kumquats for garnish

Preheat oven to 350°F. Sift together flour, baking powder, and salt and set aside. In a medium-sized mixing bowl, beat the eggs until they are thick and lemon colored. With a portable mixer, beat in the sugar, a little at a time, then continue to beat for 3 to 5 minutes (the mixture should be very thick). At low speed, beat in the flour mixture just until smooth. Add the orange peel and juice, and beat just until combined. Pour into an ungreased 8-inch tube pan and bake for 45 minutes, or until cake tester inserted in pan comes out clean. Place the pan (cake side up) over the neck of a bottle and allow to cool completely before removing cake from pan. Frost with Orange Frosting Supreme and garnish with fresh kumquats.

NOTES: Remove cake from pan by gently running a table knife around the edge of the cake. Invert the cake pan and rap it firmly but gently on the kitchen counter. The cake should drop out of the pan.

    As the cake serves 4, you will have some left over, which may be frozen for the next time you have a guest. Or you can freeze it in slices so you can have a slice whenever you wish. Freeze the cake, then remove from the freezer, cover with plastic wrap, and place back in the freezer. Remove wrapping before thawing so icing will not stick to it.

Orange Frosting Supreme

Frosts an 8-inch tube cake

3 tablespoons butter or margarine,
   softened
1 egg yolk

1 tablespoon grated orange peel
3 cups sifted confectioners' sugar
2 tablespoons fresh orange juice

In a medium-sized bowl, beat the butter until light and fluffy. Add the egg yolk and orange peel and beat to combine. Beat in the confectioners' sugar, 1 cup at a time, alternating with tablespoons of the orange juice. Beat until light and fluffy. If the frosting is too stiff to spread, beat in a little more orange juice.

NOTE: Freeze the leftover egg white to use in preparing Apricot Whip (page 155).

Celebration À Deux

Chicken Broth Florentine

Scallops Provençal

Neapolitan Spumoni

Demitasse

The dishes on this menu, with titles evocative of the Continent, are simple to prepare right here at home—for luncheon or an evening meal. A perfect menu to prepare for a friend (or a family member) returning for a visit from college or a home in another town, this is equally appropriate if you wish to provide a meal for a friend before a play, concert, or other special event you will attend together. Only the dessert requires time for its preparation, and you can do that early, or even the day before. To streamline the process even further, prepare the spinach for the broth and the vegetables for the main dish earlier in the day and refrigerate until cooking time. Demitasse is a strong-bodied after-dinner coffee served in small (demitasse) cups. It should be freshly brewed and is usually served black. You may, however, offer sugar and cream with it. French roasted coffee (a dark, strong-flavored bean), or coffee blends using French beans, are especially good to use for demitasse. Though best freshly brewed, there are several strong-bodied instant coffee blends available for demitasse. Although demitasse provides an extra special touch, coffee or tea will also do nicely if you prefer.

Scallops Provençal.

Chicken Broth Florentine

Serves 2

2 cups chicken broth
1 cup fresh spinach leaves, washed
   and cut into strips, if large
Grated cheese *or* garlic-flavored
   croutons

In a medium-sized saucepan, heat the broth until it is steaming hot. Stir in the spinach and pour into two heated soup bowls. Sprinkle with cheese or croutons.

NOTE: Heat the bowls in a warm oven (150°–200°F).

Scallops Provençal

Serves 2

½ pound sea scallops, cut in half if large
1½ tablespoons lemon juice
¼ pound mushrooms, sliced
¼ cup scallions, with green tops, sliced
3 tablespoons olive oil

1 tablespoon chopped fresh parsley
¼ teaspoon dried oregano
1 large tomato, peeled and coarsely chopped, *or* ¾ cup canned tomatoes, chopped
Parsley for garnish

In a small bowl, marinate the scallops in the lemon juice, and set aside. In a medium-sized skillet, sauté the mushrooms and scallions in 1 tablespoon of the olive oil until golden. Add the parsley, oregano, and tomato. Simmer gently for 5 minutes and set aside. In another skillet, sauté the scallops in the remaining olive oil until golden and cooked through (about 3 to 5 minutes). Combine the scallops with the sauce. Garnish with parsley to serve.

Neapolitan Spumoni

Serves 2 to 4

½ pint chocolate ice cream
½ pint strawberry ice cream
½ pint vanilla ice cream
1 teaspoon brandy
2 tablespoons chopped candied mixed fruit

½ cup heavy cream
1 tablespoon confectioners' sugar
1 small plain chocolate bar

Soften ice creams slightly. Spoon the chocolate ice cream into the bottom of a 1¾- to 2-cup bowl or round mold and spread evenly. Spread the strawberry ice cream over the chocolate. Blend the brandy and the mixed fruit into the vanilla ice cream and spread the mixture over the strawberry ice cream. Cover with plastic wrap and freeze until firm. Beat the cream and sugar until stiff. Unmold the ice cream onto a small round serving platter (to loosen the ice cream, run a knife around the edge of the ice cream and dip mold briefly into warm water up to the rim). Spread two-thirds of the whipped cream over the unmolded ice cream. Place the rest of the whipped cream in a pastry bag fitted with a star tip and decorate the spumoni. Garnish with chocolate shavings. Place in freezer. For ease in cutting, remove from freezer 10 minutes before serving.

NOTES: Make chocolate shavings by scraping the edge of the candy bar (at room temperature) with a vegetable peeler.

If you cannot find ice cream in ½ pint containers, buy pint containers and make two ice cream molds. Wrap one tightly in plastic wrap after unmolding, and store in your freezer for up to 4 weeks.

Good Neighbors

Egg Drop Soup

Stir-fry Shrimp and Vegetables

Oriental Rice

Apricot Whip

Chinese Tea

When you meet your new neighbor from across the hall in the elevator (or from down the street in the supermarket or the post office) invite her (or him) to your home for an Oriental supper. Less time in the kitchen means more time at the table to get to know one another, and these dishes can be made in minutes if you take the time to plan, and do ahead of time the things that can be done to make last-minute assembly and quick cooking a breeze. The dessert needs time to chill, so you can make it well ahead of serving time. Though it is not Oriental in origin, it is a lovely light complement to Oriental cuisine. Preparing Egg Drop Soup is almost as easy as boiling water, combining liquids with one another just before serving. Stir-fry Shrimp and Vegetables is easy too, once the cleaning and slicing have been done ahead of time. Heighten the Oriental ambience by serving tea throughout the meal, rather than at its close.

Stir-fry shrimp with vegetables.

Egg Drop Soup

1 tablespoon cornstarch mixed with 2 tablespoons water
1 teaspoon soy sauce
1 (10¾-ounce) can chicken broth
1 cup water

1 egg, beaten
1 tablespoon sherry
Chopped scallions *or* chopped parsley

In a medium-sized saucepan, combine the cornstarch mixture with the soy sauce, chicken broth, and water. Combine the egg and the sherry. Bring the soup to a boil and add the egg and sherry while stirring constantly with a fork. Garnish with chopped scallions or parsley.

Stir-fry Shrimp and Vegetables

12 medium-sized shrimp, peeled and deveined
2–3 tablespoons vegetable oil (corn oil or peanut oil)
¼ pound mushrooms, sliced
¼ pound snow peas, stem end snipped
¼ pound broccoli florets
2 stalks celery, sliced on the diagonal

½ red pepper, sliced into ¼-inch strips
¾ cup hot water
3 tablespoons soy sauce
1 tablespoon cornstarch
2 tablespoons cold water
¼ cup water chestnuts, sliced (optional)
3 scallions with green tops, cut into 1-inch pieces

In a wok or heavy skillet, stir-fry shrimp in 1 tablespoon of the oil for 2 minutes, or until cooked (they will be pink). Remove shrimp from wok and set aside. Add more oil to wok, if necessary, and stir-fry mushrooms. Remove mushrooms from wok and set aside with shrimp. Add 1 tablespoon oil to wok and stir-fry snow peas, broccoli, celery, and red pepper for 2 minutes. Add hot water, cover, and steam vegetables for 3 to 5 minutes, or until almost tender. Mix soy sauce and cornstarch with cold water. Add to vegetable mixture and stir. Add water chestnuts, scallions, reserved shrimp, and mushrooms. Stir-fry for 2 minutes more to heat the mixture and thicken the sauce.

Oriental Rice

Serves 2

1 cup long-grain white rice
1½ cups water

Place the rice in a 2-quart saucepan, fill the saucepan with cold water, and wash the rice by rubbing it between your fingers. Gently pour off the water (the rice will sink to the bottom of the pan). Repeat this process several times, until the water stays clear. Drain the rice and return it to the saucepan. Add the 1½ cups water, cover, and bring to a boil over medium heat. Reduce the heat and simmer, stirring once or twice, for 15 to 20 minutes, or until the rice is tender and the water has been absorbed. The rice should be soft and translucent, with separate grains.

Apricot Whip

Serves 2

¼ cup chopped dried apricots
½ cup plus 2 tablespoons water
1 teaspoon unflavored gelatin
2 egg whites

2 tablespoons sugar
2 dried apricot wedges *or* 2
   tablespoons Sweetened
   Whipped Cream

In a small saucepan, bring the apricots and ½ cup water to a boil. Simmer, covered, for 15 minutes. Dissolve gelatin in 2 tablespoons cold water, and stir into warm apricot mixture to dissolve the gelatin completely. Puree the mixture in a food mill or blender and cool to room temperature. Beat egg whites with an electric mixer until soft peaks form when the beaters are slowly lifted. Add sugar, ½ tablespoon at a time, beating well after each addition. Beat until stiff. Fold the apricot puree into the beaten egg whites. Pour apricot whip into 2 parfait glasses and chill for at least 2 hours. Garnish with a dried apricot wedge or Sweetened Whipped Cream.

FESTIVE FARE FOR FOUR TO EIGHT

Among Friends

Onion Soup

Baked Whole Fish

Turkish Cucumber Salad

Chocolate Fondue

Coffee or Tea

This menu, planned for six, is perfect for late fall or winter dining. A warming and nutritious meal, it has an additional virtue, that of economy. Even the impressive chocolate fondue can be an economical dessert, especially if made with well-drained canned fruits rather than fresh, and with cake left over from another meal (or meals).

Some preparation time in the kitchen is required prior to serving for the soup and the Baked Whole Fish, but since you will be among friends, perhaps someone will keep you company in the kitchen. You can, however, prepare the salad ahead of time, and the fruits and cake for fondue can be prepared earlier as well.

Onion soup.

Onion Soup

Serves 4 to 6

2 tablespoons butter
4 medium-sized onions, thinly
  sliced
1 teaspoon flour
6 cups beef stock *or* bouillon made
  from 4 cubes with 6 cups water,
  heated
½ cup dry red or dry white wine
  (optional)

Salt and freshly ground black
  pepper
6 slices French bread, lightly
  toasted
3 tablespoons grated Gruyère
  cheese

In a large saucepan, melt the butter and sauté the onions until golden. Stir in the flour and cook, stirring, for 5 minutes. Stir in the stock, add wine if desired, and season with salt and pepper to taste. Simmer, partially covered, for 30 minutes. Adjust the seasoning as desired. Place the bread slices in the bottom of a casserole or in individual ovenproof bowls and pour in the soup. Sprinkle grated cheese over the bread and put the casserole or bowls in a hot oven or under the broiler until the cheese is melted. Or put a slice of bread in each bowl, sprinkle it with grated cheese, and pour the hot soup over it. The bread will rise to the surface.

157

Baked Whole Fish

⅓ cup butter
2 medium-sized onions, chopped
6 stalks celery, chopped
3 tablespoons chopped parsley
1 teaspoon savory
½ teaspoon salt
⅛ teaspoon white pepper
6 cups day-old bread cubes

1 (4-to 5-pound) fish (striped bass, cod, haddock, red snapper, or bluefish), cleaned
Lemon Basting Sauce (recipe follows)
½ teaspoon cracked pepper
1 lemon, sliced

Preheat oven to 400°F. Melt the butter in a medium-sized skillet. Add the onion and celery and sauté until tender. Add the parsley, savory, salt, and white pepper. Pour butter, vegetables, and herbs over the bread cubes in a large bowl and toss to combine. Wash the cleaned fish with cold water and pat dry. Stuff the fish loosely and sew the opening closed with a large needle and string (or use skewers to close the opening). Brush the underside of the fish with lemon basting sauce and place on a large roasting pan. Brush the basting sauce on the top of the fish and sprinkle with cracked pepper. Bake for 35 to 40 minutes, or until fish flakes easily when tested with a fork. Baste occasionally to prevent drying. Before serving, remove the string or skewers, place baked fish on serving platter, and garnish with lemon slices.

NOTE: If you have an ovenproof platter, you may bake the fish right on it, eliminating the transfer of fish from the roasting pan to a serving platter.

Lemon Basting Sauce

2 tablespoons lemon juice
¼ cup olive oil

½ teaspoon grated onion
¼ teaspoon savory

Combine all ingredients in a small bowl and use to baste fish.

Turkish Cucumber Salad

Serves 6

4 cups plain yogurt
1 tablespoon olive oil
3–4 medium-sized cucumbers, peeled, seeded, and cut into ¼-inch slices

1 clove garlic, finely chopped
2 tablespoons finely chopped mint leaves
Salt to taste
Mint sprigs

In a large bowl, whisk the oil slowly into the yogurt until well blended. Add the cucumbers, garlic, mint, and salt and mix gently. Chill for at least 2 hours before serving. Garnish with mint sprigs.

Chocolate Fondue

8 ounces semisweet baking chocolate
⅓ cup Vandermint, Sabra, *or* white crème de menthe
1 (5-ounce) can evaporated milk
Assorted fruits (fresh fruit should be washed and chilled, canned fruits should be well drained and chilled)

Assorted cakes cut into 1¼-inch squares (pound cake, fruitcake, nut cake, or any other firm-textured cake)

In a medium-sized saucepan or fondue pot, combine the chocolate, liqueur, and evaporated milk. Cook over very low heat until chocolate is melted, stirring occasionally. Arrange the fruit and cake on a platter and serve with the chocolate mixture. Each person spears his own pieces of fruit and cake and dips them in the chocolate.

The Boss Comes to Dinner

Smoked Salmon Canapés with Horseradish Sauce

Roast Beef

Pan-roasted Potatoes and Carrots

Boston Lettuce Mimosa

Open Fresh Fruit Tart

Coffee or Demitasse

Roast Beef is one of the easiest main dishes a host or hostess can prepare and serve, for the vegetables cook right along with it and you needn't tend to it once it's in the oven. Directions are provided here for two different cuts of meat—roast prime ribs are an impressive (though simple) main dish, but it is the most expensive cut available, because of the amount of weight that is bones and fat; a sirloin tip roast, virtually waste-free, is also a good tasting, tender cut, and much less costly per serving. The canapés assemble easily, and the sauce for them is easy too—just remember the sauce needs an hour in the refrigerator for the flavors to blend. The salad, too, is easy. The Fresh Fruit Tart requires some time and attention, but will come together beautifully if you carefully follow directions—a dessert as good to look at as it will be to eat.

Smoked Salmon Canapés

Makes 20 canapés

5–10 slices rye bread (depending on size)
Softened butter
¼ pound smoked salmon, in thin slices

Horseradish Sauce (recipe follows)
Fresh dill *or* very thin slices of lemon cut into triangles

Cut the bread into 20 (2-inch) squares and spread with butter. Place a square of salmon on each buttered square and top with a dollop of Horseradish Sauce. Garnish each square with a sprig of fresh dill or a very tiny lemon triangle.

Horseradish Sauce

Makes ⅓ cup

⅓ cup sour cream
1 tablespoon prepared horseradish

1 teaspoon minced onion
Dash of salt

Combine all ingredients and refrigerate, covered, for 1 hour to blend the flavors.

Roast Sirloin Tip

Serves 4 to 6

1 (3-pound) sirloin tip roast

Salt and pepper to taste

Preheat oven to 325°F. Rub roast with salt and pepper and place, fat side up, on a rack in a roasting pan. Insert a meat thermometer in the thickest part of the roast. Roast for 1½ to 2 hours, or until the thermometer reaches 140°F. Remove roast from oven and let stand for 15 minutes before carving. Carve on the diagonal, in ¼-inch slices.

Roast Prime Ribs

Serves 4

1 (4- to 5-pound) standing rib roast

Salt and pepper to taste

Preheat oven to 325°F. Rub the roast with salt and pepper and place, fat side up, in a roasting pan (the bones form a rack). Insert a meat thermometer into the thickest part of the roast, being careful to keep it from touching the bone. Roast for about 1¾ hours for rare (140°F), or about 2¼ hours for medium (160°F). Remove from the oven and let rest for 15 minutes before carving.

Open fresh fruit tart.

Roast Potatoes and Carrots

Serves 4 to 6

1¼ pounds tiny new potatoes, scrubbed, *or* medium-sized regular potatoes, peeled and quartered

1 pound baby (1- to 1½-inch) carrots, scrubbed, *or* regular carrots, peeled, halved, then quartered lengthwise
2 tablespoons vegetable oil

Place potatoes and carrots in a large mixing bowl, drizzle the oil over the vegetables, and toss until they are coated. About 1 hour before the roast will be done, add the vegetables to the roasting pan and cook with the meat. Stir the vegetables occasionally and baste them with pan juices. If meat is on a rack (as with sirloin tip roast), place the vegetables in another pan and bake alongside the roast. You may still use the drippings from the roast to baste the vegetables. Keep the vegetables warm while the meat rests for 15 minutes before carving. If the vegetables are not quite tender, they can continue cooking in the oven for this additional time.

Boston Lettuce Mimosa

Serves 4 to 6

1–3 heads Boston lettuce
(depending on size)

4 hard-cooked egg yolks
Chopped fresh parsley

Wash lettuce and dry completely. Do not break up the heads. Return to refrigerator to crisp until ready to serve. Gently open heads from the middle and press down slightly onto a platter to form open "wells" inside each head. Crown the centers with freshly sieved egg yolk and sprinkle with parsley. Serve with a light vinaigrette dressing (page 251).

Open Fresh Fruit Tart

Serves 4

1 sheet prerolled puff pastry
(9 × 10 inches)
1 egg yolk, mixed with 1
tablespoon water
¾ cup milk
1 tablespoon cornstarch
2 tablespoons sugar
1 egg yolk, slightly beaten

¼ cup heavy cream
½ pint strawberries, washed,
hulled, and halved lengthwise
Small bunch of green grapes
1 kiwi fruit, peeled, sliced, and each
slice cut in half
¼ cup apple jelly
1 tablespoon water

Preheat the oven to 450°F. Thaw the pastry as directed on the package and cut a sheet in half lengthwise. Place one half on a cookie sheet and brush with the egg yolk-water mixture. On the other half, mark a line an inch from each side. With a sharp knife, cut out the center rectangle, leaving a 1-inch "frame." Place the frame on the half you have brushed with egg yolk, lining up the sides evenly. With a very sharp knife, gently score the frame with large X's. Brush with egg yolk. Bake for 15 minutes, or until pastry is puffed and golden. From the remaining pastry, cut 4 large leaves and 2 flower shapes. Brush with egg yolk and bake for 10 to 15 minutes. Combine the milk, cornstarch, and sugar in a small saucepan. Slowly heat to the boiling point, stirring. When thickened, remove from the heat, and spoon a little of the milk mixture into the egg yolk. Stir the egg into the milk mixture in the saucepan, and heat just until the mixture starts to boil. Pour into a small bowl and refrigerate, covered with plastic wrap placed directly on the custard. Whip the cream until stiff, then fold into the custard. Pour the custard into the puff pastry shell. Arrange strawberries, grapes, and kiwi on the top of the custard. Melt the jelly with the water in a small saucepan over low heat. Brush the fruit with the melted jelly.

NOTE: Freeze the egg whites for another use (Amaretto Meringues, page 214).

Guest of Honor

Caviar Cocktail Mold

Veal Roulade Oregano

Mediterranean Salad

Chocolate Mousse

Coffee or Demitasse with "Spirits"

P lanned for six persons, this elegant menu to honor a special guest requires very little last-minute attention, and your guests can enjoy your company as well as your cuisine. If you entertain on a Saturday evening, you can prepare these dishes in a leisurely fashion and take time during the day to purchase fresh flowers and perhaps arrange them yourself in a favorite vase or other container of your own.

Prepare and assemble the molds early on, so they will have time to set and chill. Chocolate Mousse should probably be first, as it requires several hours in the refrigerator. Prepare the whipped cream later in the day, and pipe it on at the last minute before serving. Put together the Caviar Cocktail Mold, place it in the refrigerator to chill also, then prepare vegetables for the veal dish and for your salad. Serve your coffee or demitasse, with spirits for a special touch, as a separate course, after the dessert.

Veal Roulade Oregano.

Caviar Cocktail Mold

Serves 6

1 envelope unflavored gelatin
½ cup cold milk
1 cup mayonnaise
1 tablespoon fresh lemon juice

1 cup heavy cream, whipped
1 tablespoon finely chopped onion
1 cup black lumpfish caviar
Crackers

In a saucepan, soften the gelatin in the milk for 3 to 5 minutes. Cook the mixture over low heat, stirring, until the gelatin dissolves completely. Let the mixture cool and stir in the mayonnaise, lemon juice, whipped cream, onion, and caviar. Pour into a lightly oiled 1-quart fish-shaped mold and chill until firm. Unmold onto a platter and serve with the crackers.

Veal Roulade Oregano

Serves 6

1½ pounds veal for scallopini (6 large scallops)
Salt and pepper
¼ pound prosciutto (6 thin slices)
3 tablespoons olive oil
1 clove garlic, crushed
3 medium-sized onions, sliced thin
½ pound mushrooms, sliced
1 teaspoon dried oregano
½ teaspoon dried basil
2 teaspoons chopped fresh parsley
½ cup dry vermouth
2 cups canned Italian tomatoes, broken into pieces

With a flat-headed meat mallet, gently pound each scallop to flatten slightly. Sprinkle with salt and pepper and top each scallop with a slice of prosciutto. Roll up and fasten with toothpicks. Repeat for each roulade. In a large skillet, sauté the veal rolls in olive oil until browned, then remove from skillet and set aside. In the same skillet, sauté the garlic, onion, and mushrooms until golden—about 5 minutes. Add the oregano, basil, parsley, vermouth, and tomatoes. Return the roulades to the skillet and simmer, covered, for 45 minutes, or until the veal is cooked through.

NOTE: Chicken broth may be substituted for the dry vermouth.

Mediterranean Salad

Serves 6

⅓ cup olive oil
¼ cup lemon juice
1 clove garlic, crushed
Freshly ground black pepper to taste
1½ cups cooked artichoke hearts, sliced in half
1 medium-sized head Boston lettuce
1 small bunch chicory (½ pound)
½ pound fresh spinach
½ cup sliced scallions
5 plum tomatoes, thinly sliced, *or* 1 pint cherry tomatoes
1 medium-sized cucumber, peeled and sliced
1 green pepper, seeds removed and sliced
1 cup black olives

In a medium-sized bowl, combine the olive oil, lemon juice, garlic, pepper, and artichokes. Stir to mix well, cover with plastic wrap, and refrigerate. Wash the lettuce, chicory, and spinach, pat dry, break into bite-sized pieces, and refrigerate in a plastic bag. To serve, place greens, scallions, tomatoes, cucumber, green pepper, and black olives in a large salad bowl. Pour the artichoke mixture over the salad and toss lightly.

Chocolate Mousse

Serves 6

6 ounces semisweet chocolate pieces
½ cup milk, heated
½ cup butter, softened
4 eggs, separated

1 teaspoon vanilla
Dash of salt
¼ cup granulated sugar
½ cup heavy cream
1 tablespoon confectioners' sugar

Place chocolate pieces in a blender and pour in the hot milk. Cover and blend until chocolate is melted and mixture is smooth. Add the butter, egg yolks, vanilla, and salt. Blend until smooth. In a large bowl, beat the egg whites with an electric mixer until soft peaks form. Add the granulated sugar, 1 tablespoon at a time, beating well after each addition. Continue beating until stiff peaks form when beaters are slowly raised. Fold the chocolate mixture into the egg whites, then pour into an attractive ½-quart serving bowl. Refrigerate for several hours. Beat the cream and confectioners' sugar together until stiff. Spoon whipped cream into a pastry bag fitted with a large star tip, and pipe decorative rosettes on the mousse.

Coffee or Demitasse with "Spirits"

Brew your favorite coffee and add 1 to 2 tablespoons liqueur to each cup. Serve black. Some tasty additions include brandy, whiskey, Amaretto, cognac with orange, Irish Whiskey, Lochan Ora, and Vandermint.

For demitasse, see page 150. Add ½ to 1 tablespoon liqueur and serve black.

Easter Breakfast

Orange Pineapple Juice or *Orange Blossoms*
Quiche Lorraine
English Muffins or *Croissants*
with Marmalades and Jams
Coffee

You will want to make the English muffins (if you are serving them, rather than croissants, which you can buy) the night before, and you can do the quiche then, also, if you wish, and simply warm it the next morning before serving.

To make Orange Pineapple Juice, simply combine the juices in equal amounts (or another proportion, if you prefer). Canned or frozen pineapple juice is practical and economical, but you might want to squeeze fresh orange juice for an extra pleasant touch. If you and your guests would prefer Orange Blossoms, omit the pineapple juice, add gin to taste (up to 1½ ounces per serving), and garnish each glass with a slice of fresh orange.

Quiche with ham.

Quiche Lorraine

Serves 6

1 Rich Pastry for Quiche (recipe
 follows)
1 egg white
1 tablespoon water
4 eggs, lightly beaten
2 cups light cream
½ teaspoon salt

Pinch of cayenne *or* nutmeg
2 cups grated Swiss, Jarlsburg, or
 Gruyère cheese (about ½
 pound)
1 tablespoon butter
½ pound bacon, cooked until crisp
 and crumbled

Place pastry on a lightly floured pastry board and roll out to a 13-inch circle. Carefully fit the crust into a 9-inch diameter, 1½-inch deep ceramic quiche pan or casserole. Trim the pastry off around the top of the quiche pan. Mix the egg white with the water and brush it over the entire surface of the pastry. Refrigerate pastry-lined casserole for 30 minutes to prevent shrinkage. Preheat oven to 375°F. In a large bowl, combine the eggs, cream, salt, and cayenne. Sprinkle the cheese over the bottom of the quiche shell. Pour the egg mixture over the cheese and dot with the butter. Bake for 40 minutes, or until golden. The quiche is fully cooked when a knife blade inserted 2 inches from the edge of the quiche comes out clean. Sprinkle with the crumbled bacon and serve.

Honeydew melon balls with kiwi.

Honeydew Delight

Serves 8

3 honeydew melons, halved, and
   seeds removed
4 kiwi fruits, chilled

Cut 1-inch balls from the melons with a spoon or melon baller and chill.
To serve, peel and slice the kiwi fruits, then cut each slice in half. Divide
the melon balls among 8 dessert bowls and arrange slices of kiwi around
the sides.

Crown of Shrimp in Aspic

Serves 8

1½ tablespoons unflavored gelatin
½ cup dry white wine
3 cups hot whitefish stock *or*
   canned chicken broth
Few drops of fresh lemon juice
2 egg whites, beaten until frothy
4–5 ripe tomatoes, peeled, seeded,
   and quartered

1 pound cooked shrimp, shelled
   and deveined
Watercress
2 cups mayonnaise, flavored with a
   little tomato paste or tomato
   juice

In a small bowl, soften the gelatin in wine for 3 to 5 minutes. In a saucepan, heat the stock or broth over low heat until hot, add the gelatin, and stir until it is completely dissolved. Add the lemon juice and egg whites and bring to a boil, whisking constantly. Remove the pan from the heat without disturbing the mixture and let it stand for 5 minutes. Bring the mixture to a boil again, whisking, remove it from the heat, and let it stand for 5 minutes. Repeat the process one more time. Strain the mixture through a double layer of cheesecloth into a bowl and let it cool. (The mixture must remain liquid, if it starts to thicken, heat it slightly over low heat.)

Cover the bottom of a lightly oiled 1½- or 2-quart mold with a layer of aspic and chill until partially set. Arrange the tomato quarters, rounded sides down, in the aspic and cover with more aspic. Chill until partially set. Arrange some of the shrimp on the aspic and chill. Continue to fill the mold, alternating layers of aspic and shrimp, chilling the mold each time a layer of aspic is added. Chill, covered, until firm.

Before serving, unmold the salad and fill the center of the ring with watercress. Serve with the tomato-flavored mayonnaise.

Watercress Butter
Makes ½ cup

¼ pound (1 stick) unsalted butter
½ bunch watercress, leaves only, minced
1 tablespoon lemon juice

1 teaspoon salt
Freshly ground black pepper to taste

Place the butter in a bowl to soften. When it is soft, cream the butter by mashing it against the sides of the bowl with a wooden spoon until it is light and fluffy. Add the other ingredients, blending well.

NOTE: Watercress butter will keep in the refrigerator, in a tightly covered container, for 2 weeks. It can be shaped into a cylinder by rolling in a sheet of waxed paper. Refrigerate to harden slightly, or freeze until needed.

Sherbet Parfaits
Serves 1

To make each sherbet parfait, layer slightly softened sherbet and fresh fruit in a parfait glass, beginning and ending with the sherbet. Garnish the top with a piece of fresh fruit. It is nice to serve one or two small cookies with each parfait. Some tasty sherbet and fruit combinations include:

Orange sherbet with orange sections or fresh pineapple cubes
Lemon sherbet with strawberry halves or raspberries
Raspberry sherbet with raspberries or sliced peaches (toss sliced peaches with a little orange juice to prevent discoloration)

NOTE: If you do not have parfait glasses, use wineglasses or tall bar glasses.

Iced Coffee

Serves 8

Brew a large pot of your favorite coffee (about 12 cups). Pour the coffee into a heat-resistant glass pitcher or carafe. (If you have a drip- or filter-type coffeemaker that allows the coffee to drip into its own carafe, this is fine.) Cover the pitcher and cool the coffee to room temperature. To serve, pour over lots of ice in tall bar glasses or tumblers. Pass sugar and cream, for those who prefer their coffee sweet or light. Iced-tea spoons are just right for stirring.

Fourth of July Picnic

Gazpacho Soup
Crudités (Crisp Fresh Vegetables)
Easy Oven-fried Chicken Legs
Nutty Brownies   Assorted Fresh Fruits
Lemon-Iced Tea

The Fourth of July and picnics are natural go-togethers. If you and your family (and/or friends) traditionally join others in your town or city at a gathering place to watch the evening's fireworks display on our country's birthday, take this picnic along for supper. If you spend the day at the beach, take it along for lunch.

All of these foods pack and travel well. Take the Gazpacho and the tea along in thermos jugs to keep them cool, and pack the vegetables, chicken, and brownies in their own separate plastic containers. Choose any fruits in season of which your family or group is fond; wash and dry them well before packing them, and take care not to choose any that are very ripe, or they may be bruised along the way. Be sure to take ice along in a picnic cooler to keep the tea cold when you serve it. If you pack the ice carefully you can store the other foods in the cooler as well to keep them chilled.

175

Crispy fried chicken, crudités, fresh fruit, nutty brownies.

Gazpacho

.2 cups tomato juice
1 cup tomatoes, peeled, seeded, and finely chopped
½ cup finely chopped green pepper
½ cup finely chopped peeled cucumber
½ cup finely chopped celery
¼ cup minced onion

1 tablespoon chopped parsley
1 teaspoon chopped fresh chives
1 small clove garlic, crushed
1 tablespoon tarragon vinegar
1 tablespoon olive oil
½ teaspoon salt
¼ teaspoon freshly ground black pepper
Croutons (optional)

In a large bowl, combine all ingredients except the croutons and chill the soup for at least 4 hours. If you prefer a smooth soup, puree the mixture in a food mill, blender, or food processor for 10 seconds before chilling. Reserve some chopped tomato, cucumber, pepper, and celery as garnishes, if you wish. Serve chilled, garnished with chopped vegetables and/or croutons as desired.

Crudités

1 pint cherry tomatoes
1 small head cauliflower
2 medium-sized zucchini

3 large carrots, scraped
4 large stalks celery

Wash cherry tomatoes and place in a plastic container (or bag). Refrigerate covered, until serving time. Wash the cauliflower and break into florets. Wash the zucchini and cut into ¼-inch slices. Place cauliflower and zucchini in a plastic container, cover, and refrigerate. Make carrot curls by scraping slices off the length of the carrot with a vegetable peeler. Roll into curls, secure with toothpicks, and drop into a bowl of ice water. Refrigerate for several hours. Cut the celery into celery frills as directed on page 208. To serve, drain the carrots and celery, remove the toothpicks from the carrot curls, and place in a plastic container or serving dish with the cauliflower, zucchini, and tomatoes.

Easy Oven-fried Chicken Legs
Serves 6

1½ cups prepared seasoned bread
crumbs
¼ cup grated Parmesan cheese

½ cup butter or margarine, melted
18 chicken legs (or 9 legs with
thighs, separated)

Preheat the oven to 375°F. Combine the bread crumbs and cheese in a pie plate. Roll each chicken leg in the butter, then in the bread crumb mixture. Place the legs on a large, low-sided broiler pan and bake for 30 minutes, or until the outside is golden and the juice runs clear when pierced with a fork.

NOTE: Chicken breasts may be baked in the same manner. Separate the wings from the breasts and cut each breast into 2 pieces for uniform size.

Nutty Brownies
Serves 6

½ cup shortening
¼ cup butter or margarine
3 squares (ounces) unsweetened
chocolate
1¼ cups flour
1 teaspoon baking powder

½ teaspoon salt
3 eggs
1½ cups sugar
1½ teaspoons vanilla
2 cups chopped walnuts

Preheat oven to 350°F. In a small saucepan, melt the shortening, butter, and chocolate over low heat. Cool. Sift together the flour, baking powder, and salt. In a large bowl, beat the eggs until light and lemon colored. Beat in the sugar, chocolate mixture, and vanilla. Stir in the flour, then 1½ cups of the walnuts. Pour into a lightly greased 9-inch-square baking pan and sprinkle the top with the remaining nuts. Bake for 40 to 50 minutes, or until a cake tester inserted into the brownies comes out clean. Let cool, then cut into 12 pieces.

Lemon-Iced Tea
Serves 6

Place 6 tea bags in a heat-resistant 1-quart measure. Pour boiling water to the 1 quart line. Let stand for 5 minutes, then remove the tea bags. Pour in more water to make 1 quart. Let cool, covered, to room temperature. Do not refrigerate; this will cloud the tea. To serve, fill tall bar glasses or tumblers with ice. Pour the tea over the ice and stir 2 to 3 teaspoons of fresh lemon juice into each glass. Garnish each glass with a lemon slice.

NOTE: For a very thirsty group, double this recipe.

Thanksgiving Buffet

Relish Tray
Roast Breast of Turkey
Acorn Squash stuffed with Small Whole Onions and Peas
Wild Rice Casserole
Pumpkin Tarts
Coffee and After-dinner Liqueurs

This Thanksgiving meal is designed for carefree serving; host or hostess can enjoy the company of guests throughout the meal, and need spend no time in the kitchen except to put the coffee on. Pastry for the tarts can be made ahead of time and refrigerated. The tarts themselves can be made early and left to cool in the kitchen until serving time. Whipped cream topping for the tarts can be made ahead as well, and refrigerated; it won't be quite so stiff, but it will taste just fine. Make the baked acorn squash ahead, too, or bake with the turkey breast. The Wild Rice Casserole needs only thirty minutes in the oven, so space within won't be a problem if you plan well. Breast of turkey gives you the advantage of ease in carving, and there is no waste. You could, however, use the wild rice mixture to stuff a turkey, if you like.

179

Roast breast of turkey.

Relish Tray

Serves 8

2 bunches of celery, well washed,
   leaves removed
1 large can jumbo or colossal black
   olives, well drained

1 large jar jumbo or colossal whole
   green olives, well drained

Trim the ends of the celery stalks so the root ends are clean and rounded.
Cut each bunch of celery into fourths or eighths, as you prefer. Use an
attractive long shallow serving dish (relish dish) as your tray. Pat the celery
dry and arrange it on the dish. Place the olives in two clusters at the same
end of the dish. If you are serving the relish before the meal, you may want
to use a deeper dish and place some crushed ice under the celery and
olives to keep them chilled.

Roast Turkey Breast

Serves 8

1 (5-pound) turkey breast
Salt and pepper

½ cup butter or margarine
½ teaspoon crushed rosemary

Preheat the oven to 325°F. Place the turkey breast, skin side down, on a rack in a broiler pan. Rub it well with salt and pepper. In a saucepan, melt the butter and add the rosemary. Baste the turkey with the melted butter and place in the oven. Roast for 50 minutes, basting occasionally. Turn the breast skin side up and baste again. Continue to roast the turkey breast, basting frequently, for about 60 minutes longer, or until the internal temperature reaches 180°F.

Stuffed Baked Squash

Serves 8

4 small acorn squash
¼ cup plus 2 tablespoons butter or
  margarine, melted

2 (1-pound) packages frozen peas
  and baby onions
3 large lettuce leaves
½ teaspoon sugar

Preheat oven to 325°F. Cut each acorn squash in half and remove seeds. Brush the insides with the ¼ cup melted butter and place, cut side down, on a baking sheet. Bake for 40 minutes, or until tender. Cook the peas and onions in a medium-sized saucepan according to package directions, adding the lettuce and sugar to the saucepan. When cooked, drain the pea mixture, remove lettuce leaves, and stir in the 2 tablespoons of butter. Spoon the peas and onions into the baked squash shells.

NOTE: The acorn squash may be baked at the same time as the turkey or they may be baked ahead and reheated. To reheat, brush again with butter, place cut side down on a baking sheet and bake until heated through (10 to 15 minutes in a 325°–350°F oven).

Wild Rice Casserole

Serves 8

6 ounces wild rice
6 cups chicken broth
¾ cup long-grain white rice
2 cups sliced scallions, including
  green tops, *or* chopped onion
2 green or red peppers, chopped
1 clove garlic, crushed

⅓ cup olive oil
½ cup chopped fresh parsley
½ teaspoon salt
⅛ teaspoon pepper
2 tablespoons lemon juice
⅓ cup pignola nuts

Rinse wild rice and place in a large saucepan with the chicken broth. Bring to a boil over high heat, then reduce the heat and simmer the rice, covered, for 25 minutes. Add the long-grain rice and simmer for 20 minutes longer, or until the rice is just tender and the broth is absorbed. In a medium skillet, sauté the scallions, green or red pepper, and garlic in the olive oil until tender, then stir in parsley, salt, pepper, lemon juice, and nuts. Combine with rice and pour into a 2-quart casserole and refrigerate. Put casserole in a preheated 350°F oven 30 minutes before serving.

NOTES: This recipe may be used to stuff a turkey.
Wild Rice Casserole is delicious served cold as a salad.

Pumpkin Tarts
Serves 8 (about 20 tarts)

1 Basic Pastry (recipe follows)
2 small eggs, lightly beaten
1 (18-ounce) can pumpkin pie filling

1¼ cups light cream
1 cup heavy cream
2 tablespoons confectioners' sugar

Roll half of the prepared pie crust dough to a thickness of ⅛-inch. Using a cookie cutter, cut the pastry into 3½-inch rounds. Carefully fit the rounds into the cups of a muffin tin (or use small tart pans, if you have them). Repeat with the remaining dough, gently rolling out the scraps to use all the dough. Refrigerate the prepared tart shells for 1 hour. Preheat the oven to 425°F. In a medium-sized bowl combine the eggs, pie filling, and light cream. Spoon the filling into the tart shells, then bake for 20 minutes, or until the pastry is browned and the filling is cooked. Let cool for 10 minutes before removing the tarts from the muffin tins to a wire rack. Let cool completely. In a medium-sized bowl, beat the cream with the sugar until stiff. Serve tarts at room temperature with a dollop of the sweetened whipped cream on each.

Basic Pastry
For a 2-crust 9-inch pie, or 20 tart shells

1⅓ cups flour
½ teaspoon salt

½ cup shortening
4–5 tablespoons ice water

In a medium-sized bowl combine the flour and salt. Using a pastry blender or 2 table knives, cut the shortening into the flour until the pieces are the size of small peas. Sprinkle 3 tablespoons of the ice water over the mixture. Gently stir with a fork to moisten the flour mixture. Push the moistened parts to one side of the bowl. Sprinkle another tablespoon of water on the dry portion and stir to moisten. Repeat with the remaining tablespoon of water, if necessary. Shape the pastry into a ball and flatten it slightly. Cover the dough with plastic wrap and refrigerate for 30 minutes, or until ready to use.

Autumn Formal Dinner

Puree of Apple Soup
Crown Roast of Pork with Peas
Oven-roasted Parmesan Potatoes   Hot Dinner Rolls
Pecan Pie topped with Chocolate and Whipped Cream
Coffee

Nothing warms a home faster on a chilly autumn day than the smells of good food cooking in the kitchen. You could make the dessert the day before if you wish, as it needs time to chill, and whip the cream just before serving. If you set aside the day for cooking, however, start with the pie, so it can cool, then chill, while the roast is in the oven and the soup is on the stove. If your butcher will prepare the crown roast for you, roasting is easy. If you have to make the crown roast yourself, be sure to ask the butcher to crack the bones at the base of each rib, which will make it easy to serve. Remove as much fat from the bones as possible, score the ribs about 1½ inches down from the ends and cut away the meat to the mark. Sew the two loins together, largest ends touching, with a large kitchen needle and twine. Bring the other ends together, sew them as well, and tie a string around the crown for security.

Crown roast of pork with peas.

Puree of Apple Soup

Serves 8

4 tablespoons butter
1 small onion, finely chopped
6–7 apples, unpeeled, cored, and sliced
Salt and freshly ground white pepper

4 cups beef broth
4 tablespoons dry sherry
1¼ teaspoons arrowroot, mixed with 1 tablespoon water
⅓ cup blanched, sliced almonds, sautéed in 2 teaspoons butter

In a large saucepan, melt the butter and cook the onion until it is golden. Add the apple slices and salt and pepper to taste and cook the mixture until the apples are tender. Add the broth and sherry, bring to a boil, and simmer for 15 minutes. Stir in the arrowroot mixture and cook the soup, stirring, until it is thickened. Adjust the seasonings. Strain the soup through a fine sieve into another pan and reheat it. Serve the soup in warmed bowls and sprinkle with the almonds.

Crown Roast of Pork with Peas

Serves 8

1 crown roast of pork (2 full loins)
Salt and pepper
2 packages frozen peas

1–3 tablespoons butter
Paper frills or spiced crab apples

184

Preheat oven to 325°F. Sprinkle the roast all over with salt and pepper. Place the roast, bone ends down, on a shallow roasting pan and bake for 2¾ to 3 hours, or until a meat thermometer placed in the thickest part of the meat (not touching a bone) registers 170°F. Cook the peas according to package directions. Drain, then toss gently with the butter. Place the roast, rib ends up, on a serving platter. Spoon the peas into the center and place a paper frill or spiced crab apple on the end of each rib.

NOTES: Sliced water chestnuts or sautéed sliced mushrooms may be added to the peas for an extra special touch.

To make each paper frill, fold a 5 × 8-inch sheet of paper in half lengthwise. Make 1½-inch cuts in the folded edge at ⅛-inch intervals to make a fringe. Wrap a frill around each bone and secure with transparent tape.

Parmesan Potatoes
Serves 8

3 pounds small new potatoes, peeled

3–4 tablespoons grated Parmesan cheese

About 1¼ hours before the roast will be done, place the potatoes in the roasting pan with the meat. Roll the potatoes in the meat drippings and roast for 45 minutes, basting occasionally. Sprinkle with the Parmesan cheese and continue to roast until tender.

Pecan Pie
Serves 8

1 (9-inch) unbaked pie shell (see page 182 for pastry recipe)
¾ cup sugar
1 tablespoon flour
¼ teaspoon salt
¾ cup light corn syrup
4 eggs, lightly beaten

¼ cup butter
2 cups pecan halves
6 ounces semisweet chocolate pieces
⅓ cup heavy cream
Sweetened Whipped Cream

Refrigerate the pie shell until the filling is ready. Preheat oven to 350°F. In a large bowl, combine the sugar, flour, and salt. Stir in the corn syrup, eggs, and butter. Add the pecans and pour the mixture into the prepared pie shell. Bake for 55 minutes, or until set. Remove the pie from the oven and place it on a wire rack to cool. In a small saucepan, over low heat, melt the chocolate pieces with the cream. Stir to combine, then spread the chocolate mixture over the top of the cooled pie. Serve the pie chilled, topped with Sweetened Whipped Cream.

Winter Formal Dinner

Hot Tomato-Clam Broth with Breadsticks

London Broil

Baked Potatoes with Sour Cream

Green Beans with Mushrooms

Catalonian Crème

Coffee

S tart preparing the meal the day before, and you will get a bonus dish for a meal that day. Make the tomato-clam broth with fresh littleneck clams; only the broth is used in the recipe, and the clams can be enjoyed the day before with melted butter. Cool the broth slightly, strain it, let it cool completely, then refrigerate. On the day you plan to serve, simply combine the broth and the tomato juice, and warm them together. Crème Fraîche to garnish the soup should be made the day before as well; it needs to chill in the refrigerator for at least 8 hours.

The meat and vegetables for this meal are simple and quick to prepare. The dessert will take time to prepare and to bake, but directions are easy to follow. Melting the sugar for the caramel garnish is easy if you do it slowly. Directions for easy cleanup of the caramel pan are provided, too.

Catalonian creme.

Tomato Clam Broth

Serves 6 to 8

2 quarts littleneck clams in their shells
1 medium-sized onion, chopped
1 stalk celery, chopped
1 carrot, chopped
4 sprigs parsley

3 cups water
2 cups tomato juice
Crème Fraîche for garnish (recipe follows)
Chopped chives for garnish

Scrub the clams and put them in a soup pot with the remaining ingredients except the tomato juice, Crème Fraîche, and chives. Cook the mixture, covered, for 10 minutes, or until the clam shells open. Discard any clams that do not open. Reserve the clams; you can serve them as they are with a sauce of melted butter.

Strain the broth through a fine towel or a double thickness of cheesecloth into a bowl. Add the tomato juice. Serve hot or cold, garnished with the Crème Fraîche and chives.

Crème Fraîche

Makes 2 cups

1 cup heavy cream   1 cup sour cream

In a bowl, mix the heavy cream with the sour cream until well blended. Cover and let stand at room temperature overnight. Stir and refrigerate for 8 hours before using.

NOTES: Soup to which Crème Fraîche has been added can be brought to a boil without danger of curdling.

Crème Fraîche keeps, covered, in the refrigerator for at least a week. Use as a garnish on soups as well as on stews and on fresh fruit.

London Broil

Serves 8

1 cup dry red wine
½ cup vegetable oil
1 medium-sized onion, chopped
1 clove garlic, pressed

¼ teaspoon freshly ground pepper
4 pounds boneless round or shoulder steak, 1½ inches thick

Early in the day, combine the wine, oil, onion, garlic, and pepper in a pan slightly larger than the steak. Place the steak in the marinade, turn once, cover with plastic wrap, and refrigerate for at least 4 hours, turning the steak several times. Remove the steak from the marinade, place on a broiler pan, and adjust the shelf so that the steak is about 4 inches from the heat. For rare steak, broil about 12 minutes on each side; for medium, about 14 minutes on each side (these times will vary depending on the thickness of the steak and the type of broiler). To serve, place the steak on a cutting board and slice on the diagonal, ¼ inch thick.

NOTES: To assure tender meat, use unseasoned meat tenderizer, as the label directs, just before broiling.

Chopped fresh parsley, crushed bay leaf, or crushed rosemary may be added to the marinade to give it additional flavor.

Baked Potatoes with Sour Cream

Serves 8

2 cups sour cream
¼ cup chopped scallions (with green part)

8 medium-sized baking potatoes
½ pound bacon strips

Preheat oven to 425°F. Combine the sour cream and scallions in a small bowl, cover with plastic wrap, and refrigerate. Scrub the potatoes and pierce them in several places with a fork. Bake for 1 hour, or until they feel soft when gently squeezed (be sure to use a potholder to squeeze the potatoes). Fry the bacon until crisp, drain, and crumble into a small serving dish. To serve, slash a large X in the top of each potato and pinch the sides together so that the potato "fluffs out." Pass the sour cream and bacon separately at the table.

Green Beans with Mushrooms
Serves 8

2–3 cups water
2 pounds fresh green beans, stem end removed, and cut in half
½ pound fresh mushrooms, sliced

¼ cup butter or margarine
Pinch of marjoram
Salt to taste

Place water in a large skillet. Bring to a boil and add the green beans. Cover the skillet and boil gently for 12 to 15 minutes, or until tender. Meanwhile, in a medium-sized skillet sauté the mushrooms in butter until golden, about 5 minutes. Drain the water off the beans, then add the mushrooms and their butter, marjoram, and salt. Toss gently, then turn into a serving dish.

Catalonian Crème (Flan)
Serves 8

4 eggs, slightly beaten
1 (14-ounce) can sweetened condensed milk
2 cups milk

3 tablespoons Tuaca Demi Sec liqueur *or* apple brandy (optional)
¼ cup sugar

Preheat oven to 375°F. In a large bowl combine the eggs, condensed milk, milk, and liqueur. Pour into a 9-inch shallow baking casserole. Place the casserole in a larger baking pan and pour hot water around the casserole to a depth of 1 inch. Bake for 50 minutes, or until a knife inserted 2 inches from the edge of the flan comes out clean. Remove the flan to a wire rack to cool. Just before serving, melt the sugar in a small saucepan, stirring to prevent burning. When the sugar is melted and golden brown, remove it from the heat and drizzle it over the top of the flan.

NOTE: To clean the pan used to caramelize the sugar, add hot water, and boil until all the sugar is dissolved.

Christmas Dinner

Oyster Stew

Glazed Whole Ham trimmed with Fruit

Sweet Potatoes   Molded Whole Cranberry Salad

Yule Log Cake (Buche de Noël)

Coffee

A traditional meal from start to finish, this Christmas dinner features a dessert well worth your spending the time it takes to make and assemble it. Yule Log Cake is a French holiday specialty your family and friends may look forward to as an annual experience. Once made, the finished, decorated cake can be set aside until serving time. Molded whole cranberry salad is made ahead of time and chilled before serving. Oyster stew is quick and easy if you don't bother to chop the oysters; it will still taste as good. The sweet potatoes, too, are no trouble, especially if you leave the skins on for serving; simply wash them well, trim, and boil. Using a fully cooked bone-in ham will cut down on the roasting time for the main dish. If you buy a ham that has not been precooked, be sure to allow at least 3 hours baking time.

Glazed whole ham with fruit trim.

Oyster Stew

Serves 8 to 12

6 cups shucked oysters, with their
    liquor
4 cups milk
2 cups light cream

Salt and freshly ground white
    pepper
Butter
Paprika

Strain the liquor from the oysters, combine it with the milk and cream in a large saucepan and bring the mixture to a boil. Add the oysters, whole or coarsely chopped, and simmer for 1 minute, or until the oysters become plump. Season with salt and pepper to taste. Serve the stew in warmed bowls with a pat of butter and a sprinkling of paprika on each.

Sweet Potatoes

To cook sweet potatoes, scrub them and remove the bruised spots and root ends. Place the potatoes in a large saucepan and cover them with boiling water. Cook, covered, for about 40 minutes, or until tender. Drain and peel (holding each potato with a fork and scraping the hot skin away with a sharp knife), or serve with skins on.

Molded Whole Cranberry Salad   *Serves 8*

1 envelope unflavored gelatin
¾ cup cold water
3 cups cranberries, picked over
   and rinsed

2 cups sugar
1 cup fresh orange juice
Salad greens for garnish

In a small bowl, soften the gelatin in ¼ cup of the water. In a saucepan combine 2 cups of the cranberries with the remaining ½ cup water and cook, covered, over moderate heat for about 15 minutes, or until the skins pop. Force berries with the liquid through a sieve into a saucepan and add the sugar, orange juice, and remaining cup of cranberries. Bring the mixture to a boil and simmer it over low heat for 5 minutes. Add the gelatin and stir gently until it dissolves. Remove the pan from the heat and remove the whole berries with a slotted spoon. Arrange the berries in the bottom of a lightly oiled 1-quart mold, pour in enough of the berry liquid to just cover them, and chill until partially set. Add the remaining liquid and chill, covered, until firm.

Before serving, unmold onto a platter lined with salad greens.

Baked Ham   *Serves 8 to 12*

1 (8–10 pound) ham, bone-in,
   fully cooked
¾ cup brown sugar, firmly packed
½ cup pineapple juice (drained
   from pineapple slices)

8–10 pineapple slices
8–10 spiced crab apples

Preheat the oven to 325°F. Place the ham, fat side up, in a roasting pan. Insert a meat thermometer in the thickest part of the ham, away from the bone. Bake for 1¾ hours. Remove the ham from the oven and cut away the rind (if necessary). Combine the brown sugar and pineapple juice and brush over the ham. Arrange the pineapple slices over the ham, fastening each with a toothpick, if necessary (to be removed before serving). Return the ham to the oven and bake, basting occasionally with brown sugar mixture, for another 30 to 40 minutes, or until internal temperature reaches 140°F. Garnish with spiced crab apples.

NOTE: A bone-in whole ham that has not been precooked *must* bake for 2¾ to 3¼ hours, or until the internal temperature reaches 160°F.

Yule Log Cake
Serves 8

1 cup flour
1½ teaspoons baking powder
¼ teaspoon salt
4 eggs
1 cup sugar
¼ cup water

1 teaspoon vanilla
Confectioners' sugar
Rum Syrup (recipe follows)
Mocha Frosting (recipe follows)
Candy Holly (recipe follows)

Preheat the oven to 425°F. Grease an 11 × 17-inch jelly roll pan, line it with waxed paper, then lightly grease the waxed paper. Sift together the flour, baking powder, and salt and set aside. In a large bowl, beat the eggs with an electric mixer until very thick and lemon colored. Beat in the sugar, 2 or 3 tablespoons at a time, and continue beating for 2 more minutes after all the sugar has been added. At low speed, beat in the water, then the flour mixture and the vanilla, just to combine. Pour the batter into the prepared jelly roll pan, and bake for 12 to 15 minutes. When cake is done, turn out immediately onto a clean tea towel that has been sprinkled with confectioners' sugar. Remove the waxed paper and trim the ends of the cake with a sharp knife. Roll cake up *with* the tea towel, to form a 17-inch-long roll, and cool on a wire rack. When cool, unroll and brush the cake with half the Rum Syrup. Spread with one-third of the Mocha Frosting and reroll the cake, removing the tea towel as you roll. Place the cake on serving platter, cut off both ends of the cake diagonally, and place on the rolled cake to look like branches or knots. Brush the top and sides of the cake (not the cut ends) with the remaining Rum Syrup. Frost with the remaining frosting, being careful not to frost the ends of the log. Run the tines of a fork lengthwise along the cake to give the frosting the appearance of bark. Decorate with Candy Holly.

Rum Syrup
Makes ¹/₂ cup

¼ cup sugar
¼ cup water

2 tablespoons dark rum

Boil the sugar and water in a small saucepan until syrupy (about 3 mintues). Cool, then add the rum.

Mocha Frosting
Makes 3¹/₂ cups, enough to frost a 9-inch cake

2 cups heavy cream
⅓ cup confectioners' sugar
¼ cup unsweetened Dutch-process
   cocoa powder

1 tablespoon instant coffee
1½ tablespoons dark rum

Combine all the ingredients in a large bowl, blending thoroughly, and refrigerate for 1 hour. Remove from the refrigerator and beat until stiff.

Candy Holly

Small spearmint candy leaves (the
   green jelly type)

Red cinnamon decors

Slice several small spearmint leaves in half and arrange, sugared side down, in groups of 2 or 3 leaves on the Yule Log. Place 1 or 2 red cinnamon decors at the base of the leaves to complete the holly.

New Year's Eve Supper

Cheese Platter and Cocktails
Boeuf Bourguignon
Brussels Sprouts
Fruitcake Slices with Brandy Sauce
Coffee

This New Year's Eve Supper is planned for twelve guests. Serve your cheese platter with whatever drinks your guests may favor, dine later, toast the New Year with champagne if you like, and save the dessert and coffee 'til last. The main dish is best made ahead of time; it is tastier if the flavors in the sauce can blend overnight. Be sure to follow directions; the last ingredient (cornstarch) is not to be added until just before serving. The only time you need to spend in the kitchen on party day is a few minutes before dinner time to prepare and boil the brussels sprouts, and a few minutes before dessert time to whip up the brandy sauce for the fruitcake.

Boeuf Bourguignon.

Cheese Platter

An attractive arrangement of cheeses is a delicious yet easy appetizer to serve your guests with cocktails. Offer a variety of textures and flavors and you will surely please everyone. Usually a selection of soft, semisoft, and semihard to hard cheese will do nicely. Arrange your choices on a large platter or cheese board with a variety of crackers. Be sure to have at least one cheese knife or server for each cheese.

Below are several tasty choices in each category.

SOFT
Boursin—an unripened cheese with a creamy herb or garlic flavor
Neufchâtel—an unripened cheese with a very mild flavor
Brie—a ripened cheese with a relatively strong flavor
Camembert—a ripened cheese with a strong flavor

SEMISOFT
Bonbel—smooth with a mild flavor
Muenster—mild flavor
Roquefort—blue veined with a sharp flavor
Stilton—blue veined with a sharp flavor

SEMIHARD TO HARD
Cheddar—mild to sharp
Edam—mild, nutty flavor
Monterey Jack—mild

The fresh, soft cheeses (Boursin and Neufchâtel) should be served chilled. All other cheeses should be served at room temperature.

Boeuf Bourguignon   *Serves 12*

4 pounds boneless beef bottom round, cut into 1¼-inch cubes
¼ cup vegetable oil
2 pounds small white onions, peeled
2 pounds mushrooms, cut in half if large
2 (10½-ounce) cans beef broth

3 cups Burgundy wine
1 (8-ounce) can tomato sauce
1 bay leaf
⅛ teaspoon freshly ground black pepper
3 tablespoons cornstarch
¼ cup water

In a large Dutch oven, brown the meat a little at a time in the oil, removing the meat as it is browned. When all the meat has been browned and removed, brown the onions and remove, then the mushrooms. When the mushrooms are golden, return the browned meat and onions to the pot along with the broth, wine, tomato sauce, bay leaf, and pepper. Simmer, covered, for 1½ hours, or until the beef is tender. Mix the cornstarch and water and stir into the pot. Continue cooking until the mixture is thickened and the broth is translucent. If a thicker sauce is desired, mix more cornstarch and water and add to the Boeuf Bourguignon.

NOTE: This is best made a day ahead. Cook as directed until the beef is tender, but *do not* add the cornstarch. Before serving, heat the Boeuf Bourguignon, then add the cornstarch as directed above.

Fresh Brussels Sprouts

Serves 12

3 pounds fresh brussels sprouts
1 teaspoon salt

3 tablespoons butter, melted

Wash brussels sprouts well. Cut off the stem ends and remove any discolored leaves. Soak in cold water to cover for 15 minutes. Drain, then place the brussels sprouts in a large saucepan or a Dutch oven with the salt and pour in boiling water to 1 inch. Cover tightly and simmer for 15 to 20 minutes, or until tender. Drain, pour into serving dish, and top with butter.

Fruitcake with Brandy Sauce

Serves 12

At this time of the year, wonderful fruitcakes abound in specialty shops, bakeries, and even the neighborhood grocery store. Buy a large one and give it your own "special" touch. Soak a large piece of cheesecloth in several tablespoons of brandy. Wrap the cheesecloth around the fruitcake, then place in a plastic food-storage bag, close, and seal. The next day, resoak the cheesecloth in brandy and rewrap the cake. Repeat 1 more day, then store tightly wrapped in the refrigerator for up to a month. To serve, remove the cheesecloth, cut the fruitcake into thin slices, and top with Fluffy Brandy Sauce (recipe follows).

Fluffy Brandy Sauce

Makes about 1½ cups

½ cup butter or margarine,
    softened
2 cups confectioners' sugar

1 tablespoon brandy *or* dark rum
¼ teaspoon vanilla

In a small bowl, combine all ingredients and beat with an electric mixer until the sauce is light and fluffy.

SPECIAL OCCASIONS

Housewarming

French Peasant Vegetable Soup
Barbecued Spareribs
Baby Lima Beans
Corn Bread Sticks
Cinnamon-Rice Pudding

This housewarming menu was created with portability in mind—you can prepare this meal, planned for eight, and take it with you when you visit a new family on the block. All of these foods—from soup to dessert—can be prepared at home, packed in tightly-sealed containers, taken along, and reheated when you arrive. Sharing a meal with friends is a very pleasant way to "warm" a new house, and these home-style dishes seem especially appropriate.

You can, of course, prepare this menu in your own new home and invite friends over to share it with you, once you have unpacked and put your kitchen and china closet in order. The pleasant kitchen aromas filling the house will make it seem like home right from the beginning.

Rice pudding.

French Peasant Vegetable Soup

Serves 8

5–6 large potatoes, sliced
3 tomatoes, quartered
3 leeks (white parts only), sliced
4–5 carrots, quartered
5–6 celery stalks with leaves, sliced
3 medium-sized onions, sliced
4–5 lettuce leaves

Bouquet garni: 1 bay leaf, ½
teaspoon dried thyme, and 6
sprigs parsley
Salt and freshly ground black
pepper
Grated Gruyère cheese

Put all the vegetables and the bouquet garni in a large enamel or stainless-steel saucepan. Add water to cover, bring to a boil, and simmer, covered, for 1 hour. Remove the pan from the heat and discard the bouquet garni. Season to taste with salt and pepper. Serve the soup in warmed bowls, sprinkled with the cheese.

Barbecued Spareribs with Baby Lima Beans

Serves 8

1 cup ketchup
½ cup water
¾ cup chili sauce
3 tablespoons vinegar
1 tablespoon Worcestershire sauce
2 tablespoons brown sugar

1 teaspoon salt
1 teaspooon dry mustard
6–8 pounds spareribs, cut into
    serving-sized pieces
3 large onions, chopped
Baby Lima Beans (recipe follows)

Preheat oven to 325°F. In a medium-sized saucepan, combine the ketchup, water, chili sauce, vinegar, Worcestershire sauce, sugar, salt, and mustard. Bring to a boil, reduce heat, and simmer, uncovered, for 5 minutes. Layer half the ribs in a large roasting pan, sprinkle with half the onions, and spoon half the sauce over them. Repeat the layers. Cover the pan tightly with aluminum foil. Bake for 1½ hours, uncover, and bake for 30 minutes longer, or until tender. To serve, mound the ribs in the center of a large serving platter or tray. Spoon the baby lima beans around the ribs. Spoon the fat off the sauce in the roasting pan and pour the sauce over the lima beans.

NOTE: If the sauce is thin, pour it into a saucepan, and boil to thicken it slightly.

Baby Lima Beans

Serves 8

1 pound dried baby lima beans*
6 cups of water

1 teaspoon salt
2 tablespoons butter or margarine

Place the lima beans in a large bowl and cover with the water. Refrigerate, covered, overnight. The next day, pour the beans and liquid into a large kettle, add the salt, and bring to a boil. Turn the heat down and simmer the beans, covered, for about 1 hour, or until tender and most of the liquid has been absorbed. Pour off the excess liquid, if necessary. Stir in the butter, and serve with the Barbecued Spareribs.

*An alternate method for softening the lima beans would be to cover them with cold water in a large soup pot, bring the water to a boil, simmer for 3 minutes, turn off the heat, and let stand for 1 hour.

Corn Bread Sticks

Serves 8

1 cup yellow cornmeal
½ cup flour
2 tablespoons sugar
1½ teaspoons baking powder
½ teaspoon salt

2 eggs
½ cup milk
¼ cup vegetable oil

Preheat oven to 425°F. In a bowl, combine the cornmeal, flour, sugar, baking powder, and salt. Add the eggs, milk, and oil, beating just until smooth. Pour into a lightly greased 9-inch square baking pan, and bake for 15 minutes or until a cake tester inserted in the center comes out clean. To serve, cut the bread in half, then cut each half into 8 (1-inch) sticks.

Cinnamon-Rice Pudding

Serves 8

6 cups milk
1 cup rice
1 (1-inch) piece of stick cinnamon
3 eggs
1 cup sugar

½ teaspoon vanilla
½ teaspoon ground cinnamon, mixed with 1 tablespoon sugar
Additional stick cinnamon for garnish (optional)

In a heavy, medium-sized saucepan, over low heat, warm the milk until bubbles form around the edge of the pan. Add the rice and stick cinnamon. Cover and cook, stirring occasionally, until the rice has absorbed all the milk. Remove from heat and discard the cinnamon stick.

Preheat oven to 350°F. In a medium-sized bowl, beat the eggs until light and lemon colored. Add the sugar and vanilla, beat 1 minute longer, then stir into the cooked rice. Pour the mixture into a buttered 2- to 2½-quart casserole and bake for 30 minutes, stirring occasionally. Serve hot or cold, sprinkled with the cinnamon-sugar mixture. Garnish with stick cinnamon, if desired.

Reception at Home

Easy Finger Sandwiches

Liver Pâté en Gelée

Champagne Punch

Tiny Cookies

Tea and Coffee

If you are celebrating a graduation, honoring the arrival of respected visitors, or observing a holiday in any season, you will find this an appropriate menu. As right for early evening as for an afternoon, this menu will also be equally suitable indoors or out.

The festive champagne punch is elegant and easy. The Liver Pâté en Gelée requires work and patience, but it should be prepared the day before you plan to serve, so you will not be overwhelmed by a complex task on party day. The attractive party sandwiches are not difficult to assemble, and it is as easy to make many as it would be to make a few. For those guests who may prefer sweets, provide a tray or two of cookies. Many fine commercial ones are now available; the crisp little Danish cookies sold in tins would be an especially good accompaniment.

Easy Finger Sandwiches

Cut an assortment of thinly sliced bread (white, whole-wheat, rye, pumpernickel) into fancy shapes, using 2½-inch cookie cutters. Spread a thin layer of softened butter on each bread cutout. Spread one of the fillings described below on a buttered bread cutout and place another cutout of the same shape on top (butter side down) to make a sandwich. Repeat with the remaining bread cutouts. Sandwiches may be garnished with whole olives, small pickles, or ham and cheese cubes fastened to the top of a sandwich with a fancy toothpick. You may also butter the edges of some sandwiches and dip them in finely chopped parsley or watercress. Arrange attractively on a large tray.

Shrimp Filling

Makes 15 2½-inch sandwiches

1 cup chopped, cooked shrimp
¼ cup chopped celery
1 tablespoon chopped parsley

1 teaspoon lemon juice
Salt to taste
3 tablespoons mayonnaise

Combine all ingredients in a small bowl.

Egg Salad and Watercress Filling

Makes 15 2½-inch sandwiches

3 hard-cooked eggs, finely
    chopped
3 tablespoons chopped watercress

1 teaspoon minced onion
2 tablespoons mayonnaise
Salt and cayenne to taste

Combine all ingredients in a small bowl.

Ham Salad Filling

Makes 10 2½-inch sandwiches

1 (4½-ounce) can deviled ham
2 tablespoons sweet pickle relish

1 tablespoon mayonnaise
1 teaspoon sloe gin (optional)

Combine all ingredients in a small bowl.

Pâté en gelée.

Pâté en Gelée

Serves 18 (½-inch slices)

½ pound bacon
1 pound chicken livers
2 tablespoons butter or margarine
1 medium-sized onion, chopped
2 cloves garlic, chopped
2 eggs
3 tablespoons brandy
½ cup fresh bread crumbs
1 pound pork, ground
1 pound veal, ground
1 teaspoon salt
Pepper to taste
½ teaspoon nutmeg

½ teaspoon allspice
½ teaspoon dried thyme
1 pound boneless chicken breasts, skin removed, cut in strips lengthwise
1 (10¾-ounce) can chicken broth
3 tablespoons dry sherry
1 envelope unflavored gelatin
2 hard-cooked eggs
Pimiento
Black olives
Watercress for garnish
Radish roses for garnish

Line a 9 × 5 × 2¾-inch loaf pan with strips of raw bacon. In a large skillet, sauté the chicken livers in butter. Place sautéed chicken livers in a food processor with the onion and garlic and puree the mixture. Add the eggs, brandy, and bread crumbs, and run the processor for a few seconds to combine the mixture. In a large bowl, combine the processed chicken-liver mixture with the ground pork, veal, and spices.

205

Preheat oven to 375°F. Layer liver mixture and chicken strips in the prepared loaf pan, beginning and ending with the liver. Cover the pan tightly with aluminum foil, place in a larger baking pan and pour 1 inch of hot water into the larger pan. Bake for 1½ hours, or until the juice runs clear when the loaf is pierced. Remove from the oven, pour off the fat, replace the foil and place a weight on the pâté (canned vegetables work nicely). Refrigerate overnight.

Next day, combine chicken broth and sherry in a small saucepan. Sprinkle gelatin over the mixture and let stand for 5 minutes to soften the gelatin. Gently heat until the gelatin is dissolved. Place the saucepan in a bowl of ice water and chill, stirring occasionally, until the mixture is the consistency of uncooked egg white. Set a wire rack on a tray or jelly-roll pan. Unmold the pâté onto the rack and remove the bacon. Spoon the gelatin over the top and sides of the pâté and refrigerate for 10 minutes. Cut the egg white, pimiento, and black olives into decorative shapes and place on top of pâté. Spoon more gelatin over the pâté and refrigerate. Repeat the coating process 1 or 2 more times. If gelatin becomes too thick, reheat and chill as directed above (gelatin which has dripped into the pan under the pâté may be scraped off and added). Place the pâté on a serving platter (a large spatula will enable you to do so easily) and garnish with watercress and radish roses.

NOTES: Make the pâté the day before you wish to serve it.

To make radish roses, slice thin petals around the sides of each radish with a small paring knife, starting at the pointed end. Place in ice water for 1 hour to open.

Champagne Punch   *Serves 20*

6 lumps sugar   1 cup fine cognac
Dash of orange bitters   3 bottles chilled brut champagne

Put the sugar lumps in a punch bowl and add a dash of bitters. Add the cognac, and stir to dissolve the sugar. Just before serving, add a large block of ice, and pour in the champagne. Garnish, if you like, with fresh fruits in season.

Gala Open House

Fresh Tomatoes and Celery Vinaigrette
Bouillabaisse
Home-baked French Bread
Cheese and Fruit Dessert with Wine
Coffee

This open house menu is designed to give you, the host or hostess, the freedom to enjoy your guests as they enjoy your hospitality.

The ingredients for the salad can be prepared ahead of time and assembled when you are ready to put the salad on the buffet. Guests attend to the dressing. As party time approaches, bouillabaisse can cook atop the stove while bread is baking within. Your dessert, also, can be prepared and put away earlier in the day, as you will not be cutting the fruit. Just remember to remove cheese from the refrigerator to bring it to room temperature for serving, and to open the wine in enough time for it to "breathe" a bit.

Bouillabaisse.

Tomato and Celery Vinaigrette

This impressively attractive salad is wonderfully simple to make. Arrange slices of ripe tomato and frills or cuts of celery on a bed of Boston or other leaf lettuce. Sprinkle with chopped fresh herbs—basil, oregano, and parsely are complementary—and serve with oil (corn, olive, or safflower) and vinegar (white wine or tarragon). For a smaller number of guests, this salad can be presented in the same fashion on individual plates. The celery frills must be prepared in advance.

To make celery frills: Cut celery stalks into 1½-inch pieces. Cut each piece down lengthwise 1 inch then make 3 to 4 crosswise cuts of equal depth on each of the two sides. Place in ice water for several hours for the frills to open up. Drain to serve.

Bouillabaisse

Serves 8

⅓ cup olive oil
2 large onions, finely chopped
2 cloves garlic, crushed
¼ teaspooon saffron
8 tomatoes, peeled and chopped
¼ cup chopped parsley
1 teaspoon thyme
1 bay leaf
Salt and pepper to taste
2 cups fish stock or clam juice

2 cups white wine
2 cups water
1½ to 2 pounds fish fillets (cod or haddock), cut into serving-size pieces
24 shucked clams or mussels
24 medium shrimp
2 large (or 4 to 6 small) lobster tails, cut into pieces

In a Dutch oven, combine the olive oil, onion, garlic, and saffron and sauté until vegetables are soft. Add the tomatoes, parsley, thyme, bay leaf, salt, pepper, fish stock, wine, and water. Simmer, covered, for 20 minutes. Add the fish fillets, clams or mussels, shrimp, and lobster tails, and simmer for 15 minutes longer. Serve in a tureen for guests to help themselves, or in deep individual serving bowls.

NOTES: To serve a larger number of guests, make two or more batches.

If using frozen fish or other frozen ingredients, thaw first and drain well before adding.

French Bread

Makes 2 loaves

1½ cups warm water (105°F to 115°F)
1 package active dry yeast
1 tablespoon sugar

1 tablespoon shortening, softened
2 teaspoons salt
3½ to 4 cups unsifted flour
2 tablespoons cornmeal

Pour the water into a large mixing bowl. Sprinkle the yeast over the water, then stir to dissolve. Add the sugar, shortening, and salt. Stir in the flour, 1 cup at a time, adding more if necessary (if dough is too sticky to handle). Knead the dough on a lightly floured surface until it is smooth and elastic, about 10 minutes.

Place the dough in a lightly greased large bowl. Brush the top of the dough with shortening, cover the bowl with a towel, and let rise in a draft-free place until doubled in bulk, about 1½ hours.

Punch down the dough, and turn it out onto a lightly floured surface. Divide the dough in half, and roll each half into an 8 × 12-inch rectangle.

Lima Bean Soup

Serves 8

½ cup chopped onion
¼ cup chopped carrot
¼ cup chopped celery
4 tablespoons corn oil margarine
2 cups dried baby lima beans, soaked overnight in water to cover*

1 teaspoon thyme
2 teaspoons dried cilantro *or* several sprigs fresh cilantro
1 teaspoon salt
2 cups light cream
Chopped cilantro or parsley for garnish

In a large saucepan or soup pot, sauté the onion, carrot, and celery in 2 tablespoons of the margarine until the onions are soft but not browned. Drain the lima beans and reserve the liquid in a 2-quart measuring cup (add water to the bean liquid to make 8 cups). Add the lima beans, water and bean liquid, thyme, cilantro, and salt to the onion and vegetables in the pot. Simmer until the beans are tender, about 1 hour. Puree the mixture, in batches if necessary, in a food mill, food processor, or blender. Rinse the pot and return the soup to it. Add the cream and the remaining 2 tablespoons margarine. Heat gently before serving. Garnish the individual servings with chopped cilantro or parsley.

NOTE: Cilantro is also known as coriander leaf.

*An alternate method for softening the lima beans would be to cover them with cold water in a large soup pot, bring the water to a boil, simmer for 3 minutes, turn off the heat, and let stand for 1 hour.

Ziti Casserole

Serves 8

1 cup chopped onion
2 cloves garlic, minced
2 tablespoons olive oil
6 cups canned Italian plum tomatoes
2 teaspoons salt
⅛ teaspoon pepper
1 teaspoon oregano

1 teaspoon dried basil
1 pound mozzarella cheese
1 pound ricotta cheese
1½ cups cooked spinach, well drained
2 eggs, lightly beaten
½ cup Parmesan cheese
1 pound ziti, cooked and drained

In a large skillet, sauté the onion and garlic in olive oil until golden. Add the tomatoes, 1½ teaspoons of the salt, pepper, oregano, and basil. Simmer for 1 hour, stirring occasionally. Cut one-third of the mozzarella cheese in thin slices and reserve. Cut the remaining cheese into small cubes and combine in a large mixing bowl with the ricotta cheese, spinach, eggs, Parmesan cheese, and the remaining ½ teaspoon salt.

Vegetarian ziti casserole.

Preheat the oven to 375°F. Spoon a little of the sauce over the bottom of a large baking pan or casserole. Layer with half the ziti, all of the cheese filling, and half the sauce. Add the remaining ziti and lightly toss with 2 forks to distribute the cheese and spinach filling throughout the casserole. Spoon the remaining sauce over the ziti, and place the reserved mozzarella slices in a decorative pattern on top. Bake for 45 minutes.

NOTE: Two smaller baking pans or casseroles may be used.

Zesty Tossed Salad

Serves 8

¼ cup vegetable oil
¼ cup white wine vinegar
1 tablespoon grated Parmesan cheese
2 teaspoons Dijon mustard
1 teaspoon sugar
½ teaspoon salt
Dash of pepper

2 medium heads leaf lettuce, torn into bite-sized pieces
½ cup sliced scallions
1 green pepper, seeded and cut into ½-inch pieces
3 cups mandarin orange sections, drained
1 cup walnut pieces

Using a fork or wire whisk, combine the oil, vinegar, Parmesan cheese, mustard, sugar, salt, and pepper in a small bowl. Refrigerate, covered, until ready to serve the salad. Combine the lettuce, scallions, and green pepper in a large plastic bag and place in the refrigerator to crisp until serving time.

To serve: Place the lettuce mixture, orange sections, and walnuts in a large salad bowl and toss lightly with the dressing.

Amaretto Meringues

Serves 8

4 egg whites, at room temperature
¼ teaspoon cream of tartar
Dash of salt
¾ cup granulated sugar

2 cups heavy cream
¼ cup confectioners' sugar
2 tablespoons Amaretto
½ cup sliced almonds, toasted

Preheat oven to 275°F. In a large mixing bowl, beat the egg whites with cream of tartar and salt until soft peaks form when the beater is slowly raised. Beat in the granulated sugar, 2 tablespoons at a time. Beat until the meringue is stiff and all the sugar has dissolved. Cover a baking sheet with parchment or brown paper, and divide the meringue onto it in 8 mounds. With the back of a spoon, shape the mounds into little "nests" (be sure to leave room for the "nests" to expand during baking). Bake for 1 hour, then turn the oven off and leave the meringues in the oven for another hour to dry. In a medium-sized bowl, chill the cream, confectioners' sugar, and Amaretto while the meringues are baking. To serve: Whip the cream mixture until stiff, and spoon the mixture into the meringue "nests" (or pipe it in with a pastry bag fitted with a large star tip). Garnish with toasted almond slices.

BRUNCHES

English Breakfast

Fruit Juice
Mixed Grill with Cheese-scrambled Eggs
Toast with Marmalade and Black Currant Jam
Tea with Lemon or Hot Milk and Sugar

You can prepare a quite authentic English breakfast here at home, thanks to the availability, even in supermarkets, of the well-known English marmalades and jams, and teas. There is even a blend of tea called "English Breakfast," an obvious choice for our menu. Another suitable blend would be "Earl Grey"—and there are others, too. Choose any one that appeals to you. Among the available imported marmalades, in addition to the traditional orange, are such exotica as the grapefruit and three-fruit marmalades; this choice, too, is yours. Black currant jam is an English favorite, so you will probably want to include that in any selection you provide. Though you probably think of English tea as being served with milk, for breakfast lemon is just as appropriate. Sugar is provided, of course, in either case. The "main dish" combination on this menu is substantial, another feature of traditionally hearty English breakfast fare.

Mixed grill with scrambled eggs.

Mixed Grill

Serves 4

½ pound calves' liver
½ cup milk
½ pound bacon
4 lamb chops (1-inch thick)

½ pound breakfast link sausage
  (about 8)
½ cup water

Cut the calves' liver into 4 pieces, place in a bowl, and pour the milk over it. Marinate for 30 minutes. Sauté the bacon until crispy and drain on paper towels. If desired, before draining roll bacon strips immediately on the tines of a fork to form curls. Drain all except 2 tablespoons of bacon fat from the skillet and set the skillet aside for later use.

Meanwhile, place the lamb chops on a broiler rack 4 inches from the heat and broil for about 8 minutes on each side. Place the sausage and water in another skillet. Bring to a boil, then simmer, covered, for 5 minutes. Drain the water off, then sauté for 10 minutes, or until golden brown. Drain on paper towels. Drain the liver and pat dry with paper towels. Sauté in the skillet with reserved bacon fat over medium heat for about 3 minutes on each side, or until pink inside. Put paper frills on the lamb chop bones, if desired (see page 185 for directions). Place all the meats on a serving platter or in a chafing dish (this will keep everything piping-hot) and serve with Cheese-scrambled Eggs.

Cheese-scrambled Eggs

Serves 4

6 eggs
2 tablespoons light cream *or* milk
1 tablespoon dry sherry
¼ teaspoon dried oregano

Salt and pepper to taste
½ cup grated cheese (Edam, Swiss,
  or American)
2 tablespoons butter or margarine

In a medium-sized bowl, combine the eggs, cream, sherry, oregano, salt, and pepper. Stir in the cheese. Melt the butter in a medium-sized skillet over medium heat and add the egg mixture. Use a wooden spoon or metal spatula to gently scramble the eggs, pushing scrambled egg aside as it cooks on the bottom. Repeat until the mixture is cooked the way you like it.

Home for the Holidays

Buttermilk Pancakes with Whipped Honey Butter
Canadian Bacon
The Ultimate Strawberry (Strawberries in Champagne)

This is a holiday menu of comforts and delights, of nostalgia and extravagance. A brunch to pamper family members or to honor guests, its elements are traditional and contemporary. You can, of course, serve an alternate fruit course and offer a hot beverage (coffee or tea) or milk with the pancakes and bacon—or put the fruit in the pancakes, as suggested in the recipe variation provided in the menu. Blueberry pancakes with fresh blueberries are a cinch all year 'round—even at Thanksgiving, Christmas, or New Year's—if you have learned a simple trick: fresh blueberries can be easily prepared for freezing, and stored until you wish to serve them out of season as a special treat. To do this, pick over the berries carefully, removing the stems and discarding those that are badly bruised or overripe. If you wash them, drain them well and let them dry completely before spreading them out on a cookie sheet or metal tray. Freeze them on the tray, remove them, pack them in plastic bags (they will be individually frozen), and store them in your freezer for future use.

Buttermilk Pancakes

Serves 6

2¼ cups flour
2 teaspooons baking powder
2 teaspoons baking soda
3 tablespoons sugar
1 teaspoon salt

3 eggs, well beaten
2¼ cups buttermilk
¼ cup vegetable oil
Whipped Honey Butter (recipe
  follows)

In a medium-sized bowl, sift together the flour, baking powder, baking soda, sugar, and salt. Add the eggs, oil, and buttermilk all at once. Stir just to combine all the ingredients (the batter will be lumpy). For each pancake, pour about ¼ cup batter onto a preheated griddle, lightly greased. Cook until bubbles form on the surface and the edges look dry. With a large pancake turner, gently turn the pancake and cook until it is nicely browned on the underside and cooked throughout. Make as many pancakes at one time as will fit on your griddle without running together. Keep the pancakes hot in a warm oven or serve them as they come right off the griddle. Top each pancake with a dollop of Whipped Honey Butter.

NOTE: The griddle should always be heated slowly. It has reached the proper temperature when a little cold water dropped on the hot griddle sizzles and rolls off in little drops.

Blueberry Pancakes

Follow the recipe for Buttermilk Pancakes (above) but before turning the pancakes, sprinkle each with some blueberries. Turn the pancakes and proceed as directed.

Whipped Honey Butter

Makes 1 cup

½ cup butter

¾ cup honey

Let the butter soften in a small bowl to room temperature. Beat until light and airy, then slowly beat in the honey.

Sautéed Canadian Bacon

Serves 6

12 slices Canadian bacon

In a heavy skillet, sauté bacon slices over low heat for about 5 minutes, turning occasionally. The bacon is cooked when the lean part is a red-brown color and the fat is golden brown.

Strawberries in champagne.

The Ultimate Strawberry

Serves 6

½ cup sugar
1 cup water
3 pints strawberries, washed and
   hulled

1 (750 ml) bottle dry champagne,
chilled

In a medium-sized saucepan, bring the sugar and water to a boil, and boil for 5 minutes to make a syrup. Refrigerate to chill.For serving, arrange the strawberries in 6 stemmed goblets or saucer champagne glasses. Spoon 2 tablespoons of the syrup over each serving of strawberries. Carefully pour the champagne to fill the glasses.

NOTE: Try to choose beautiful, well-shaped strawberries, whether large or small. You might want to leave the stems on 6 of them to garnish the tops of the servings.

Sunday Sophisticate

Screwdrivers or *Freshly Squeezed Orange Juice*
Broiled Baby Lamp Chops and Herbed Tomatoes
Asparagus Tips Vinaigrette
Miniature Danish Pastries
Coffee

This elegant brunch or luncheon menu requires very little time in the kitchen before serving, so you will be as relaxed as your guests, and enjoy the event as fully as they will. You can prepare the asparagus the day before, allowing you to select it the day it is cooked so it will be its freshest. Refrigerate it, covered, overnight. Prepare the vinaigrette on Saturday, too, to give it time for the flavors to blend. You could also trim the chops ahead of time to make cooking easier; remember to wrap them well before refrigerating overnight. The tomatoes are best prepared shortly before serving, but they do not require much time; bake them, of course, before you will need the broiler for the chops, and keep them warm. If you decide to serve miniature Danish pastries, buy them at a local bakery; bread or rolls could be substituted, if you prefer. Offer coffee at the close of the meal, especially if you do not serve an alcoholic beverage.

Baby lamb chops with herbed tomatoes.

Screwdriver

Makes 1 drink

2 ounces vodka
Freshly squeezed orange juice
1 slice of orange

Pour vodka over ice in a highball glass. Add orange juice and stir gently.

VARIATIONS: A screwdriver can also be made with rum or tequila.
    For an extra-special brunch treat, float 1 teaspoon of Cointreau on the top of each drink just before serving.

Broiled Baby Lamb Chops
Serves 4

8 rib lamb chops, 1 inch thick, with the fat scraped from the tips of the bones

2 tablespoons melted butter or margarine
Herbed Tomatoes (recipe follows)

Brush the lamb chops with the butter and place on the rack of a large broiler pan. Broil 4 inches from the heat for about 8 minutes, turn, brush with more butter and broil for about 8 minutes longer. The chops should be medium-rare. Place a paper frill (see page 185) on the bone end of each chop. Serve with Herbed Tomatoes.

Herbed Tomatoes
Serves 4

4 medium-sized tomatoes
Salt
1 clove garlic, crushed
1 tablespoon minced onion

3 tablespoons butter or margarine
1 tablespoon chopped parsley
½ teaspoon dried basil
2 cups day-old bread cubes

Preheat oven to 375°F. Slice the tops off the tomatoes and scoop out the pulp to ¾-inch down. With a sharp knife, cut a ½-inch deep zigzag border around each tomato. Sprinkle with salt, turn upside-down onto paper towels, and set aside. Sauté the garlic and onion in the butter until soft. Stir in the parsley and basil. Pour the seasoned butter over the bread cubes in a medium-sized bowl and toss to combine. Spoon mixture into the tomatoes, mounding slightly. Bake for 20 minutes and keep warm until the lamb chops are broiled.

Asparagus Tips Vinaigrette
Serves 4

1½ pounds asparagus
3 tablespoons white wine vinegar
¼ cup vegetable oil
¼ cup sliced scallions (with some green tops)

1 tablespoon chopped parsley
1 teaspoon sugar
Salt and pepper to taste
Leaf lettuce (Boston or romaine)

Wash the asparagus and break off the tough ends. With a vegetable parer, remove the scales and skin from the lower portion of each stalk. Place asparagus in a steamer over boiling water, cover, and steam for 15 minutes, or until just tender. Plunge the asparagus into a large bowl of ice and water to chill it quickly and stop the cooking. Drain the asparagus and refrigerate, covered, until serving time. Combine the vinegar, oil, scallions, parsley, sugar, salt, and pepper in a small bowl. Refrigerate, covered, for at least 1 hour. To serve, arrange the asparagus on a bed of lettuce and spoon the vinaigrette dressing over it.

TEAS AND COFFEES

Afternoon Choice

Tea with a Choice of Flavorings
Hearty Tea Sandwiches
Petits Fours
Mint Crèmes

This menu for afternoon tea is a perfect one to plan on serving at or after a meeting held in your home, or a gathering of your bridge club or sewing circle. It is also appropriate for a gathering of friends or family on a weekend afternoon. The sandwiches are simple, and assemble in little time. The mint crèmes can be stored in an airtight container, so you can make them well ahead of time. The major effort is, of course, the Petits Fours. As the frosting that covers each cake will seal in some of the moisture, you can make these the day before if you wish, decorate them, and set them aside. However, you will not want to stack or layer them, as the decorations might be disturbed that way—and you wouldn't want to leave them out, uncovered, for long—so it might be best to make them in the morning. They will then be perfect, and absolutely fresh, for your afternoon event.

Petits fours.

Tea with a Choice of Flavorings

When you brew a pot of full-bodied, satisfying tea, provided you have not chosen a flavored one such as mint, or one to which spices or citrus have already been added, you can offer your guests a choice of flavorings to add themselves.

Provide standard accompaniments such as lemon slices, milk, and sugar, and add to the selection thin slices of orange, sticks of cinnamon, whole cloves, even jams, and fresh fruits—slices of banana or apple, sections of tangerine or mandarin orange (clementine). Such flavored teas are delightful; guests place the flavoring ingredient of their choice in the cup, pour the tea over, and allow it to stand a minute or two.

Hearty Tea Sandwiches   *Makes 1*

For each sandwich, trim the crusts from two slices of bread (or leave it on if you wish) and spread with softened butter. Place a filling on a slice of buttered bread, top with another piece of bread, press firmly, and cut the sandwiches in half. These sandwiches are attractive piled high in a basket or arranged on a tray. Some delicious combinations include:

> Cream cheese and jelly on whole-wheat or nut bread
> Ham and cheese (Swiss or Muenster) on rye bread
> Tongue and Horseradish Sauce (page 161) on pumpernickel bread
> Roast beef or corned beef and mustard on rye
> Chicken or turkey with mayonnaise and watercress on white or
>   whole-wheat bread

NOTES: All the meats and cheeses for these sandwiches should be sliced very thin.

Watercress Butter (see page 173) or Herb Butter (see page 148) are excellent spreads for chicken or turkey sandwiches.

Petits Fours

Makes about 30

1 (16-ounce) package pound cake
mix
1 cup raspberry jelly
¼ cup granulated sugar

4 cups confectioners' sugar
1½ tablespoons kirsch
⅓ cup boiling water (approximate)

Preheat the oven to 350°F. Make the pound cake according to package directions. Bake in a lightly greased and floured 9-inch square pan for 30 minutes, or until a cake tester inserted in the cake comes out clean. Cool the cake for 15 minutes, then remove it from the pan and cool completely on a wire rack. With a sharp knife, cut the cake into 1½-inch squares, diamonds, and triangles.

In a small saucepan, over medium heat, melt the raspberry jelly. Stir in the granulated sugar until it dissolves. Bring the mixture to a full boil and remove it from the heat. Dip the top of each piece of cake into the glaze and place jelly side up on a cake rack, with a cookie sheet under it to catch the drips. For a thicker glaze, dip each cake a second time. Place the confectioners' sugar in a medium-sized bowl. Add the kirsch and enough boiling water to make a frosting of dipping consistency. If desired, tint the frosting with one or two drops of food coloring. Using a fork, pierce the bottom of a piece of cake to hold it. Dip the cake into the frosting to coat the top and sides of the cake. If the frosting becomes too thick, place the bowl over boiling water until it returns to the proper consistency. Place each piece back on the cake rack to allow excess frosting to drip off. When the frosting is set, decorate as desired.

NOTE: You may decorate Petits Fours with chopped nuts, chocolate shot (sprinkles), candied lilacs, or drizzled chocolate. For drizzled chocolate, melt 4 ounces sweet baking chocolate with 2 tablespoons butter. Drizzle on tops in a zigzag pattern.

Mint Crèmes

Makes about 24

1 tablespoon egg white
½ tablespoon green crème de
menthe

1½ cups confectioners' sugar
Whole unsalted nuts (cashews,
almonds, walnuts, or pecans)

Combine the egg white and liqueur in a medium-sized bowl. Add one-half cup of the sugar, stirring until smooth. Stir in remaining 1 cup sugar, a little at a time. When the dough becomes too stiff to stir, knead in remaining sugar with your hands. Roll into 1-inch balls, flatten slightly, and press a whole nut into the top of each. Store in an airtight container until ready to serve.

Summer Pickup

Fruit Juice Refreshers

Assorted Finger Sandwiches:

Dill Cream Cheese Squares

Open-face Tarragon Chicken Sandwiches

Watercress Rolls

Ice Cream

T hese Fruit Juice Refreshers are so simple, and so delightful, that if you are not familiar with them you will wonder why it took you so long to come upon them. Fresh fruit juices, if you have the time to prepare them, make these drinks even better—and the fresh fruit garnishes suggested in the recipe make them as attractive as they are delicious. A sprig of fresh mint would add a colorful (and fragrant) touch to any or all of these drinks.

The Finger Sandwiches are as light as the season suggests they should be, but a selection substantial enough to provide some sustenance; even in the summer, when we perhaps have smaller appetites, we still need nourishment and energy. If you and your guests enjoy sweets, ice cream is the perfect summer dessert, cool and easy.

Fresh fruit ice cream.

Fruit Juice Refreshers

What better way to cool off on a hot summer day than to drink a tall, refreshing fruit punch? Pour chilled juices and carbonated mixers into tall glasses over lots of ice. To make your drinks more elegant, garnish each with an orange slice, cherry, or strawberry. Try one of these combinations for a start, then create your own!

    1 part orange juice, 1 part grape juice, 2 parts ginger ale
    1 part orange juice, 1 part pineapple juice, 2 parts ginger ale
    1 part grapefruit juice, 1 part club soda
    1 part grape juice, 1 part club soda

Dill Cream Cheese Squares

Makes 16 cocktail sandwiches

4 ounces cream cheese, softened
2 tablespoons finely chopped fresh
  dill
4 very thin slices of rye bread, cut

into fourths, *or* 16 small square
  slices of party rye bread
16 small sprigs dill, for garnish
  (optional)

Combine the cream cheese with the dill. Refrigerate overnight to enhance the flavor. Let dill cream cheese come to room temperature and spread it on the rye squares. Garnish with dill sprigs, if you wish.

Open-face Tarragon Chicken Sandwiches

Makes 8 sandwiches

8 slices firm-textured white bread,
  crusts removed
½ cup Tarragon Butter (recipe
  follows)

24 thin slices of chicken breast
Minced parsley for garnish

Toast the bread slices on one side only, if you wish. Spread the untoasted sides of the bread slices with the Tarragon Butter, and arrange the chicken slices on top. Sprinkle with parsley.

Tarragon Butter

Makes ½ cup

¼ pound (1 stick) unsalted butter

1 tablespoon dried chopped
  tarragon *or* 2 tablespoons fresh

Place butter in a small bowl and let soften. Cream butter by mashing against the sides of the bowl until it is light and fluffy. Add the tarragon and blend well.

Watercress Rolls

Makes 12 tea sandwiches

1½ bunches watercress
12 very thin slices white bread,
  crusts removed

6 tablespoons butter *or* cream
  cheese, softened

Wash the watercress in cold water and pat dry. Remove and discard the stems.

Flatten the bread with a rolling pin, then spread generously with butter or cream cheese. Place several sprigs of watercress at one end of each slice of bread and roll the bread up around the watercress. For attractive sandwiches, let some of the leaves stick out a bit from either end, so they show when the sandwiches are rolled. To keep sandwiches firmly rolled, wrap them in plastic wrap or a damp tea towel and chill before serving.

229

Chocolate Layers

Makes 2 (9-inch) layers

⅔ cup unsweetened cocoa for
   baking
1¾ cups flour
1½ teaspoons baking soda
¼ teaspoon baking powder
¼ teaspoon salt

⅔ cup butter
1½ cups sugar
3 eggs
1 teaspoon vanilla
1¼ cups milk

Preheat oven to 350°F. Sift the cocoa, flour, baking soda, baking powder, and salt together, and set aside. In a large bowl, beat the butter and sugar together. Beat in the eggs and vanilla. Add the flour mixture and the milk alternately, beginning and ending with the flour mixture. Beat well after each addition. Pour the batter into 2 lightly greased and floured 9-inch round pans. Bake for 25 to 30 minutes, or until a cake tester inserted in the center comes out clean. Cool for 10 minutes in the pans, then turn out onto a wire rack to cool completely.

Creamy Chocolate Frosting

Makes enough to fill and frost a 9-inch cake

¼ cup butter
3 ounces unsweetened chocolate
2½ cups confectioners' sugar
1 egg

½ teaspoon vanilla
Dash of salt
¼ cup cream

In a small saucepan, melt the butter and chocolate over low heat. Pour the chocolate mixture into a bowl with 1 cup of the confectioners' sugar and beat until combined. Beat in the egg, vanilla, and salt. Add the remaining 1½ cups confectioners' sugar alternately with the cream, beating until the frosting is creamy and a good consistency for spreading.

Winter Warm-Up

Chocolate Brownie Torte
Irish Coffee

This second company coffee menu features another rich and elegant dessert, and an especially satisfying, warming coffee delight. Long a traditional favorite, Irish Coffee combines full-bodied coffee with Irish whiskey for a drink that is truly greater than the sum of its parts, topped with rich whipped cream to drink it through. For an added element to the presentation, top each serving of whipped cream with a roasted coffee bean. And of course, Irish Coffee mugs, if you have them, show off this special drink to its very best advantage. One note of caution: if you are serving this wonderful beverage to occasional imbibers, or to guests who have never tasted its delights before, be sure to warn them that Irish whiskey—though the flavor it adds to the coffee is a subtle one—is a strong alcoholic drink, and the effects may not become obvious quite soon enough. Irish Coffee is so delicious it is hard to stop after just one; anyone who has more than one, though, should drink slowly—savoring the delights.

Irish coffee.

Chocolate Brownie Torte

Serves 4 to 6

1 (15-ounce) package brownie mix
½ cup walnuts
Confectioners' sugar
1½ cups heavy cream

⅓ cup confectioners' sugar
2 tablespoons Amaretto
  liqueur
¼ cup toasted sliced almonds

Preheat oven to 350°F. Make the brownie mix according to package directions for a cake-type brownie, adding the walnuts. Grease a 13 × 9 × 2-inch baking pan and line it with waxed paper. Spread the brownie mixture evenly in the prepared pan and bake for 15 minutes, or until a cake tester comes out clean when inserted into the cake. Let cool in the pan for 10 minutes. Sift a little confectioners' sugar onto a tea towel. Turn the cake out onto the sugared towel and remove the waxed paper. Cool completely. Meanwhile, combine the cream, ⅓ cup confectioners' sugar and liqueur in a medium-sized bowl and refrigerate for 1 hour. Whip the cream mixture until stiff. Cut the brownie layer into thirds (three 9 × 4½-inch layers). Place one layer on a serving plate and spread with one-third of the whipped cream mixture. Repeat with the other two layers and the remaining whipped cream. Sprinkle toasted almond slices over the top.

NOTES: This cake is best if assembled 4 to 5 hours before serving. Slice with a very sharp knife.

   If you prefer not to use a liqueur, add ¼ teaspoon almond extract instead.

   To toast sliced almonds, place on a cookie sheet in a preheated 350°F oven. Roast, stirring frequently, until golden brown.

Irish Coffee

Serves 1

1½ ounces Irish whiskey
Strong hot black coffee

Chilled whipped cream

Pour the whiskey into a stemmed, heat-resistant glass. Fill to within ½ inch of the top with the coffee. Cover the surface of the coffee, to the brim of the glass, with the whipped cream.

Iced Coffee with a Twist

Iced Coffee with Ice Cream and/or other Flavorings
Platter of Cookies
Peanut Butter Cookies   *Almond Spritz Cookies*
Spritz Sandwich Cookies   *Coconut Meringues*
Vanilla-glazed Chocolate Drops

This coffee event is a lovely idea for an afternoon or evening get-together in the late spring, all summer, or the very early fall. Flavored coffee is an idea that has become more popular in recent years, and it can be a real delight. For the simplest, easiest flavored iced coffees, just provide complementary ice creams and offer guests their choice. Standby favorites, of course, would be vanilla, chocolate, and coffee ice cream. Others you might want to try include mint, chocolate mint, perhaps one of the newer "gourmet" flavors, such as honey vanilla. Another way to provide a choice of flavors is to prepare flavored whipped creams—using vanilla, almond, or orange extracts, for example. These flavored whipped creams can be dolloped onto the iced coffee—attractive, and delicious.

All of these cookie recipes bake up quickly, so the kitchen shouldn't get too hot or stay too hot if you bake from scratch, but bakery cookies would be okay, too, if chosen with care.

Peanut Butter Cookies

Makes 48 small cookies

1½ cups flour
½ teaspoon baking soda
¼ teaspoon salt
¾ cup chunk-style peanut butter
⅓ cup butter
¼ cup sugar

¼ cup honey
½ teaspoon vanilla
1 egg
Semisweet chocolate pieces
Chopped peanuts

Preheat oven to 375°F. Sift together the flour, baking soda, and salt, and set aside. Beat together the peanut butter, butter, and sugar until creamy, then beat in the honey, vanilla, and egg. Gradually stir in the flour mixture. Using your hands, roll the dough into ¾-inch balls. Place on a cookie sheet and press with a fork to flatten slightly. Sprinkle each cookie with chocolate pieces or chopped peanuts. Bake for 8 to 10 minutes.

Almond Spritz Cookies

Makes 30 small cookies

1½ cups flour
¼ teaspoon salt
½ cup butter or margarine, softened

½ cup sugar
1 egg yolk
¼ teaspoon almond extract

Preheat oven to 375°F. Sift together the flour and salt and set aside. Cream together the butter and sugar, then beat in the egg yolk and almond extract. Stir in the flour, one third at a time (the dough should be stiff). Fill a cookie press with the dough and press out the desired shapes onto a cookie sheet. Bake for about 8 minutes (the cookies should not be brown).

Spritz Sandwich Cookies

½ cup semisweet chocolate pieces
2 tablespoons butter

Almond Spritz Cookies, baked

In a small saucepan, over low heat, melt the chocolate pieces with the butter, stirring to combine. Spread on a cookie and top with a second to make a sandwich cookie. For another variation, drizzle the chocolate over the tops of the cookies in a zigzag design.

Iced coffee and assorted cookies.

Coconut Meringues

Makes 24 small cookies

2 egg whites from jumbo eggs, at
   room temperature
½ teaspoon vanilla
½ cup confectioners' sugar
1 cup flaked coconut

¼ cup flour
Additional flaked coconut for
   garnish
Glacéed cherries for garnish

Preheat oven to 325°F. In a medium-sized bowl, beat the egg whites until stiff peaks form. Add the vanilla, then beat in the sugar, 1 tablespoon at a time, beating well after each addition. Fold in the 1 cup coconut and the flour. Butter and flour a cookie sheet. Drop a scant teaspoonful of dough for each cookie onto the cookie sheet. Sprinkle a little coconut on the tops of half the cookies and place small pieces of glacéed cherry in the centers of the other half. Bake for 18 to 20 minutes, or until lightly browned.

Chocolate Drops

Makes 48 small cookies

2½ cups flour
2 teaspoons baking powder
½ teaspoon salt
½ cup shortening
1 cup sugar
2 eggs

3 ounces unsweetened chocolate,
  melted
½ cup milk
1 teaspoon vanilla
Vanilla Glaze (recipe follows)

Preheat oven to 375°F. Sift together the flour, baking powder, and salt and set aside. Cream together the shortening and sugar, then beat in the eggs and chocolate. Add the flour mixture and milk alternately, beginning and ending with the flour mixture. Stir in the vanilla. Drop by teaspoonfuls onto a lightly greased cookie sheet, 2 inches apart. Bake for 15 minutes, or until set. Remove to a wire rack to cool. Frost the tops with Vanilla Glaze.

Vanilla Glaze

1½ cups confectioners' sugar
Dash of salt

½ teaspoon vanilla
1–2 tablespoons milk

In a medium bowl, beat all ingredients together until smooth. Spread on Chocolate Drops.

LATE AFTERNOON PARTIES

Summer Cooler

Open-face Danish Sandwiches
Prosciutto and Cream Cheese Squares
Cucumber Salmon Triangles
Caviar Fingers   Salami Rolls
Fruit Salad with Sour Cream and Honey Dressing
Summer Punch Cooler or *Sparkling Melon Punch*

This menu of satisfying and refreshing summer foods has an added virtue. The quantities can easily be increased to accommodate even the largest of summer gatherings. As an option for a larger party format, an alternate punch recipe is included—one that serves 40 (and even that could be doubled!). For a small gathering of friends you've invited over for a dip in the backyard pool, just adjust the sandwich quantities up or down as needed. Fruit salad and dressing quantities can be easily modified, too. The selection of sandwiches is broad enough to provide for all tastes, and an additional option is yours to exercise if you wish: select either the Danish or the cocktail sandwiches, instead of providing all.

Open-face Danish Sandwiches

Thin slices of square dark
  pumpernickel bread, crusts
  removed
Thin slices of square rye bread,
  crusts removed
Unsalted butter
Thin slices of smoked salmon

Boneless, skinless sardines
Canned baby asparagus spears,
  drained
Small, thin slices of red onion
Freshly ground black pepper
Thin slices of lemon
Small sprigs of fresh dill

Spread the bread slices with a thin layer of the butter. Cover some of the slices with thin slices of smoked salmon, others with drained sardines. Garnish salmon sandwiches with small lengths of asparagus, lemon slices, and fresh dill. Season the sardine sandwiches with twists from the pepper mill and garnish with slices of onion, lemon slices, and sprigs of dill.

Prosciutto and Cream Cheese Squares

Makes 12 sandwiches

12 ounces cream cheese, softened
12 slices rye or pumpernickel
  bread

12 thin slices prosciutto
12 black olive rounds

Spread the cream cheese on the bread slices, then top each with a slice of prosciutto folded back on itself. Crown each sandwich with a round of black olive.

Cucumber Salmon Triangles   *Makes 16 sandwiches*

1 cucumber, peeled and thinly
  sliced
8 very thin slices square
  pumpernickel bread, crusts
  removed

½ cup Salmon Butter (recipe
  follows)

Place cucumber slices in a colander and salt generously. Set aside for at least 30 minutes to remove excess water. Dry the cucumber slices on paper towels.

Spread the bread slices with the Salmon Butter. Cover 4 slices of the buttered bread with cucumber slices, and top with the remaining slices of buttered bread. Cut into triangles.

241

Salmon Butter

Makes ½ cup

¼ pound (1 stick) unsalted butter
¼ pound smoked salmon, finely
chopped

Freshly ground black pepper to
taste

Place the butter in a bowl and let soften. Cream the softened butter by
mashing it against the sides of the bowl with a wooden spoon until it is
light and fluffy. Add the salmon and pepper to taste, blending well.

Caviar Fingers

Makes 16 sandwiches

4 square slices pumpernickel
bread
1 (2-ounce) jar red, black, or
lumpfish caviar

½ cup sour cream
1 hard-boiled egg, chopped fine
Paprika

Toast the bread on one side. Gently mix the caviar and the sour cream
together, and spread on the untoasted sides of the bread. Cut each slice
into fourths and garnish with sprinklings of chopped egg and paprika.

Salami Rolls

Makes 16 sandwiches

1 (8-ounce) package cream cheese,
softened
2 tablespoons prepared
horseradish, drained

16 very thin slices salami
4 very thin slices square
pumpernickel bread, cut
into quarters

Blend the cream cheese with the horseradish and spread generously on
the salami slices. Reserve about a tablespoon of the spread. Roll the salami
slices into cones, and place on the bread squares, securing each roll with a
tiny dab of the reserved spread.

Fruit Salad with sour cream and honey dressing.

Fruit Salad Platter

Serves 12

Romaine lettuce
6 grapefruits, sectioned
10 oranges, sectioned
6 tangerines, sectioned
1 pineapple, pared, cored, and cut
   into spears
4 apples, peeled, cored, sliced
   lengthwise, and sprinkled with
   lemon juice

Nuts (optional)
Coconut (optional)
Sour Cream and Honey Dressing
   (recipe follows)

Line a serving platter with the lettuce and arrange the fruit in a decorative pattern. Sprinkle with nuts and coconut, if you wish. Serve with the dressing in a separate bowl.

NOTE: Keep the fruit platter in the refrigerator, covered, until ready to serve.

Sour Cream and Honey Dressing   *Makes 1 cup*

1 cup sour cream
2 tablespoons honey

1½ teaspoons fresh lemon juice
Salt

In a bowl combine all the ingredients, except the salt, and mix until blended. Add salt to taste, chill. Serve with fruit salads.

Summer Punch Cooler   *Serves 12*

3 cups apricot nectar
2 pints orange sherbet

1 bottle chilled brut champagne
2 ounces Grand Marnier

Blend apricot nectar and orange sherbet in several batches in an electric blender until smooth. Let mixture stand in the refrigerator until ready to serve. Place a block of ice in a large punch bowl, and pour the mixture over it. Add the champagne and Grand Marnier and stir gently.

Sparkling Melon Punch   *Serves 40*

1 fifth Midori melon liqueur
1 fifth light rum
12 ounces crème de banane
1 (46-ounce) can unsweetened
   pineapple juice

12 ounces Rose's lime juice
1½ quarts chilled club soda
1 lime, thinly sliced (optional)
1 pint strawberries, sliced
   (optional)

Pour all ingredients into a large punch bowl and stir to combine. Add a large block of ice to the bowl. Garnish with the sliced fruit.

For a spectacular summertime presentation of this punch, make a watermelon punch bowl. Slice off the top third of a large watermelon, and scoop out the flesh. Save it for another use. Chill the "punch bowl" for several hours. Mix the punch, as directed, in a large bowl and ladle it into the cold melon shell over large chunks of ice.

In From the Cold

St. John's Soup with Potato Croquettes
French Peasant Pâté with Warmed Breads
Nutty Rum Balls
Mulled Wine

This hearty menu for entertaining on winter afternoons or early evenings is perfect fare to serve after strenuous outdoor cold weather sports—skiing, sledding, ice skating, hockey, and the like. All preparation can be done ahead of time, and food can be warming on the stove while friends are warming themselves in front of the fireplace (if you are fortunate enough to have one). You may want to serve mulled wine when you first arrive home, and supper a little later on, or save the warm beverage to have with dessert. Mulled wine is a friendly, warming drink at any time, and takes just a few minutes to prepare. You can serve the soup, crouquettes, pâté, and breads buffet style, or as a sit-down meal, depending on the size of the group and your table capacity. For a small group, either service would be appropriate; for a group larger than six or eight you will probably find buffet service more convenient. Food quantities can be multiplied, of course, by preparing more than one batch of any food (or foods) you choose.

Hearty beef soup and potato croquettes.

St. John's Soup (Hearty Beef Soup)   *Serves 10*

2 pounds boneless beef (stew beef), cut into 1½ inch pieces
10 cups water
½ cup pearl barley *or* rice
3 tablespoons butter
2 carrots, peeled and diced
2 medium onions, coarsely chopped

½ cup diced white potato (optional)
2 stalks celery
Salt and freshly ground white pepper

Put the beef in a large soup pot, add the water and barley, and bring the mixture to a boil. Simmer, covered, for about 2 hours, or until the meat is very tender. Remove the meat and break it into smaller pieces, if desired, then set meat aside.

In a skillet melt the butter and cook the vegetables very slowly for 15 minutes. Add the meat and vegetables to the soup pot and cook the mixture for an additional 30 minutes. Season with salt and pepper to taste, and serve.

NOTE: You can, of course, make the soup ahead of time and heat just before serving almost to a boil; or proceed with the recipe until the meat has cooked in the broth and reserve the remaining steps until 45 minutes or so before serving time.

Potato Croquettes

Serves 8 to 10 as an accompaniment

2 cups mashed potatoes (recipe below)
2 eggs

¼ cup flour
½ cup vegetable oil (or more if deep frying)

Beat one egg, and add it to the Mashed Potatoes, mixing well. Shape the mixture into 16 to 20 small balls, flatten each slightly with the heel of a hand, place them on waxed paper and place in refrigerator to chill. Beat the other egg, dip the croquettes in the egg, then into the flour, then set aside. Heat the oil in a skillet or deep fryer to a medium-high temperature. Add the croquettes to the oil, allowing enough room to turn them as they brown. Brown on each side, turn over, brown on the second side, remove, and keep warm until all have been browned.

Mashed Potatoes

4–6 white potatoes, washed, peeled, and quartered
6 tablespoons milk

Butter or margarine to taste (optional)
Salt to taste

Boil potatoes until a fork inserted goes in easily. Drain, place in bowl of electric mixer, add 3 tablespoons of milk and a tablespoon of butter or margarine if desired. Using electric mixer on low speed, blend until potatoes have softened and other ingredients begin to combine with them. Add more milk and/or butter if necessary, and salt to taste. Continue mixing until mashed potatoes are the consistency you desire.

NOTE: For use in the Croquette recipe, you will want the mixture to be firm.

French Peasant Pâté

Serves 6 to 8

4 tablespoons butter
¼ cup onion, minced very fine
1 pound chicken livers, well cleaned and drained
¼ cup brandy

¼ cup heavy cream
2 tablespoons minced parsley
Salt and freshly ground black pepper

In a medium-sized skillet melt the butter and cook the onions until they are soft but not brown. Add the livers and cook for 5 minutes. Add the brandy, touch a match to the mixture, and allow the alcohol to burn off. Add the cream, salt, and pepper to taste. Puree with the parsley in a food processor or blender until the mixture is liquid. Pour into a serving dish, cover tightly, and chill. Serve with warm bread or crisp crackers.

NOTE: This pâté is best if made at least 24 hours ahead.

247

Nutty Rum Balls

Makes 36 rum balls

2 cups finely chopped pecans
2 cups crushed vanilla wafers
2 cups confectioners' sugar
3 tablespoons unsweetened cocoa

¼ cup melted butter
½ teaspoon vanilla
¼ cup dark rum
Confectioners' sugar (optional)

In a large bowl, combine the pecans, vanilla wafers, 2 cups sugar, and cocoa. Stir in the butter, vanilla, and rum. Shape into 1-inch balls and roll in additional confectioners' sugar, if desired.

Mulled Wine

Serves 12

1 quart burgundy
Peel from 1 lemon and 1 orange
3-inch stick of cinnamon

1 whole nutmeg, crushed
6 whole cloves
1 tablespoon superfine sugar

Combine all ingredients in a stainless-steel pot and simmer gently for 8 minutes. Strain and serve in warmed mugs.

MEALS IN THE OPEN AIR

Patio Salad Bar

Mixed Greens with Accompaniments and Dressings
Succulent Cabbage Salad
24-Karat Salad   Nizza Salad
Serve-yourself Sandwiches
Assorted Fruit Juices, Soft Drinks, Iced Tea

You could serve this light and easy summer meal indoors, but it is really perfect for patio or poolside entertaining. Set out the buffet, and have fun with the crowd—this menu is suitable for all ages, afternoon or evening. Teenagers will love these wholesome foods, and could even put together this buffet on their own for friends. For younger children, you will probably want to mix a green salad and dress it for them beforehand, and make the sandwiches for them, too. The younger ones will probably find the other salads too sophisticated for their tastes, but the green salad and sandwiches will be a well-balanced meal in themselves.

You may want to omit mayonnaise-based salad mixtures from your sandwich offerings in the heat of summer: sliced meats and cheeses are just as nourishing and will stay appealing on the platter longer.

Nizza salad.

Green Salad Bar

Use the following greens and accompaniments in a combination of your choice. Make sure the greens are well washed and carefully dried to preserve their texture. Chill well after drying. Do not cut greens for salads; gently tear them into bite-sized pieces.

Iceberg lettuce—good texture, keeps well
Boston lettuce—smaller head, delicate texture and flavor
Romaine lettuce—long, broad leaves, good flavor
Escarole—curly, and strong in flavor
Spinach—long stemmed and dark green, strong but satisfying flavor
Whole cherry tomatoes, or tomato wedges
Herbs—chop and sprinkle some fresh herbs over the top of your bowl of greens. Parsley, chives, dill, basil, and tarragon all add interesting individual flavors; choose one or more
Onions—finely chopped or sliced red or yellow onions add flavor and texture.

Russian Dressing

Makes 1½ cups

½ cup mayonnaise
½ cup sour cream
3 tablespoons chili sauce
3 tablespoons fresh lime juice

2 tablespoons finely chopped fresh
  chives
¼ teaspoon salt

In a bowl combine all the ingredients and stir until well blended. Refrigerate before serving. This dressing is a pleasing complement to a green salad.

Vinaigrette

Makes ½ cup

2 tablespoons red or white wine
  vinegar
6–8 tablespoons olive oil
½ teaspoon salt

¾ teaspoon Dijon mustard
2 teaspoons finely chopped
  shallots (optional)
Freshly ground black pepper

Blend all the ingredients, except the pepper, in a blender or food processor, or shake in a jar with a tight-fitting lid, until the mixture is well combined. Transfer to a container and add pepper to taste.

NOTE: For a lighter dressing, combine 3–4 tablespoons olive oil and 3–4 tablespoons corn oil.

VARIATIONS:

With garlic: In a blender or food processor, blend 1 cup vinaigrette with 1 clove garlic for 10 seconds. Or let the garlic marinate in the dressing in the refrigerator overnight. Remove the garlic before serving.

Tarragon vinaigrette: Substitue tarragon vinegar for the red or white wine vinegar.

With herbs: Add 3 sprigs parsley, finely chopped, 1 teaspoon dried tarragon, and 1 teaspoon fresh basil *or* ½ teaspoon dried to 1 cup vinaigrette.

Succulent Cabbage Salad

Serves 8

1–2 oranges, peeled
1 medium-sized head red cabbage,
  quartered and cored

½ leek, sliced crosswise
Orange juice (optional)

Cut the orange sections into bite-sized pieces, being careful to reserve the juice. Slice the cabbage thinly. In a salad bowl, combine the oranges, cabbage, leek, and juice. Toss lightly and serve. Use additional orange juice, if more dressing is desired.

251

24-Karat Salad

Serves 8 to 12

8 large carrots, shredded
½ cup salad oil
3 tablespoons fresh lemon juice
4 teaspoons sugar or honey

¾ teaspoon salt
½ cup raisins
½ cup chopped walnuts

In a bowl, combine all the ingredients except the walnuts, and adjust the seasoning. Marinate the mixture at room temperature for 1 hour. Just before serving, add the walnuts and toss gently.

Nizza Salad

Serves 8 to 10

¾ pound string beans, well washed and trimmed
¾ pound (3 medium) tomatoes, cut into small wedges (eighths)
¾ pound (about 6) small boiled potatoes, peeled (or cut into fourths or eighths if large)

Vinaigrette marinade (recipe follows)
1 small can black olives *or* small jar of green olives
12–18 boneless sardines
Capers for garnish

Prepare the marinade. Place beans, tomatoes, and potatoes in separate bowls. Divide the marinade among them, pouring ⅓ of the mixture over the contents of each bowl. Let vegetables soak in the marinade for at least 1 hour.

Drain the ingredients, reserving the marinade, and arrange vegetables attractively in bowl or platter. Garnish the salad with the olives, capers, and sardines, then pour the reserved marinades over it.

Vinaigrette marinade

2 tablespoons wine vinegar
6 tablespoons vegetable oil

½ teaspoon salt
½ teaspoon black pepper

In a small bowl, combine the ingredients and mix well.

Serve-yourself Sandwiches

If you wish to provide something substantial in addition to hearty salads, a tray of thin slices of assorted breads, and a selection of thinly sliced meats and cheeses is always appropriate. Slices of chicken breast, boiled ham, Muenster, and Swiss cheese would be a good combination.

Such fillings as tuna or chicken salad, egg salad and the like should probably be avoided when the weather is warm and you are serving outside, but if you have a younger crowd you might want to provide crocks of jelly and peanut butter, and slices of apple or banana, accompanied by whole-grain breads.

Portable Party

Thermos of Yogurt-Cucumber Soup
Pita Bread Pockets with Hot Beef Filling
Party Cheesecake
Rum Fruit Punch
Coffee

E xcept for the cheesecake, this entire menu consists of foods that can be packed in containers to keep them cold (or hot). That makes it very convenient to take along almost anywhere. A useful accessory to add to your stock of picnic gear—if you enjoy eating in the outdoors in the spring, summer, and fall; hiking, tailgating at sports events, day trips at a lake or pool—is one shown here, a pie-basket for carrying freshly baked goods. You can also use this basket year-round to protect pies and cakes baked for friends, and for community suppers, church or school events. Many of these have compartments under the pie shelf that can be used for sandwiches, so you could take a picnic in one of these alone, except for a thermos of drinks. Do not carry things that should be kept cool, though, in any container that cannot also hold ice. This rule is especially important in the summer.

Party Cheesecake.

Yogurt-Cucumber Soup

Serves 4

½ cup raisins, soaked in ½ cup
  warm water
2 cups plain yogurt
1 large cucumber, peeled, seeded,
  and grated
1 small onion, grated
1 clove garlic, crushed (optional)
1½ teaspoons salt

¼ teaspoon freshly ground white
  pepper
2 cups milk
½ cup sour cream (optional)
2 teaspoons chopped fresh dill *or*
  ½ teaspoon dried
Cucumber slices for garnish

In a large bowl or saucepan, combine all ingredients except the cucumber
slices (be sure to include the water in which the raisins have soaked). Chill
for at least 3 hours. Serve in chilled bowls and garnish with cucumber
slices.

Hot Beef Filling for Picnic Pitas *Serves 4 to 6*

1½ pounds lean ground beef
(ground round or sirloin)
1 medium-sized onion, chopped
1 medium-sized green pepper,
chopped
1 clove garlic, peeled (optional)

Salt and freshly ground black
pepper
Ketchup (optional)
Worcestershire sauce (optional)
4–6 pitas

Crumble up the ground beef into a medium-sized skillet and sauté over medium heat, stirring constantly, until the meat is browned. Drain off most of the fat, reserving 2 to 3 tablespoons. Keep cooked meat warm. Sauté onion, green pepper, and garlic in the reserved fat, until the pepper is soft and the onion has begun to brown. Remove garlic and discard. Combine browned meat with sautéed vegetables and cook slightly to combine and reheat. Flavor with salt and pepper, ketchup or Worcestershire sauce, if desired. Pack the mixture in a large thermos.

To serve, slice pitas open at one end, and fill with the mixture.

Party Cheesecake *Serves 8 to 10*

1 cup graham cracker crumbs
1 cup plus 2 tablespoons sugar
2 tablespoons butter or margarine,
melted
3 (8-ounce) packages cream
cheese, at room temperature
2 tablespoons flour
1 tablespoon grated lemon peel

2 tablespoons lemon juice
½ teaspoon vanilla
5 eggs
1 cup heavy cream
¼ cup pineapple preserves
1 cup crushed pineapple, drained
1 pint blueberries
¼ cup blueberry jam

In a small bowl, mix together the graham cracker crumbs, the 2 tablespoons sugar, and the butter. Press the mixture into the bottom of a 9-inch springform pan and refrigerate it while the filling is prepared.

Preheat oven to 350°F. In a large bowl, beat the cream cheese, 1 cup sugar, flour, and lemon peel until smooth. Beat in the lemon juice, vanilla, and eggs. Add the cream and beat until well blended. Pour into the prepared pan and bake for 50 minutes, or until almost firm. Remove from the oven to a wire rack. Carefully run the tip of a sharp knife around the side of the cake, next to the pan. Cool cake completely, then refrigerate, loosely covered, for 4 hours or overnight.

In a small saucepan, melt the pineapple preserves. Add the crushed pineapple, and let the mixture cool. In another small saucepan, melt the blueberry preserves. Add the blueberries and let cool. Remove the side of the springform pan. Using a toothpick, mark the top of the cake into 8 wedges. Carefully spoon the pineapple and blueberry topping onto alternate sections.

Rum Fruit Punch

Makes 1¼ gallons

1½ quarts orange juice, chilled
1 quart grapefruit juice, chilled
3 cups light rum

½ cup curaçao
2 (12-ounce) bottles ginger ale, chilled

At least one day before you will be serving, combine 2 cups of the orange juice with 1 cup of the grapefruit juice, pour into ice cube trays and freeze. To serve, combine the remaining orange juice, grapefruit juice, rum, and curaçao in a 1½-gallon punch bowl. Add the ginger ale and fruit-juice "ice" cubes. Stir gently to combine.

NOTES: For a picnic, combine the orange juice, grapefruit juice, rum, curaçao, and fruit juice cubes in a large picnic jug. Carry the ginger ale in a picnic cooler. Add the ginger ale to the punch just before serving.

You can make ice for your picnic cooler by freezing water in a large plastic drink container with a top that seals tightly. Take the ice along right in the container. As the ice melts, you have fresh ice water to drink.

Pack Up and Go

Sandwich Ingredients and Fillings with
Assorted Fresh Breads
Ham with Pineapple Chunks
Apple and Celery Salad
Fresh Fruits
Raisins and Nuts
Iced Soft Drinks

This picnic menu is far less sophisicated than our Portable Party, and much easier to assemble than the Fourth of July Picnic. In fact, this is basically an impromptu occasion menu, designed to provide guidelines for those times you will be traveling with children, so that you can conveniently satisfy their hunger and thirst.

If you normally travel with your children in the family car, just assembling the ingredients for sandwiches and fresh breads is most convenient; there will be no leftover sandwiches (you will make what you need at the time), and the ones you make will be absolutely fresh—breads will stay firm even if you make sandwiches with moist ingredients, like tuna or deviled ham spread. If you will be traveling by train or other public conveyance, it would be best to make sandwiches ahead of time. Stay away from moist ingredients if possible, or protect breads from moist spreads by placing lettuce leaves between bread and spread.

Sandwich makings, ham with pineapple chunks, apple and celery salad.

If you are traveling and the weather is mild, you might want to consider packing the "fixings" for a roadside picnic. Some sandwich fillings to use, in your favorite combinations, include:

Peanut butter   Lettuce
Jelly   Cold cuts
Deviled ham   Apple and Celery Salad (recipe follows)
Canned tuna   Ham and Pineapple Chunks (recipe fol-
Sliced cheese   lows)

Apple and Celery Salad

Wash and core several apples and cut them into ½-inch pieces. Slice several stalks of celery and add to the apples. Toss with your favorite Italian dressing. Pack in an airtight container and carry in a picnic cooler.

Ham and Pineapple Chunks

Cut a precooked ¼-inch ham slice into cubes. Add a small can of drained pineapple chunks. Toss and pack in an airtight container. Carry in a picnic cooler.

258

Tennis Buffs' Buffet

Assorted Appetizers:

Miniature Quiches   *Shrimp Salad Tarts*

Double-cheese Canapes   *Ham Salad Puffs*

Ziti Salad with Peppers

Sangria or Fruit Punch

You can spend the late morning or early afternoon on the court and entertain your tennis-playing friends later in the day for a relaxed—and relaxing—meal with foods keyed to the day's strenuous exercise, designed to renew energy spent.

Double-cheese Canapes can be assembled almost in seconds. (Make the Cutouts ahead of time, of course.) Miniature Quiches can be made ahead and warmed again before serving. Ziti Salad should be made ahead and chilled. The Shrimp Salad Tarts and Ham Salad Puffs can be left for you to fill just before serving if you want to present them at their very best.

You can make Sangria (if you are serving it) ahead of time and the flavors will marry in the interim, but do not add ice before the event. The same, of course, would be true of a nonalcoholic punch. Fruit juices or iced tea could also be substituted for the Sangria or punch.

Miniature Quiches

Makes 24

1 Basic Pastry (see page 182)
1 egg white, mixed with 1
    tablespoon water
2 eggs, lightly beaten
1 cup light cream

Dash of salt
1 cup grated Swiss-type cheese
¼ pound bacon, cooked, drained,
    and crumbled
Dash of nutmeg

Roll half of the prepared piecrust to ⅛-inch thickness. Using a cookie cutter, cut the dough into 3½-inch rounds. Carefully fit each round into a muffin-pan cup. Repeat the procedure with the remaining dough. Brush each pastry shell with the egg-white mixture and refrigerate until ready to fill. Preheat oven to 400°F. In a small bowl, combine the eggs, cream, salt, and nutmeg. To bake, sprinkle some grated cheese into each tart shell; spoon the egg and cream mixture over the cheese, and bake for 20 minutes, or until the crust is golden and the filling is slightly puffed. Cool the quiches in the pans for 10 minutes, then remove them to a serving tray and sprinkle them with the bacon.

Shrimp Salad Tarts

Makes 24

1 Basic Pastry (see page 182)
1 egg yolk, mixed with 1
    tablespoon water
1 (3-ounce) package cream cheese,
    softened
1 tablespoon lemon juice
1 teaspoon finely chopped fresh
    dill

1 teaspoon grated onion
¼ teaspoon Worcestershire sauce
1 cup chopped cooked shrimp
24 small whole shrimp for garnish
Fresh dill sprigs for garnish

Make tart shells as directed in the recipe for Miniature Quiches (above). Prick the surface of the shells with the tines of a fork and refrigerate for 30 minutes.

Preheat oven to 450°F. Brush each shell with the egg-yolk mixture and bake for 8 to 10 minutes, or until nicely browned. Cool, then remove shells from the muffin pans. In a medium-sized bowl, combine the cream cheese, lemon juice, dill, onion, and Worcestershire sauce, stirring until smooth. Fold in the chopped shrimp and chill.

To serve, spoon the filling into the pastry shells and garnish each with a whole shrimp and a sprig of dill.

Ham salad in pastry puffs, miniature quiches, double-cheese canapés, shrimp salad tarts.

Double-cheese Canapés

Makes about 20

1 cup Cheddar cheese spread, softened

Cheese Pastry Cutouts
(recipe follows)
Sliced stuffed olives

Spoon the cheese spread into a pastry bag fitted with a large star tip. Pipe cheese swirls on each cracker and garnish each with an olive slice.

NOTE: Serve remaining Cutouts plain, in a bowl or basket.

Cheese Pastry Cutouts

Makes 48

1¼ cups flour
½ teaspoon salt
Pinch of cayenne
¼ cup shortening, chilled

1 (3-ounce) package cream cheese, chilled
1 tablespoon ice water
1 egg yolk, mixed with
1 tablespoon water

Sift together into a medium-sized bowl the flour, salt, and cayenne. With a pastry blender or 2 knives, cut the shortening and cream cheese into the flour until the pieces are the size of small peas. Quickly stir in the water to moisten. Gather the dough together to form a ball. Flatten slightly, wrap in plastic wrap, and chill for ½ hour. Preheat oven to 425°F. Roll the dough to a ⅛-inch thickness and cut into fancy shapes with 1½-inch cookie cutters. Place on a cookie sheet, brush with the egg yolk mixture, and bake for 10 minutes, or until nicely browned.

261

Ham Salad Puffs

Makes 20

¼ cup butter, melted
½ cup water
½ cup flour
⅛ teaspoon salt

Dash of cayenne (optional)
2 eggs
Ham Salad Filling (recipe follows)

Preheat oven to 400°F. In a small saucepan, bring the melted butter and water to a boil. Remove from the heat and add the flour, salt, and cayenne all at once, stirring to combine. Place over low heat and continue stirring until the dough leaves the sides of the pan and forms a ball. Remove from the heat and add the eggs, one at a time, beating well after each addition. Drop the dough by rounded teaspoonfuls on a cookie sheet, 2 inches apart. Bake for 25 minutes, or until puffed and nicely browned. Cool on a wire rack. To serve, slice the tops off with a sharp paring knife, fill each with a rounded tablespoon of Ham Salad Filling, and replace the tops.

Ham Salad Filling

Fills 20 puffs

1 cup chopped cooked ham
½ cup chopped celery
¼ cup chopped green pepper

1 teaspoon minced onion
2 to 3 tablespoons mayonnaise
2 teaspoons sloe gin (optional)

Combine all ingredients in a small bowl and refrigerate, covered.

Ziti Salad with Peppers

Serves 4 to 6

1 green pepper, coarsely chopped
1 red pepper, coarsely chopped
2 tablespoons chopped scallions (include some green tops)
2 tablespoons finely chopped parsley

3 cups cooked ziti *(al dente),* drained and slightly cooled
¾ cup Sour Cream Dressing (recipe follows)

Combine all ingredients in a bowl and chill, covered, for 1 hour before serving.

Sour Cream Dressing

Makes 1½ cups

½ cup mayonnaise
1 cup sour cream
½ cup chopped parsley
2 tablespoons cider vinegar or
　white-wine vinegar

1 small onion, chopped
Salt and freshly ground white
　pepper
Worcestershire sauce

Blend all the ingredients in a blender or food processor until well combined. Serve with a vegetable, potato, or pasta salad.

Sangria

Serves 8

1 bottle Spanish red wine
1 orange, thinly sliced
6 lemon slices
1½ ounces cognac or brandy
1 ounce Triple Sec

1 ounce maraschino
1 tablespoon superfine sugar (or to
　taste)
6 ounces sparkling mineral water

Put all the ingredients except the water into a large pitcher and stir to dissolve the sugar. Let the flavors marry for at least an hour. Just before serving, add sparkling mineral water and ice cubes to the pitcher and stir gently. Pour into chilled wineglasses.

White Wine Sangria

Serves 8

1 bottle dry white wine
1 orange, thinly sliced
2 slices lemon
2 slices lime
1 ounce brandy

2 tablespoons superfine sugar
3-inch stick of cinnamon
10 large strawberries, halved
6 ounces sparkling mineral water

Put all ingredients except the water into a large pitcher and stir to dissolve the sugar. Let the flavors marry for at least an hour. Just before serving, add sparkling mineral water and ice cubes to the pitcher and stir gently. Pour into chilled wineglasses.

Weekend Windup

Blueberry Soup
Chicken Liver Sauté
Wilted Lettuce Salad
Pecan Waffle Sundaes
Coffee

T his hearty menu is planned for a meal which doesn't fall easily into a standard category. Heartier than a brunch, and composed of more courses than generally served at such a meal, it may, in fact be eaten at a time when brunch might normally be served. It is intended as a farewell send-off for weekend guests. If they have a long trip ahead of them, you will want to serve them a hearty meal before they depart to sustain them. If they are leaving in the early afternoon, an additional very light breakfast of coffee or tea, fruit or juice, toast (or hot rolls or croissants) would be appropriate for early risers—to tide them over until your Weekend Windup.

The Blueberry Soup, which should be served chilled, is to be made ahead of time. You can also make the waffles and the chocolate sauce for the Pecan Waffle Sundaes, and reheat them to serve. The whipped cream can be made a little ahead of time, too, and stored in the refrigerator, covered, until serving time.

Blueberry Soup

Serves 6

4 cups water
3 tablespoons or more sugar
3 cups blueberries

2 tablespoons arrowroot, mixed
   with 6 tablespoons water
½ cup heavy cream, whipped

In a saucepan, bring the water to boil and add the sugar and fruit. Simmer for 3 minutes, or until fruit is tender. Stir in the arrowroot paste and heat until the soup is thickened, about 1 minute. Add more sugar, if desired. Chill the soup and serve with dollops of whipped cream.

Chicken Liver Sauté

Serves 6

½ pound bacon
1 pound mushrooms, sliced
1½ pounds chicken livers, cleaned
   and halved
1 cup sliced scallions, (include
   some green tops)

2 tablespoons chopped parsley
1 cup dry red wine
½ cup chicken broth
Salt and freshly ground pepper to
   taste
Toast points

Cut the bacon into 1-inch pieces and sauté in a medium-sized skillet until crisp. Remove the bacon with a slotted spoon and set aside. Sauté the mushrooms in the skillet until golden and set aside with the bacon. Spoon 2 tablespoons of bacon fat into a large skillet and sauté the chicken livers until golden on the outside and just pink on the inside.

Meanwhile, pour out all of the bacon fat in the medium skillet except 2 tablespoons. Sauté the scallions and the parsley in the bacon fat for 1 minute, add the wine and chicken broth and boil to reduce to about half, about 5 minutes. Add the reserved bacon and mushrooms, sautéed chicken livers, salt, and pepper to the sauce. Heat gently to blend the flavors, about 3 minutes. To serve, pour carefully into a chafing dish. Garnish with several toast points and serve additional toast points in a basket.

NOTE: To make toast points, trim the crusts from 10 slices of white bread and place on a cookie sheet. Bake in a preheated 450°F. oven for 4 minutes, then turn and bake for another 4 minutes or until golden. Slice in half on the diagonal for large triangles or slice in fourths on the diagonal for small triangles.

Wilted Lettuce Salad

Serves 6

4 slices bacon
2 heads lettuce (romaine, Boston, escarole) *or* 1 pound spinach, well washed and dried
3 tablespoons finely chopped scallions (include some of the green tops)
3 hard-cooked eggs, chopped

4 tablespoons vinegar *or* fresh lemon juice
1 teaspoon sugar
½ teaspoon Dijon mustard
Salt and freshly ground black pepper to taste

In a skillet, cook the bacon until crisp and reserve the fat. Drain the bacon on paper towels and crumble it.

Crisp the lettuce or spinach, wrapped in paper towels or a kitchen towel, in the refrigerator. Break the leaves into pieces and put them in a chilled salad bowl with the scallions, eggs, and bacon. To the reserved fat in the skillet add the vinegar, sugar, mustard, salt, and pepper and heat until the sugar dissolves. Pour the heated dressing over the salad, toss, and serve immediately.

Pecan Waffle Sundaes

Serves 6

6 Pecan Waffles (recipe follows)
Vanilla ice cream

Chocolate Sauce (recipe follows)
Sweetened whipped cream

Place a Pecan Waffle on a dessert plate. Add a large scoop of vanilla ice cream. Spoon on Chocolate Sauce and top with a generous swirl of Sweetened Whipped Cream.

Pecan Waffles

Makes 10 (4½-inch) waffles

3 eggs
1 cup flour
¾ cup finely grated pecans
¼ teaspoon salt

½ teaspoon baking soda
¼ teasooon baking powder
½ cup light cream
⅓ cup melted butter or margarine

In a medium-sized bowl, beat the eggs until thick and lemon colored. Combine the flour, pecans, salt, baking soda, and baking powder, blending thoroughly. Add the flour mixture and cream alternately to the eggs, beginning and ending with the flour mixture. Stir in the butter. Use about ¼ cup batter for each waffle (they should be small). Pour the batter onto the bottom half of a preheated waffle iron. Lower the top half and cook until the waffle iron stops steaming. Raise the top and remove the waffle.

NOTE: These waffles may be made ahead, cooled on a wire rack, and wrapped in plastic wrap. To serve, remove wrap, place on a cookie sheet, and warm in a 325°F oven.

Pecan waffle sundae.

Chocolate Sauce

Makes about 1 cup

6 ounces semisweet chocolate
  pieces
1½ tablespoons butter or
  margarine

1 tablespoon light corn syrup
½ cup heavy cream

In a double boiler, over hot water, melt the chocolate pieces and butter. Remove from the heat and stir in the corn syrup and cream.

NOTE: Sauce may be made ahead and warmed in a double boiler over hot water at serving time. If sauce is too thick, thin with a little more cream.

267

CHILDREN'S PARTIES

Bib-and-Tucker Birthday

Citrus Sparkle
Party Sandwiches
Birthday Cupcakes
Ice Cream

T his menu, designed for a party to celebrate a toddler's or small child's birthday, is an easy one, composed of children's traditional party favorites. To give a healthful touch to the soda children love, Citrus Sparkle is made by adding orange juice to a fruit-flavored soda of your choice (or giner ale, for more sophisticated young tastes). There are directions here for frosting preparation—and cross-references for those in other menus, as well as a cross-reference for a chocolate cake batter that can be used for cupcakes—but more important are the suggestions for cupcake decorations to delight young guests (and guests of honor). The cupcakes can also be made from any cake mix you like to use; the idea here is to spend your time, energy, and creativity on the decorations. Recipes for sandwiches have not been provided; you know your child's personal favorites, and preparing those for a birthday celebration will make the honored guest feel even more special. You might cut the sandwiches in interesting shapes (triangles, circles, etc.), for an extra presentation touch.

Birthday cupcakes.

Citrus Sparkle

Makes 1 drink

3 ounces orange juice
Lemon or lemon-lime soda or
   ginger ale
1 slice of orange

Pour ingredients over ice and stir. Garnish with the orange slice.

NOTE: You can combine the juice and soda, in any proportion you think pleasing, in a pitcher, for ease in serving.

Birthday Party Cupcakes

Makes 24 cupcakes

24 cupcakes (from a mix, your favorite recipe, or use the recipe for chocolate layers—see page 235)

Creamy Chocolate Frosting (see page 235)

Vanilla Butter Cream Frosting (recipe follows)

Food colors
Nonpareil decors
Chocolate shot decors (sprinkles)
Rainbow mix shot decors (sprinkles)

Frosting swirls: Spoon frosting into a pastry bag fitted with a large star tip. Pipe frosting onto the cupcakes in a circular motion, to form a tall swirl. Sprinkle with nonpareil decors, chocolate shot decors, or rainbow mix shot decors.

Baseball mitts, baseballs, and happy faces: Frost the cupcakes with Creamy Chocolate Frosting, or Vanilla Butter Cream Frosting, making the frosting as smooth as possible. Use a toothpick to outline a mitt, baseball, or face on each cupcake, as pictured. Spoon frosting of a contrasting color into a pastry bag fitted with a round writing tip. Pipe the frosting over the outlines.

Fancy tops: Frost the cupcakes with Creamy Chocolate Frosting, or Vanilla Butter Cream Frosting. Using food colors, tint Vanilla Butter Cream Frosting bright shades of red, yellow, and blue. Use one color at a time in a pastry bag fitted with a small star tip to pipe decorative designs and edgings on cupcakes.

Vanilla Butter Cream Frosting

Frosts 24 cupcakes, or fills and frosts a 9-inch cake

½ cup butter or margarine
½ cup vegetable shortening
¾ teaspoon vanilla

1 pound confectioners' sugar
2–4 tablespoons milk

Beat together the butter and shortening until well combined. Add the vanilla, then beat in the sugar and milk alternately. Continue beating until light and fluffy.

NOTE: If you are using the frosting to *decorate* the cupcakes, use *only* 2 tablespoons of milk. If you are using the frosting to *frost* the cupcakes, use 4 tablespoons of milk. The frosting should be stiffer for decorating.

Tricksters' Treat

Witches' Brew

Jack-O-Lantern Sandwiches

Carrot and Celery Broomsticks

Vanilla Ice Cream in Orange Cup Cauldrons

Halloween Ginger Cookies

This delightful menu for a children's Halloween party is sure to please. The crowning, extra-special touch to a menu filled with surprises is the Halloween ginger cookies. Make your own patterns for witches' hats, ghosts, and pumpkins or jack-o-lanterns, and use the recipes for the dough and frostings and suggestions for decorating each variety provided here. You could also make these, of course, for your child's school Halloween party; the delight of his or her classmates at your handiwork will please your child no end. The other elements of this party menu are beautifully simple. The Witches' Brew can be mixed in a trice, and the Broomsticks are simply the celery and carrot sticks youngsters love—and are good for them, too. Jack-O-Lantern Sandwiches are easy, and wonderful fun for kids. Orange Cup "Cauldrons" to hold an ice-cream dessert are another special party touch kids will really appreciate. Your child, if he or she is old enough, might enjoy helping you prepare this party for his or her friends.

Halloween ginger cookies.

Witches' Brew

Purple or red grape juice   Ginger ale

Combine above ingredients in a proportion of your choice in a pitcher, and add ice.

Jack-O-Lantern Sandwiches   *Makes 1 sandwich*

1 slice white bread, trimmed to
   approximate a circle
1 or 2 slices of American cheese

2 slices of pitted black olive
Several black olive triangles for
   nose and teeth

Toast bread slice in oven on one side only. Remove, and place other
ingredients on untoasted side to resemble a jack-o-lantern face. Toast in
oven or under broiler until cheese is melted.

Vanilla-Ice-Cream-Filled Orange Cauldrons

1 orange for each 2 servings
1 scoop of vanilla ice cream for
   each serving

Cut each orange in half and remove the fruit carefully, keeping the shells
intact. Reserve the fruit for another use. Fill each orange-shell "cauldron"
with a scoop of vanilla ice cream.

Halloween Ginger Cookies   *Makes 30 (6-inch) cookies*

5 cups flour
2 tablespoons baking soda
1 tablespoon ginger
1 teaspoon cinnamon
1 teaspoon ground cloves
½ teaspoon salt
1 cup shortening

1 cup brown sugar
1 egg
¾ cup molasses
1 tablespoon vinegar
¼ cup water
Decorator Icing (recipe follows)

Sift together the flour, baking soda, ginger, cinnamon, cloves, and salt and
set aside. In a large bowl, cream together the shortening and sugar until
well blended. Beat in the egg, molasses, and vinegar. Add the sifted flour
mixture and the water alternately, beginning and ending with flour. Refrigerate, covered, for several hours or overnight.

   Preheat oven to 375°F. On a lightly floured pastry board roll out the
dough, one quarter at a time, to slightly more than ⅛-inch thick. Cut into Halloween shapes (see note) and place on cookie sheets. Bake for
about 8 minutes. Remove cookies to a wire rack to cool. Frost the ghosts

with white frosting, using raisins for the eyes and mouth. Frost the pumpkins with the orange frosting, using green frosting for the pumpkin's stem. Spoon the yellow frosting into a pastry bag fitted with a round writing tip. Pipe the eyes, nose, and mouth on the pumpkin. Use the yellow frosting in the pastry bag to outline the witch's hat and buckle. Allow the frosting to dry and harden, then store the cookies in an airtight container with waxed paper between the layers.

NOTE: To make halloween shapes, draw the 5- to 6-inch pumpkin, witch's hat, and ghost shapes on clean cardboard and cut out. Place the shapes on the rolled dough and cut around them with a small, sharp knife. Remove the cardboard, lift the cookie with a large spatula, and place on a cookie sheet.

Decorator Icing

1 pound confectioners' sugar   3 egg whites from jumbo eggs

In a medium-sized bowl combine the sugar and egg whites and beat until thickened (this may take about 5 minutes). Place about one third of the frosting into a small bowl and thin slightly with water (add a few drops at a time until frosting reaches the point where it will spread smoothly). In another small bowl thin one third of the frosting as above and tint it pumpkin orange. Tint 1 tablespoon of the remaining frosting green. Tint all the rest of the frosting yellow, and do *not* add water to thin. Cover all frosting with a damp paper towel until ready to use, to prevent drying out.

Teenagers' Dive-In Barbecue

Vegetable Plate to Serve with Dips

Curry Dip   Fresh Dill Dip

Hamburgers   Frankfurters

Milk or Soda

Choco-Butterscotch Bars

A menu that would travel well to the poolside or beach; teenagers will dive into this meal with enthusiasm. Easily a meal older kids can fix for themselves, this is a well balanced one—a definite plus. Teenagers may shy away from vegetables, but they will probably go for these delicious dips, and eat the vegetables along with them. If this party is to be portable, arrange the vegetables attractively in a large plastic container, and provide the dips in separate, airtight containers. See that all these items are placed in a cooler, along with the meats, of course, and milk if you will be serving it. Buns, ketchup, mustard, etc., and the Choco-Butterscotch Bars, can be carried along in a basket, as they needn't be kept cold. See that the dessert is well packed, so the bars don't become crumbs.

275

Vegetable Plate to Serve with Dips

Arrange fresh, chilled vegetables in a large bowl of ice and serve with Curry Dip (recipe follows), Fresh Dill Dip (recipe follows), or Avocado Dip. (To make Avocado Dip see the recipe for Avocado Dressing on page 144. Double all the ingredients *except* the light cream to make a tasty dip.) You may want to serve a large bowl of corn chips for dipping also. Some great "dunking" vegetables include:

Broccoli florets	Cucumber sticks or slices
Carrot sticks	Endive leaves
Cauliflower florets	Green-pepper sticks
Celery sticks	Mushroom slices
Cherry tomatoes	Scallions with green tops
Chinese pea pods	Zucchini sticks or slices

Curry Dip
Makes 1 cup

1 cup mayonnaise
1 tablespoon prepared horseradish
1 tablespoon minced onion

1 teaspoon white wine vinegar
½ teaspoon curry powder
Pinch of cayenne

Combine all of the ingredients in a small bowl and refrigerate, covered, for several hours.

Fresh Dill Dip
Makes 1¼ cups

1 cup sour cream
¼ cup finely chopped dill

2 teaspoons lemon juice (optional)

Combine the sour cream, dill, and lemon juice, if desired, in a small bowl and refrigerate, covered, for several hours.

Frankfurters

Nothing is easier or tastier than frankfurters grilled over a charcoal fire. You can grill them whole, or score or split them. A rack with a lid will make it easier to handle them once they are on the fire; they can all be turned at once and removed all at once when they are done. The rack should have an adjustable lid so that you can make sure the franks will stay put far enough apart that they will be crispy all over when cooked. Serve on plain or toasted buns, accompanied by sauerkraut, pickle relish, and mustard.

Hamburger with all the fixings.

Hamburgers

Makes 12 (¼-pound) burgers

3 pounds lean ground beef (chuck
   or round)
Salt and freshly ground black
   pepper

Dijon mustard (optional)
Worcestershire sauce (optional)

Shape the meat into 12 patties, but be careful not to handle the meat too
much; you will press out moisture and the patties will be tough. Season the
patties with salt and pepper. If you wish the burgers to have a crisp,
flavorful outer crust, combine Dijon mustard and Worcestershire in a
proportion to suit your taste and brush the burgers on both sides with the
mixture before grilling. Broil the patties over charcoal on a barbecue grill
for 3 to 6 minutes on each side, depending on how you like them. Serve on
plain or toasted buns, or on toasted English muffins.

277

Choco-Butterscotch Bars

Makes 32 bars (approx. 3 × 1-inch)

1½ cups flour
1 teaspoon baking powder
½ teaspoon salt
¾ cup butter or margarine, softened
1 cup dark brown sugar, firmly packed

3 eggs
1 teaspoon vanilla
6 ounces semisweet chocolate pieces
6 ounces butterscotch pieces
1 cup chopped walnuts

Preheat oven to 350°F. Sift together the flour, baking powder, and salt and set aside. Cream together the butter and sugar, then add the eggs and vanilla. Stir in the flour mixture until smooth. Fold the chocolate and butterscotch pieces and half the walnuts into the batter. Pour into a lightly greased 9 × 13-inch baking pan and sprinkle the remaining walnuts on top. Bake for 35 minutes, or until a cake tester inserted into the bars comes out clean. When cool, cut into bars.

Index

Make your home special

Since 1922, millions of men and women have turned to *Better Homes and Gardens* magazine for help in making their homes more enjoyable places to be. You, too, can trust *Better Homes and Gardens* to provide you with the best in ideas, inspiration and information for better family living.

In every issue you'll find ideas on food and recipes, decorating and furnishings, crafts and hobbies, remodeling and building, gardening and outdoor living plus family money management, health, education, pets, car maintenance and more.

For information on how you can have *Better Homes and Gardens* delivered to your door, write to: Mr. Robert Austin, P.O. Box 4536, Des Moines, IA 50336.

The Idea Magazine for Better Homes and Families